# Religion in International Politics and Development

# Religion in International Politics and Development

## The World Bank and Faith Institutions

John A. Rees

*Senior Lecturer in Politics and International Relations, University of Notre Dame Australia (Sydney)*

**Edward Elgar**
Cheltenham, UK • Northampton, MA, USA

Published by
Edward Elgar Publishing Limited
The Lypiatts
15 Lansdown Road
Cheltenham
Glos GL50 2JA
UK

Edward Elgar Publishing, Inc.
William Pratt House
9 Dewey Court
Northampton
Massachusetts 01060
USA

A catalogue record for this book
is available from the British Library

Library of Congress Control Number: 2011925751

ISBN 978 1 84980 308 3

Typeset by Servis Filmsetting Ltd, Stockport, Cheshire
Printed and bound by MPG Books Group, UK

# Contents

# Figures

# Tables

# Abbreviations

| | |
|---|---|
| APRODEV | Association of World Council of Churches related to Development Organizations in Europe |
| ARC | Alliance of Religions and Conservation |
| CCIA | Commission of the Churches on International Affairs |
| CDF | Comprehensive Development Framework (World Bank) |
| CGE | Centre for the Study of Global Ethics (University of Birmingham) |
| DIRGD | Guatemalan Inter-religious Dialogue on Development |
| DDVE | Development Dialogue on Values and Ethics |
| EIFDDA | Ethiopian Interfaith Forum for Development Dialogue and Action |
| FBOs | faith-based organizations |
| FC | faith community |
| FMG | Friday Morning Group (World Bank) |
| GPE | global political economy |
| HIPC | Heavily Indebted Poor Countries initiative (World Bank) |
| IBRD | International Bank for Reconstruction and Development |
| IDA | International Development Association |
| IFC | International Finance Corporation |
| IFIs | international financial institutions |
| IGO | intergovernmental organization |
| ILO | International Labour Organization |
| IMF | International Monetary Fund |
| IIPE | international political economy |
| IO | international organization |
| IR | international relations |
| LDC | less developed country |
| MAP | Multi-country AIDS Projects (World Bank) |
| MDGs | Millennium Development Goals |
| MIGA | Multilateral Investment Guarantee Agency |
| MOU | Memorandum of Understanding (WBG-WFDD) |

| | |
|---|---|
| NGO | non-governmental organization |
| PACANet | Pan-African Christian AIDS Network |
| PRSPs | Poverty Reduction Strategy Papers (World Bank) |
| RGC | responsible global capitalism |
| SAPs | structural adjustment programmes (World Bank) |
| TAP | Treatment Acceleration Program (World Bank) |
| UNCTAD | United Nations Conference on Trade and Development |
| UNDP | United Nations Development Programme |
| WBG | World Bank Group (WBG) |
| WCC | World Council of Churches |
| WDR | World Development Report |
| WFDA | Women, Faith and Development Alliance |
| WFDD | World Faiths Development Dialogue |
| WFDD-B(1–16) | World Faiths Development Dialogue Bulletins (1–16) |
| WFDD-OP(1–5) | World Faiths Development Dialogue Occasional Paper (1–5) |
| WHO | World Health Organization |
| WTO | World Trade Organization |
| WWF | World Wide Fund for Nature |

# Foreword

## Scott M. Thomas

There is now a growing literature bringing the concerns of culture and religion into our understanding of international relations, international development and international security. Where is one to begin reading, and what does one expect to find in this reading? Also, where can one go for the kind of critical engagement with this literature that encourages us to step back and ask some of the larger, harder, questions – such as, while it might be easy to recognize why the study of culture and religion were marginalized in international relations, it is particulary more troublesome to ask, given the almost inherent religiosity of the global South, why culture and religion were marginalized for so long in the study of international development? What, therefore, is the purpose of bringing religion into our understanding of international development, and who is to do it, what is the agenda, who controls it and who benefits from doing this? What does it mean to talk about religious or 'faith-based' actors, and what do they bring that secular actors do not bring to the practice of international development; or is this even the right question to ask? This book by John Rees provocatively asks these kind of questions in an engaging way, but also in a way that directly tries to link theoretical debates to a very specific and very important case study – the rise and fall of the World Bank's partnerships with religious actors, and its participation in the World Faiths Development Dialogue, as the largest multilateral development institution in international development.

The book begins by setting out a 'dynamics of religion model' – how sacred and secular elements are combined, how ideological differences separate religious actors, which maps out the terrain of the current debates, discourses and key scholars who have contributed to bringing religion into the study of international relations and international development. The book uses this model to evelute the often conflicting values, goals and assumptions behind the secular and religious organizations that have become indentified with the 'religious turn' in international relations and international development. It is then from the case study of the World Bank that the book examines many of these crucial, critical, questions, and in this way, now amidst all the concerns of policy-makers and politicians regarding religion, failed states, nation-building and terrorism, offers a much needed critical evaluation of the way religion has come into international development.

The crucial point of departure for this book is the way the dynamics of religion model is used to evaluate the World Bank's partnerships with religious actors as a type of engagement with religion from within the mainstream global development agenda. This enables the book to critically evaluate the World Bank in relation to some of the other well-known approaches to religion and development, such as the *Fes* Colloquium, the World Council of Churches and the Community of Sant'Egidio. It does so in a way that shows up the limitations that more formal relations between the World Bank and religious actors can place on enabling religious actors to contest some of the dominant ideas and practices in international development.

The problem is that the World Bank and Western donor governments are interested in religious actors at the delivery level of policy, and this can limit, or more likely exclude, the religious substance of development – core religious voices, perspectives and resources. Governments, quite understandably, aren't interested in engaging with religious organizations that are more interested in speaking truth to power, than in becoming part of the global development agenda of Western donor governments. On the other hand, this important book shows what can be done when secular organizations increasingly recognize the religiosity of the people of the global South, and their understanding of the role of religion in their own lives and in their interpretation of wellbeing and development.

**Scott M. Thomas** lectures in international relations and the politics of developing countries at the University of Bath, and is a research fellow in the Centre for Christianity and Interreligious Dialogue, Heythrop College, University of London. He is the author of *The Gobal Resurgence of Religion and the Transformation of International Relations* (Palgrave, 2005).

# Acknowledgements

I wish to thank Mr Edward Elgar and the editorial staff of Edward Elgar Publishing for their interest in my work and for guiding this project to completion.

The following people have offered indispensable advice, correction and wisdom during the research and writing of this book: sincere thanks to Marc Williams and Gavin Kitching of the School of Social Sciences and International Studies, University of New South Wales (UNSW); and Scott Thomas (University of Bath), Jeffrey Haynes (London Metropolitan University) and Anthony Langlois (Flinders University) for providing a critical and constructive assessment of the original research upon which this book is based. All lingering inadequacies that exist are mine alone.

Thanks to Katherine Marshall, former director of the World Bank Development Dialogue on Values and Ethics, and Michael Taylor and Wendy Tyndale, former directors of the World Faiths Development Dialogue, for participating in informal discussions at the preliminary stages of this research in February 2005.

I am personally and professionally indebted to Duncan McDuie-Ra, Senior Lecturer in Development Studies at the School of Social Sciences and International Studies, UNSW. Duncan's friendship is dearly held and I am honoured to include a portion of our collaborative research in this book. Thanks also to Peter Dean and my colleagues at the School of Arts and Sciences, University of Notre Dame Australia, and to Isabel Yaya for her friendship and support.

I dedicate this book to my parents Jennifer and Tudno Rees, and to my dearly loved son Patrick Phillipson Rees who gives me life and hope beyond measure.

\* \* \*

The author and publishers wish to thank the following who have kindly given permission for the use of copyright material:

- John Wiley and Sons for article 'Religious actors, civil society and the development agenda: the dynamics of inclusion and exclusion', *Journal of International Development*, (2010) **22**, 20–36.

- SAGE Publications for article 'Book reviews in religion and politics', *Millennium*, (2007) **35** (3), 813–17.
- Taylor and Francis/Routledge for article '"Really existing" scriptures: on the use of sacred text in international affairs' (2004), *The Review of Faith and International Affairs*, **2** (1), 17–26. The journal can be accessed at www.informaworld.com.

Every effort has been made to trace all the copyright holders but if any have been inadvertently overlooked the publishers will be pleased to make the necessary arrangements at the first opportunity.

**John Anthony Rees**
Sydney, August 2011

# Introduction

This book takes as its subject the discourse on religion in international relations (IR). The study of religion in IR is now as prominent as it was once neglected. Propelled by 'a cottage industry of religion-and-world-affairs conferences, hearings, publications, media coverage, and foundation grants' (Hoover, 2006, p. 1) a wave of IR analysis now seems concerned with how – not whether – research should proceed apace. The research agenda has thus moved beyond the mere 'discovery' of religion in international affairs and can be more thoroughly understood in the context of a new religionism generated by a broad spectrum of scholars who assume that religious actors and interests exist as normal rather than exotic elements in world politics. The imperative to reconsider IR concepts and methodology on the subject of religion is also strengthened at an empirical level, summarized by Jonathan Fox thus:

> A fuller picture of the world's religious economy would show secularization – the reduction of religion's influence in society – occurring in some parts of the religious economy, and sacralization – the increase of religion's influence in society – occurring in other parts. (Fox, 2008, p. 7)

Making sense of such a picture is challenging because, as the noted sociologist of religion Peter Berger succinctly attests, 'the relation between religion and modernity is rather complicated' (Berger, 1999, p. 3). It is here that IR potentially comes into its own by situating the study of religion in the analysis of global structures and interests. As Vendulka Kubalkova notes, the international context within which the worldwide resurgence of religion takes place is the primary domain of IR expertise (Kubalkova, 2000, p. 675). The new frontiers of religion research in IR will therefore be found in attempts to further analyze the perceived 'religious turn' in world politics without pushing the analysis of political religion *in toto* toward either secular or sacral poles.

A roundtable discussion at the 2006 International Studies Association (ISA) Convention addressed the topic 'Religion and the Study of International Relations' via two questions: 'Where do we go from here?' and 'Why does it matter?' (ISA, 2006, pp. 224–5). Formulating a new research agenda around such questions is difficult because the resurgence of religion in contemporary world politics presents a conceptual and methodological challenge to the secular-modern foundations of IR itself (Keddie, 2003). The first question – Where do we go from here? – must be answered at the conceptual level, heeding John Madeley's call for the development of 'alternative systems of amicable accommodation' between secular theorists and religionists as 'an urgent political priority [and] a standing challenge to political science' (Madeley, 2003, p. xxii). The second question – Why does it matter? – must be engaged at the level of methodology, a challenge succinctly problematized by Elizabeth Shakman Hurd: 'Conventional understandings of international relations . . . exclude from the start the possibility that religion could be *a fundamental organizing force* in the international system' (Hurd, 2008, p. 1, emphasis added). These new frontiers in the discipline emphasize the point that to continue 'bringing religion in' to IR will require more than simply 'adding religion' to existing discourses of the discipline (S.M. Thomas, 2005, p. 76).

## APPROACHING THE STUDY OF RELIGION

As social scientific discussions of religion are highly contested, it is important to establish some parameters for the present study. Jeffrey Haynes offers a useful three-fold starting definition of religion as follows:

> . . . religion is to do with: the idea of *transcendence*, that is, it relates to supernatural realities; with *sacredness*, that is, as a system of language and practice that organizes the world in terms of what is deemed holy; and with *ultimacy*, that is, it relates people to the ultimate conditions of existence. (Haynes, 2006, p. 223, emphasis in original)

One important addition to make to the emphasis on language and practice is the role of the social group as a constituent element in religious faith itself, thus emphasizing what Scott Thomas calls a 'social definition of religion . . . as a "community of believers" rather than as a "body of beliefs"' (S.M. Thomas, 2005, p. 24). With these introductory elements of religion now in mind, further complexities and distinctions need to be recognized.

Moving beyond generalized starting definitions of religion is difficult to achieve. An analogy from early Christian history may help to illustrate this point further. Isidore of Seville, Catholic saint from the sixth and seventh centuries, once wrote that if anyone told you he had read all the works of Augustine he was a liar (Brown, 1972, p. 25). It was a warning against the pretension to have captured Augustinian thought; not just to have read the 117 known works of this giant of late antiquity, but to know his mind. A modern Isidore might suggest it wiser to frame any treatment of Augustine within specific referents such as history, philosophy, theology, ethics or politics, all fields in which Augustinian thought remain to some degree influential. That Augustine Bishop of Hippo was a religious figure symbolizes the challenge facing any analysis of 'religion' across the myriad fields in which it can be studied. 'Which Augustine?' becomes 'which religion?', and 'which religion?' becomes 'which tradition?' and 'whose tradition practised in which place?' and 'from which sources?' and 'on behalf of whom?' and so on. These distinctions, which echo an Augustinian view about the complexity of political society itself,[1] are important for developing nuanced conceptualizations of 'religion' which are of potential value to those who participate in any political enterprise with, or as, religious actors. From both a conceptual and applied vantage any pretension to have captured 'religion' is thus countered by the imperative to engage with mere parts of it, acknowledging as Derrida once did that to read religion is 'an experience that leaves nothing intact' (Derrida, 1995, p. 120).

One conceptual approach that helps bring some order and control to the study of religion can be found in the distinction between what Lawrence Hinman has called the 'impartial' and 'particular' characteristics of moral beliefs (Hinman, 1998, pp. 14–19). Utilizing this distinction religion can be attributed with both impartial or generic characteristics common to all faiths, and particular or specific characteristics unique to some faiths and not to others (see Hinman, 1998, pp.76–119). Hence, for IR scholars such as John Esposito and Michael Watson "religion" is taken to denote the major faiths considered as "world religions", namely having today a world-wide presence and open to any human beings' within a research agenda concerned with both 'a generic focus on religion and specifically, of individual world faiths' (Esposito and Watson, 2000, pp. 2, 17–37). Carsten Bagge Lausten and Ole Waever's definition of religion also contains particular and impartial characteristics:

> Religion deals with the constitution of being through acts of faith . . . Religion is a fundamental discourse answering questions like why being, why law, why existence? It is difficult not to pose such questions. Answers to such questions have the character of transcendental justification, and do as such anchor being (and societies). (Lausten and Waever, 2000, p. 738)

Answers to 'why?' (and indeed 'why not?') questions diverge greatly between religions (that is, particularity). Yet the enacting of the answers to such questions in the political sphere often produces a continuity of response (that is, impartiality) as particular religions are aligned and realigned with others by political interests and ideology. Haynes identifies three approaches to religion useful for the purpose of social investigation:

1) from the perspective of a body of ideas and outlooks – that is, as theology and ethical code; 2) as a type of formal organization – that is, the ecclesiastical 'church', or 3) as a social group – that is, religious groups or movements. (Haynes, 2007a, p. 12)

Each of these approaches arguably has impartial and particular dimensions. Ideas and outlooks differ yet common ground between such differences is often found. At the edge of particularity lies fundamentalism that is 'to a greater or lesser degree, intolerant of differences and disagreements' (Hinman, 1998, p. 113). At the edge of impartiality lies an ecumenism characterized by a pluralism of belief and an understanding of particular traditions as fallible (Hinman, 1998, p. 113).

From the perspective of formal organization religious polity is both particular and universal. Whilst distinct ritual traditions may shape the institutional forms of religion in particular ways, mainstream institutions each share the seemingly universal organizational challenges of maintaining stable internal and external relations of power. Yet important distinctions between religions can be made against the latter criterion, notably in relation to differences in the political milieu that organized religion must operate within. Jonathan Fox's important study of religion and the state attempts to develop a scale of 'government involvement in religion (GIR)' in the period 1990–2002 that is 'based on state behaviour rather than just on whether the state has an official religion' (Fox, 2008, p. 42). At the institutional level, the study 'showed measurable differences in official [state] support between religious traditions' (2008, p. 67) and a significant increase in the level of religious discrimination (2008, pp. 69–71).

Third, at the level of the social group religion becomes closely linked to cultural practice of a formal and informal nature. The distinction between religious groups that embody dominant social values and religious movements that contest those values becomes important. The impartiality of religion can be potentially observed via the unifying effect of each position: groups of difference band together to protect common social values or to protest at the affront to those values. Particularity can equally be observed: the effect of cultural traditions to differentiate between religious groups, and also in the different nomenclatures and ritual responses religious groups bring to the social discourse in particular contexts. Yet this emphasis on the multiple socialities of religion returns us to the difficulty of a universal definition of 'religion'. As the anthropologist Talal Asad has argued, 'not only because its constituent elements and relationships are historically specific, but because that definition [of religion] is itself the historical product of discursive processes' (Asad, 1993, p. 29). This is a perennial tension that should not be lost and is one that confronts and implicates policy-makers dealing with religious actors and interests at multiple levels of politics.

## AIMS, OBJECTIVES AND ARGUMENTS

The aim of this book is to build on the established foundations of IR studies in religion to develop a new approach to the study of religion in IR at both the conceptual and methodological levels. Conceptually, I propose a new analytical approach that 'amicably accommodates' (after Madeley, 2003, p. xxii) the concomitant realities of secularization and sacralization in contemporary world politics (after Fox, 2008, p. 7). Methodologically, this new approach is operationalized as an 'organizing force' (after Hurd, 2008, p. 1) via the study of religion within the IR subfield of international development. More specifically, it is applied to a case study of interactions between the World Bank and faith institutions and communities.

I understand a discourse to comprise both normative and empirical elements and therefore grant equal legitimacy to the values that theorists hold and the data that theorists observe (Marsh and Furlong, 2002, p. 35; Pollins, 2007). The epistemological moorings of the book may therefore be described as 'interpretivist' but not without a recognition that external facts can and do influence the constructions of social theory (see Wendt, 1999, p. 90). Further discussions on religion and epistemology will tend to be bound by IR scholarship. This is employed as a mechanism of control and in recognition that the present book builds upon well-established foundations in the field.

The aim of the book is achieved via four objectives: to develop a new structure in the study of world politics; to pose a new question for religion research in IR; to construct a new model for differentiating religion in IR contexts; and to gain new insights into the impacts of religion in international development.

### (a)   A New Structure

In Chapter 1 I shall argue that there are three distinct discourses of religion inscribed upon the general discourse of IR. The secular discourse subordinates religious actors and agendas to more dominant structures and ideologies of world politics. By contrast, the sacral discourse holds religion to be the primary element in political belief and structure, thereby shaping the direction and impacts of world politics. The distinction between these discourses is effectively summarized by Jonathan Fox and Shmuel Sandler: 'while religion is sometimes a tool used by other forces, it also has an independent influence' (Fox and Sandler, 2006, p. 178). Added to the secular and sacral discourses is a third, the integrated discourse of religion in IR. In the integrated discourse the secular and sacral discourses of IR are mutually constitutive, informing and in turn being formed by the opposite approach. Ultimately, the mutual constitution of secular and sacral elements of world politics represented by the integrated discourse of IR necessitates the construction of a new analytical structure that I have simply called the religious structure of IR. Such an approach amicably accommodates co-existing evidence for secularization and sacralization.

### (b)   A New Question

Having established a new structure within which to consider the question of religion in world politics a new line of enquiry is proposed that drives the study further. I shall argue that scholars must begin with the question 'Where is religion?' in relation to the secular and sacral interests that shape world politics before asking 'What is religion?' in relation to value-driven debates such as tradition versus modernity or peace versus violence. The reflex toward the latter question is strong and stems from a long-held (and often very reasonable) secularist intention to 'contain' the negative effects of religion in the political domain. Yet posing a new question that first situates religion in world affairs allows the potential to differentiate religious elements in the international system without being constrained by prior assumptions. Religious actors and interests can be found in different places, aligned with different interests, and it is important to know why this is. Such an approach is designed to challenge a deeply rooted modernist tendency in social science that assumes to know a priori where the elements of religion are and what normative functions they carry. As Richard Roberts suggests, 'the sociological imagination as classically deployed undercuts religious and theological pretensions' (Roberts, 2002, p. 191). As a corrective to this, the extent and limits of religion will be rightly comprehended only when IR scholars situate religion within the dynamics of world politics before analysing religion in normative terms.

### (c)   A New Model

The new structure and new question help to construct a new model for analysing religion in IR that I have named the dynamics of religion model. What is a model and why is it important for the present study? Hugh Ward usefully defines social-scientific models as 'simplified representations of reality [that] force us to attend to what we want to explain, what is central to explaining phenomena we are interested in and what can be left out of the model as peripheral or unimportant' (Ward, (1995) [2002], p. 69). Whilst models in political science are popular with rational choice methodologies that proceed by 'applying logic and mathematics to a set of assumptions' (Ward, (1995) [2002], p. 69), they are also employed in fields less formed by positivist epistemologies. For instance, in religious studies John Elliott defines a social model as follows:

> An abstract selective representation of the relationships among social phenomena used to conceptualise, analyze, and interpret patterns of social relations, and to compare and contrast one system of social relations with another. Models are heuristic constructs that operationalize particular theories and that range in scope and complexity according to the phenomena to be analyzed. (Elliott, 1993, p. 132)

Rabbi and political theorist Jonathan Sacks offers a more discursive insight when he writes 'sometimes it is helpful to simplify, to draw a diagram rather than a map, in order to understand what may be at stake in a social transition' (Sacks, 1997, p. 55). This view neatly summarizes the rationale behind my construction of a model to simplify and differentiate the complex elements of religion that exist in the international system. Important qualitative questions arise from such an approach. Do social patterns and policy discourses on specific phenomena in world politics coalesce around secular theories (ones that reduce or relativize the priority of religion) in ways that are different to sacral theories (ones that attribute religion with primary agency)? Might, in turn, these patterns and policy discourses be ordered differently if we changed the phenomena we are studying? In this book the dynamics of religion model is developed by reading the phenomena of IR through the lens of the religious structure of world politics. The model differentiates the elements of religion at work in the international system and also situates those elements in relation to the dominant agendas of world politics by noting where religious actors are included in discourses of power and where they are excluded from those discourses.

### (d)   New Insights

In this book the dynamics of religion model is applied to a study of international development. Concomitant with the resurgence of religion in world politics is an emerging focus on religion in development studies. Where is religion situated in the theory and practice of development today? New insights are gained in response to this question when the divergent schools of development are situated within the religious structure of IR. Building on this, the case study considers the impact of religious agency upon the policy and practice of the World Bank, the largest multilateral development institution in world politics. The World Bank is defined in secular-sacral terms, and World Bank partnerships with religious actors in development are differentiated using the dynamics of religion model. Such an approach offers a select view of religious actors in relation to the World Bank and by inference to the global development agenda. Importantly, the model also highlights where and upon what basis religious actors and interests are included in the global development agenda and where they are excluded. I argue that without the new insights into religion in development provided by the application of the dynamics of religion model, analysis of one of the most important issues to emerge in the field of development policy and practice cannot adequately progress.

## CONTRIBUTION OF THE BOOK

This book arguably makes three distinct contributions to the study of religion in IR and development. First, it creates a new way of thinking about religion in IR. In doing so, this study answers the conceptual and methodological challenges in religion research that I have previously identified. These challenges are answered by placing a new question – 'Where is religion?' – at the centre of the research agenda, and by developing policy based on the 'spatial' differentiations of religious actors and interests within the religious structure proposed. The conceptual and methodological approaches so described do not exist in any introductory textbook of IR nor in any specialized consideration of IR and religion.

Second, this book creates new ways of thinking about religion and development and specifically a new perspective on religion and the World Bank. At the conclusion of their important study on religion and IR, Fox and Sandler suggest a core unresolved question in the field is as follows: 'How do you make a concrete study of a topic that is often ambiguous and open to multiple interpretations? In more social scientific terms, how do you put together hard data on an inherently soft topic?' (Fox and Sandler, 2006, p. 179) I answer this question by operationalizing the heuristic model through the study on religion and development. In this way the ambiguities of religion are grounded in the specific discourse of development and in the concrete institutional setting of the World Bank. What do we 'see' that we otherwise would not see by situating the World Bank in a religious analytical structure? Where is religion situated in the policy domain of the World Bank? By determining where religion 'is' can we begin to assess the impacts of religion upon the ideology of the World Bank? The present book attempts to answer these sort of questions. Of equal importance, it seeks to present a methodology than can be applied to many other sub-fields of IR beyond development.

A third contribution to knowledge is the case study of engagements with religion by the World Bank. Though a handful of studies have considered this topic the present book advances the research agenda in three ways: First, the research applies the analytical model to differentiate the distinct dynamics of religion at play to initially influence the World Bank on the question of religion, offering insights into the diverse nature of those influences. Second, the model is applied to critically differentiate the dynamics of religion between three pilot partnerships by the World Bank with religious actors in development, and to critically differentiate within an important fourth partnership involving a semi-autonomous non-government organization (NGO) known as the World Faiths Development Dialogue (WFDD). Third, the study of the World Bank and faith institutions concludes with an analysis of the dynamics of exclusion and inclusion toward religious actors in the global development agenda and the conceptual and instrumental consequences for policy that ensue from these dynamics. Such a perspective is at the frontier of new thinking about religion and development and has not emerged in the specific forms presented here.

## STRUCTURE OF THE BOOK

The opening two chapters establish the conceptual and methodological foundations of the study. The remaining chapters apply these concepts and methods to the study of religion in international development. A synopsis of each chapter follows.

Chapter 1 advances the research agenda by identifying three discourses on religion in IR. The first is simply identified as 'the secular discourse' and is the oldest and most dominant discourse on religion in the field. In the secular discourse religion is understood as a subordinate element to other more prominent factors in world politics. The second discourse is identified simply as 'the sacral discourse' in which religion is understood as a primary element that shapes the dynamics of world politics. A third discourse is named as 'the integrated discourse' and represents an emerging consensus on religion study in the field. In the integrated discourse on religion in IR, secular and sacral discourses are identified as mutually constitutive elements of political events and analysis. As the description suggests the integrated discourse links secular and sacral emphases together.

In Chapter 2 the binding effect of the integrated discourse is utilized in the construction of a simple analytical framework I have called the dynamics of religion model. The integration of the discourses of religion is examined from conceptual perspectives drawn from IR scholarship on religion, broader principles of epistemology in IR and the philosophical consideration of secularism itself. The interlinkages between secular, integrated and sacral dynamics of religion create the religious structure of world politics against which the dynamics of religion model can be applied. The model is completed when specific themes of world politics are situated within and throughout the religious structure. This approach not only differentiates the elements of religion on a given issue in international affairs, Chapter 2 also attempts to reveal where the elements of religion may lie in relation to the prevailing centres of power. The remaining chapters attempt to highlight both characteristics of religion in the theory and practice of international development.

The analysis of religion and international development occurs at three levels: discourse, institutions and policy. At the level of discourse Chapter 3 identifies the domain of international development as an appropriate sphere to further explore the contours of religion in world politics. The chapter models the 'orthodox' and 'critical' schools of development theory against the dimensions of religion model. For instance, the dynamics of religion are of secondary importance within orthodox development approaches that prioritize state power and economic measures. However, changes in the orthodox discourse of development have also seen an increased engagement with religious development organizations, at times creating an integrated dynamic between secular and sacral interests. Similarly, the dynamics of religion are of secondary importance within critical approaches that critique perceived asymmetries of power within mainstream development practice. Yet the agency of religious actors in contesting and reshaping development priorities reveals a more integrated dynamic of religion within the critical development tradition. Employed in these ways, the dynamics of religion model reorders the discourse of development. For example, it reorders the consensus on development according to the criterion of religious agency. Development approaches hitherto considered oppositional in orientation become realigned according to whether they hold religion to be a secondary, integrated or primary element in development. For instance, orthodox and critical approaches are now linked by the secular subordination of religion in some instances, and by partnerships that attempt to integrate secular and sacral religious dynamics in others. In many respects, deep cultural engagements in development that grant primary agency of religion in development remain outside different expressions of the orthodox-critical consensus. This realignment of consensus raises the possibility that differences within schools of development toward religion are important and undervalued areas of policy analysis. Applied in these sorts of ways, the dynamics of religion becomes an organizing force highlighting the differentiated nature of religion in the theory and practice of development. Situating religion throughout the development discourse increases our capacity to analyze specific contexts of religion and development.

At the level of institutions Chapter 4 focuses on the engagement with religious development actors by the World Bank Group (WBG). The WBG is defined primarily as an institutional arena of contestation between competing ideologies of development. The WBG plays a central role in negotiating and setting the global development agenda and is thus an important object of analysis. The dynamics of religion model is first applied to perceive the agency of religion in four phases of the WBG's evolution. This analysis identifies a shift from the strong subordination of religion in the early phases of the WBG to an engagement with religious actors in advocacy networks opposed to WBG policy, and finally to an engagement with religious actors and interests leading to 'faith and development' dialogues and policy partnerships. More specifically, the model helps to discern the dynamics of religion that entered the institutional domain of the WBG, differentiating secular, integrated and sacral interests at work between the 1980s and the early years of the presidency of James Wolfensohn in the mid-1990s. Secular dynamics over this period include engagements with religion modelled by other international organizations and Wolfensohn's instrumental rationale to engage religious actors in development. Integrated dynamics include the role that religious groups played in effective campaigns to influence development policy on the environment and the authority attributed to religious leaders and services in the findings of the WBG study *Voices of the Poor*. Sacral dynamics influencing WBG policy toward religion include a regular religion and ethics forum among WBG staff begun in 1981 called the Friday Morning Group and the Jubilee 2000 debt advocacy campaign. The dynamics of religion model is then employed to situate the secular, integrated and sacral dynamics of religion influencing WBG policy toward religion, and to highlight those elements that are external (and potentially disruptive) to WBG policy, from those that are internal (and potentially co-optive) to WBG policy. Applications such as these help to discern the relative agency of secular and sacral dynamics of religion upon the WBG's introductory phase in dealing with religious actors and interests. This initial modelling acts as a foundation for closer analyzes of the dynamics of religion in the policy formation process.

At the policy level, the dynamics of religion model is applied in Chapter 5 to describe and critically analyze partnerships between the WBG and faith institutions that emerged in the period 1998–2005. The study initially compares WBG partnerships with three faith institutions – the *Fes*

Festival of Sacred Music, the World Council of Churches (WCC) and the Community of Sant'Egidio. Between 2001 and 2006, the *Fes* festival hosted the *Fes* Colloquium, a forum jointly sponsored by the WBG designed for participants to engage in direct dialogue on the contentions between globalization and culture. The study employs the dynamics of religion model to describe this initiative as a harmonious partnership within the ideological sphere of the WBG where the agency of religion is secondary to other dynamics. The WBG entered into a formal dialogue with the WCC in February 2003. The dialogues that ensued were characterized by deeply rooted differences in approaches to development between the participants. The present study employs the dynamics of religion model to describe the dialogue as a conflictual partnership where both participants are attempting to integrate the dynamics of religion, but from different ideological positions. Thus, situating religion in different places within the structure of international development reinforces an oppositional dynamic that places significant obstacles in the way of partnership. The Community of Sant'Egidio is a noted actor in the area of conflict mediation and health services delivery. Using Sant'Egidio's established roots in Mozambique, the WBG established a pilot effort in the treatment of HIV/AIDS. Sant'Egidio joined the Treatment Acceleration Program (TAP) funded by the International Development Association (IDA), as part of its operation of ten day hospitals in Mozambique. However the partnership in the TAP is contrasted with a breakdown in negotiations over Sant'Egidio's participation in the IDA-funded Multi-country AIDS Projects (MAP), the main WBG strategic plan for addressing HIV/AIDS. The model is employed to observe two dynamics at work. The first represents an integrated secular-sacral approach toward HIV/AIDS patient care that builds capacity through the TAP. The second de-links the partners over the issue of prevention on religious grounds, highlighting the agency of sacral views in the service delivery of faith institutions. Only the TAP initiative can be considered a partnership. The model highlights in different ways that partnerships between religious actors and international financial institutions (IFIs) such as the WBG require integration between secular and sacral ideologies toward agreed development goals, the attainment of which can be difficult.

A modest case study in Chapter 6 attempts to differentiate the dynamics of religion in a unique partnership between the WBG and the WFDD in the period 1998–2005. The WFDD is a semi-autonomous faith-based organization (FBO) founded in 1998 following high-level networking between WBG officials and religious leaders. As such, the WBG-WFDD embodies direct policy dynamics of the WBG faith and development initiative of the Wolfensohn presidency. The dynamics of religion model highlights in specific ways the divergent elements of religion that shape the partnership and the policy formation process. The study describes and analyzes the life cycle of the WBG-WFDD partnership according to three phases: integration, contestation and disintegration. In summary, the original rationale of the WBG-WFDD partnership was to combine WBG expertise with WFDD access to grass-roots development contexts through the actions of faith communities. However the momentum of the early phase of the partnership is significantly impeded when Wolfensohn's proposal for a more expansive programme was unanimously rejected by the WBG Executive Board in late 2000. This highlights an important distinction between secular and integrated approaches to religious agency within development orthodoxy. WFDD structural and staffing problems ensued although existing reporting work is also consolidated. The work of the WFDD is sacral, producing an invaluable store of case study material on religious development activities and priorities. It is also integrated, using the development practice of faith institutions as a resource for mainstream global development approaches. Yet from 2002 there is a movement toward critical development priorities among the WFDD constituency, creating an ideological division and consolidating concerns among WFDD stakeholders concerning a lack of autonomy from the WBG. Leadership changes at the WFDD and the end of the Wolfensohn era in 2005 lead to the WBG-WFDD partnership being placed in hibernation and undergoing a period of reassessment. Using the dynamics of religion model, the study shows that each phase of the partnership shifted core elements away from the zone of integration toward distinct and eventually compartmentalized positions within the religious structure of world politics. The study therefore highlights the disintegrating dynamics that confront orthodox attempts to engage with religious actors and interests.

Chapter 7 concludes the study of the World Bank and faith institutions by combining the dynamics of religion model with assumptions drawn from the critical development school. A critical development typology classifies religious actors into one of three categories: formalized religious actors based in the 'global North', formalized religious actors based in the 'global South' and informal religious actors based in the 'global South'. Formality is measured by organizational capacity on reporting and administration relevant to the reporting demands of agenda-setting institutions such as the WBG. Formality is linked to the commonly used term faith-based organization (FBO). Informality, by contrast, is measured by localized activities of development that lack the capacity of formal reporting and procedures or grant secondary importance to the demands of formality in deference to alternative beliefs and practices. I link this definition of informality to the term faith-community (FC). FBOs and FCs associated with the WBG are categorized within a critical development typology, highlighting three characteristics. The first is a priority toward formalized organizations. The second is that engagements with religious actors categorized as informal are more problematic for the WBG. The third is that not all formalized Northern FBOs conform to the dictates of the global development agenda, thus highlighting the role religious institutions play in contesting and negotiating the development agenda in the North. Finally, the dynamics of religion model is combined to differentiate FBOs and FCs within the religious structure of international development. It is argued that secularity has a strong linkage to formality, aligning the institutional demands of development orthodoxy to FBOs that operate in a large-scale, centralized – and often monotheistic – milieu. Development partnerships bonded by secular formality are certainly breaking new ground by including religious actors in the extant development agenda. Yet such ventures place significant restrictions on the nature of faith and development partnerships by excluding FCs who cannot – or choose not to – comply to the demands of formality that the development agenda requires. Therefore, FCs are arguably the missing sacral element in the pursuit of a deeper engagement with religious actors in the practice of development. Unless this dynamic of excluding sacral communities from the development agenda can be corrected, the so-called turn to religion in development practice will remain limited.

## METHODS AND SOURCES

I shall briefly explain several aspects of the research methodology employed in the book. The first involves the construction and use of an analytical model at the forefront of the research. Once the model is established in Chapter 1 the remaining analysis is structured by that model. Put simply, a model is not an answer to a question but a tool of analysis used in pursuit of an answer. Thus the model constructed and employed in the present research is not designed to reveal what religion is in a singular sense, but rather, where distinct elements of religion can be situated in relation to the dynamics of world politics under examination. Models are also employed to reveal the limitations of research and can point to new, often modified applications. Therefore the present research seeks in no way to provide the final word on religion in IR, but instead, attempts to carry the analysis to a new stage.

The second aspect of methodology concerns the use of sources in conducting the primary study between the WBG and the WFDD. These comprised mainly of documentary resources generated by the WFDD and the

WBG. Informing my understanding of these sources were insights gained from preliminary discussions with key actors and observations from the field relevant to the WFDD. These discussions were held in February 2005 with Katherine Marshall, former director of the WBG Development Dialogue on Values and Ethics at the WBG offices in Washington, DC.[2] The WBG also granted this researcher visitor status at a forum called the Friday Morning Group.[3] The WFDD was based in the United Kingdom for the period under examination (1998–2005) and several informal discussions were held with WFDD staff and partners, including former directors Michael Taylor[4] and Wendy Tyndale[5] in Birmingham and Oxford, respectively. Despite these illuminating engagements the case study does not conform to the description of ethnography, which is more heavily reliant on 'extensive field notes' and 'relatively long-term relationships with informants' (Devine, 2002, p. 198). This limitation is partly because a preliminary field study was conducted at a time when the WFDD was classified as being 'in hibernation' awaiting decisions that would determine its future (World Bank, 2006). As such, case study research began at the end of the first incarnation of the WFDD (1998–2005). Moreover, in February 2005 the World Bank was nearing the end of the presidency of James Wolfensohn who played a central role in the WFDD initiative. The end of the Wolfensohn era marked a time of operational and missional uncertainty for the WBG. The religion and development initiative was not insulated from this, and indeed its viability was more vulnerable to change than many of the World Bank's more core operations. Quite understandably, research discussions conducted in the period reflected this caution. In sum, the case study research is informed by documentary-based analysis rather than field work observation, however the latter element provided an essential contextual frame through which to read the documentary record.

The majority of documentary sources for the description and analysis of the WFDD come from the principal partners. Whilst the existence of the WFDD is acknowledged and granted limited commentary in the emerging literature on religion and development (for example, Haynes, 2007b, p. 11; Clarke and Jennings, 2008a, p. 2) very few independent academic sources make reference to the WFDD in any substantive analytical sense (Pallas, 2005; S.M. Thomas, 2005, pp. 225–33; Clarke, 2007). Knowledge about the WFDD, therefore, is attained from WBG sources such as published conference/dialogue proceedings (for example, Marshall and Marsh, 2003; Marshall and Keough, 2005), detailed descriptive works on faith and development (Marshall and Keough, 2004; Marshall and Van Saanen, 2007), speeches (DDVE, n.d.), interviews (for example, Mumford, 2006) and articles addressing the World Bank's faiths and development programme (for example, Marshall, 2001), World Development Reports

(WDRs) and Poverty Reduction Strategy Papers (PRSPs) relevant to the WFDD (see PovertyNet, n.d.). The WFDD is the other source of primary research (WFDD, n.d. b), and includes WFDD Bulletins (for example, WFDD-B1, November 1998; WFDD-B16, March 2005) detailing decisions and programmes from November 1998 until March 2005, four occasional papers (for example, WFDD-OP1, 1998), joint publications (for example, Eade, 2002) and assessment reports.

## CONCEPTUAL ORIENTATIONS

Conceptually, the once dominant assumptions of secularization theory have come under sustained attack in the study of religion in world politics. Religious agency, observed through the growing importance of religious actors across a wide range of political contexts, challenges and reconfigures notions of the secular modern (Casanova, 1994; Bhargava, 1998; Berger, 1999; Connolly, 1999; Asad, 2003a). Religion has thus been posing an empirical challenge in the study of world politics for some time, and the discourse has now moved in important ways toward a consensus view that religious factors are an embedded component of many political dynamics in international affairs. Yet to a large degree the study of religious agency in IR has existed within the confines of an instrumental approach, perhaps reflecting what Cox famously described as 'problem solving' approaches to the world as it already exists (Cox, 1986). Beyond instrumentalism, could religion be explored at the conceptual level of IR, and would such an approach reconfigure and even disrupt understandings of the existing order of world politics? How might one do this without overemphasizing the importance of religion in a world that remains, in very fundamental ways, ordered by secular not religious influences? The most robust theoretical approaches to these empirical challenges are, it seems to me, incorporative rather than binary. Hence, Taylor's focus on the 'modes of secularism' (Taylor, 1998) and Asad's emphasis on the adaptive capacity of different notions of the secular modern (Asad, 2003) provided valuable frames for analyzing a growing body of empirical research challenging the assumption that religion was a diminishing concern in contemporary world affairs (Berger, 1999). Could these incorporative capacities be utilized in the construction of new conceptions of the international order or are they limited to observing, albeit in new ways, world politics as it already exists? The evolution of religion research in the field of IR has come to an impasse on this question. The secular moorings of IR have for some time been recognized as inadequate for the task for engaging religion (Wuthnow, 1991; Keohane, 2002; Tickner, 2006) yet these repeated assertions – as if perpetually caught in a 'ground-hog day' moment on the question of religion – only succeed in returning the discourse to the original dilemma of how to deal with religious agency in the modern world. The conceptual modelling and empirical analysis entailed in this research are designed to move the debate beyond this impasse, this moment of perpetual repetition. There are leaders in the field that have begun taking the discourse forward (for example, S.M. Thomas, 2005; Haynes, 2007a; Clarke, 2008a; Fox, 2008). The present book seeks to make a unique contribution to these efforts, strengthening the ground already laid and cutting new trails into terrain not yet fully explored.

## SCOPE AND LIMITATIONS

An inherent ambiguity exists when focusing on the dynamics of religion in IR. On the one hand, this focus refers to the treatment of religion and religious-based movements by IR scholars and those associated with a broader academic and philosophical discourse on religion and world politics. (Theologians, for instance, may not belong to the former but have certainly featured as important voices in the latter.) On the other hand, the phrase also attests to the role that religious actors and interests play in the political dynamics that IR scholars observe. Each emphasis is a component of what I mean by the term 'discourse' as the critical examination and interpretation of political dynamics in constant interaction with the dynamics themselves. The distinction between these components sets both the scope and the limitations of this study: the dynamics of religion model is conceptually grounded while the application of the model to international development connects concepts to identifiable events and organizations.

This ambiguity also determines the limitations of the book, both in a negative and positive sense. Negatively, the book is not intended to provide in-depth analysis of a broad range of religious ideas and religiously based movements at work in the international realm (or even in international development). If one is to take seriously the array of religious actors and interests that animate contemporary international affairs, such an endeavour would arguably fill a library of books and certainly not be represented in a single work. Positively, the analytical approach represented by the model is applied to a deeper exploration of a single domain of IR (religion in international development) and to specific subjects within that domain (WBG and faith institutions). Whilst the model is constructed and applied once, many other applications would be possible. Thus, while it is hoped that such an approach progresses an understanding of the dynamics of religion in a specific field, it also reminds us of how vast the horizon of religion research in world politics is and provokes further enquiry into what other applications of the ideas contained herein might be usefully attempted, either in their current or modified form.

## NOTES

1. 'We are linked to political society by something that somehow escapes our immediate consciousness, by a whole tangled skein of pressures and motives . . . Thus, Augustine will not give us a fully-worked "myth" [of the political]. Instead, he will do something more important when dealing with an intractable reality, he will tell us where it is worthwhile looking; and, in so doing, he will direct very bright beams into crucial areas of the human situation' (Brown, 1972, p. 27).
2. Discussion with Katherine Marshall (11 February 2005), Development Dialogue on Values and Ethics, World Bank, Human Development Network MSN, G6-603 (Office G6-085).
3. Friday Morning Group (11 February 2005, 7.45 am–9 am) 18th Street, Pennsylvania Avenue, Washington, DC – Private Dining Room D/E.
4. Discussion with Prof. Michael Taylor (17 February 2005), Department of Theology, University of Birmingham, Edgbaston, Birmingham, United Kingdom; discussion with Dr Christien Van Den Anker (14 February 2005), Centre for the Study of Global Ethics, University of Birmingham Priorsfield, 46 Edgbaston Park Road.
5. Discussion with Wendy Tyndale (18 February 2005), Oxford.

# 1. The discourses of religion in international politics

> We should never have known by what process truth is to be ascertained,
> if we had not previously ascertained many truths.
> John Stuart Mill, *On Liberty* (VIII, p. 833)

In Salman Rushdie's novel *Midnight's Children* the character Aadam Aziz is described as a man who was 'knocked forever into that middle place, unable to worship a God in whose existence he could not wholly disbelieve' (Rushdie, 1982, p. 12). Aziz journeyed from belief to unbelief yet ended in a psychological state somewhere in-between. This narrative serves as a metaphor about the study of religion in world politics. For IR scholars the journey has been taken in the opposite direction but the destination is the same: having emerged from securalist thought in the social sciences the contemporary resurgence of religion in world politics has knocked the discipline into a middle place where one cannot easily or quickly judge where the value and limits of religion lie. On the question of religious agency in world politics there now exist conceptual ambiguities and empirical realities that can seemingly no longer be denied. Yet despite the rise of religion as an object of analysis in IR, the terms of religion – the actors, communities, concepts and agendas that bring religion into the domain of world politics – are yet to be settled in the nomenclature of the discipline. Scholarship is therefore now moving into a new exploratory phase attempting to discover both the possibilities and limitations that religion carries for research.

In this context the present chapter develops three main arguments. First, secularism is an integral rather than an oppositional component of the study of religion, and this is important for IR approaches on the subject. Second, three distinct discourses on religion are inscribed across in the general discourse of IR of a secular, sacral and integrated nature. Third, the differentiation of religious discourses in IR leads to new methodological approaches and the creation of an analytical model applied to consider the dynamics of religion in specific domains of world politics.

## 1.1   SECULARISM AND RELIGION IN THE STUDY OF IR

My initial purpose is to emphasize the plurality of what 'secularism' means, both in theory and in practice as it relates to the study of world politics. I employ Hurd's general understanding of secularism as a 'set of discursive traditions that seeks to construct both the secular and the religious in particular ways' (Hurd, 2008, p. 44). From this plural approach we can better understand the contexts from which IR engages the question of secularism and its relation to religion in the international sphere. In what follows, I draw on recent scholarship to define secularism from a Western perspective, then reach beyond this to emphasize the global relevance of secularism and the implication that this has for the study of religion in IR.

Secularism was arguably born in Europe as one of the dominant effects of social, economic and political change that swept Europe from the fourteenth century (Kennedy, 2006, pp. 39ff.). Secularism today is variously defined as the human capacity to outgrow belief in the supernatural (Stark, 1999, p. 249), ethical discourse that is no longer framed by a theological perspective (Stout, 2004, p. 93) and the declining prestige of religious observance in scientific-industrial society (Gellner, 1992, p. 4). Yet even within these defined understandings secularism is a topic of 'staggering diversity' (Tschannen, 1991, p. 396) and this is made more so when understood from a global perspective. One notes, for instance, the qualifications and geographical shrinkage that characterize the opening sentences of Charles Taylor's seminal work *The Secular Age*:

> What does it mean to say that we live in a secular age? Almost everyone would agree that in some sense we do: I mean the 'we' who live in the West, or perhaps North-west, or otherwise put, the North Atlantic world – although secularity extends also partially, and in different ways, beyond this world. (Taylor, 2007, p. 1)

The secularism of which Taylor writes is defined as 'a move from a society where belief in God is unchallenged and indeed, unproblematic, to one in which it is understood to be one option among others, and frequently not the easiest to embrace' (2007, p. 3). From a socio-political perspective, secularism can be defined as the decline or containment of religion in society and in the minds of individuals (Berger, 1999, p. 2) such that identifiable religious ideas and traditions no longer shape the fundamental governance structures of a given polity. Such a notion underlies a Western tradition of secularism, one that Tambiah links to two interrelated processes: the impact upon scientific knowledge of theological developments associated with the Reformation, and the impact upon rational knowledge associated with the Enlightenment (Tambiah, 1998, p. 419).

Yet secularism did not mean the removal of God from the public sphere, even in the context of the rise of modernity in the West. As Taylor argued in an earlier work, whilst the modern social imaginary certainly removed one conception of God from the public sphere, even in the new world of modern nations 'the order of mutual benefit was originally seen as God-created, and its fulfilment as God-destined' (Taylor, 2004, p. 186). Such a view gives rise to civic religion in both the United States and Europe, and is accompanied by an increase in popular (and populist) spiritualities that define both the American frontier (Butler, 2000) and European romanticism. On the latter, Isaiah Berlin entertainingly wrote:

> perhaps somewhat to the surprise of people who believe the eighteenth century to have been a harmonious, symmetrical, infinitely rational, elegant, glassy sort of century . . . we find that never in the history of Europe had so many irrational persons wandered over its surface claiming adherence. (Berlin, 1999, p. 47)

Irrational or otherwise, religion in its formal and popular expressions cannot be extricated from the origins and contexts of modern secularism.

There are many alternatives to the Western conceptions of secularism described above, affirming Asad's view that 'the secular is neither singular in origin nor stable in its historical identity' (Asad, 2003a, p. 25). For instance, rather than studying secularism as a linear development within a narrow definition of modernity we begin to understand the secular as 'a concept that brings certain behaviours, knowledges, and sensibilities in modern life' (Asad, 2003a, p. 25). If European traditions emphasize the movement from belief to unbelief in the public sphere, Third World[1] understandings of secularization present a more complex view. According to one of these traditions, secularity is more akin to the notion of the equality of religions, and thereby concerned with the political status of minority religious groups rather than the diminishing of religion per se. In India, for example, the interpretation of secularism in the tradition of Gandhi and Nehru is effectively to treat religious communities in such a way that they may enjoy equality (Tambiah, 1998, pp. 420–3; Gould, 2004, p. 4). On the basis of such arguments secularism can be understood as a polysemous concept within which a diversity of assumptions and interests can operate.

Therefore, secularism is an integral rather than an oppositional component of the study of religion. This is important for appropriating voices of religious actors in a social scientific discipline such as IR. The arguments of political theologian Clodovis Boff are a valuable guide on how this might occur. Boff understands that a 'theology of the political' must engage with concepts of the political 'as articulated with the sciences of the social' (Boff, 1987, p. 51). Such an engagement should accordingly be governed by two principles: '1) respect for autonomy of the discipline in question; and 2) critique vis-à-vis all manner of dogmatism' (1987, p. 51). The autonomy that Boff attributes to social science is grounded in secularism 'which sets in relief the (relative) autonomy of earthly [that is, temporal] values'. As such secularity is linked to 'the rules relating to the evolution of a science' (1987, p. 51) and these rules should be respected:

> . . . to criticise science for bracketing realities such as God, spirit, the human being, and so on, and to accuse it of atheism, materialism, or antihumanism because it does so, is to betray an ignorance of science and of what constitutes science. It is like criticising a bird for having wings. (Boff, 1987, p. 51)

Yet the second principle for a theological engagement with social science 'refers mainly to its conclusions' (1987, p. 51) and it is here that critique by religious perspectives may legitimately occur. Whilst 'the theologian has no competency to tell the sociologist how to do sociology', for Boff, 'what the theologian may legitimately do is censure the sociologist's unwarranted premises or extrapolations' (1987, p. 52). Applying Boff's argument in the present study, we might say that it is undesirable to deconstruct the notion of secularism simply because religious voices have now, importantly and valuably, entered the conversation about world politics. Traditional secular approaches that exist at the foundations of a social science such as IR ought not therefore be revised or rejected out of hand. Despite the de-secular challenge it remains ill considered to pronounce *requiescat in pace* upon secularism as some have done (Stark, 1999, p. 270). On the other hand, it also seems legitimate for non-secular perspectives coming from theology or religious studies, and now from within sociology and political science, to critique the dogmatism of secularization as a linear schema that continues to marginalize religion in world politics in the face of contrary evidence. Connolly has identified this as one of the 'conceits of secularism' (Connolly, 1999, pp. 19–46). In this context, the theory of secularization can legitimately be reduced to the status of one concept among many (Hurd, 2008), even if secularism remains a fundamental element in the political sphere. 'To say the least', sums Berger, 'the relation between religion and modernity is rather complicated' (Berger, 1999, p. 3). This is another way of saying that the 'secular' and 'religious' exist in an ambiguous 'middle place' somewhere between belief and unbelief. Boff called his methodology 'socio-analytic mediation' (Boff, 1987, p. 10). It is in the conception of a mediatory place, between secular and sacral perspectives, that the analysis of religion in world politics is best situated. I presently suggest that the full spectrum of IR perspectives on religion therefore spans the full range of secular to de-secular views and should not be viewed within a framework that pits secular against religion in a zero-sum conflict. A more incorporative approach better informs the debate about whether religion can be employed as an organizing force in IR research as it requires a conceptual framework that both integrates and differentiates secular and sacral elements in order to deal with the analytical demands of religion in world politics today.

These characteristics serve as an introduction to religion, a topic that will be revisited in more specific ways throughout the book. To summarize, religion is a constituent feature of both secularism and non-secular alternatives to the study of world politics. Secularism does not mean the absence of religion. Rather, religion takes different forms and functions within secular and alternative conceptions of the political. In the opening pages of this book I cited Fox's observation of the world's religious economy via the concepts of secularization and sacralization (Fox, 2008, p. 7). Given the importance of religion to both secularism and its alternatives, the categories of 'secular' and 'sacral'[2] will now be employed as umbrella terms differentiating two broadly contrasting approaches toward religion in IR. Moreover, 'secular' and 'sacral' categories will also be employed as an organizing tool to order the discourses of IR on the issue of religion. Each discourse is summarized in Figure 1.1.

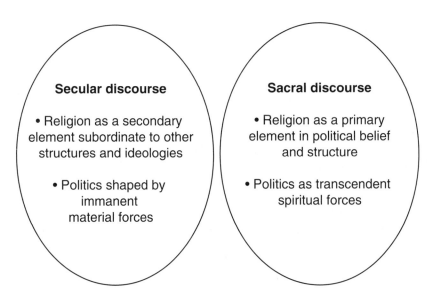

**Secular discourse**

• Religion as a secondary element subordinate to other structures and ideologies

• Politics shaped by immanent material forces

**Sacral discourse**

• Religion as a primary element in political belief and structure

• Politics as transcendent spiritual forces

*Figure 1.1    Secular and sacral discourses of IR*

The characteristics of each discourse will now be explored in more detail. I suggest that three distinct discourses on religion are inscribed upon the general discourse of IR. I begin by further identifying the secular discourse and the sacral discourse, and then introducing the integrated discourse that binds secular and sacral elements together.

## 1.2   THE SECULAR DISCOURSE OF IR

What I have termed the secular discourse of IR is the oldest and remains the most dominant discourse on religion in the discipline. As Hurd suggests, to a large extent IR still takes 'the Euro-American definition of religion and its separation of politics as the natural starting point for social-scientific inquiry' (Hurd, 2008, p. 23). The central characteristic of the secular discourse is the subordination of religion to other political actors and issues in the formation of public life. Hence, in the secular discourse religion is a secondary element in the dynamics of world politics. I shall investigate the characteristics of the secular discourse, explore possible differences within it and ask whether the secular conception encapsulates every dynamic of religion in world politics.

### 1.2.1   The *Daedalus* Compendia

The rush of interest in 'religion' today is contrasted by its slow development in the minds of scholars as a legitimate object of IR analysis. This places religion on similar ground to other 'late arriving' yet crucially important subjects in the field such as feminism (Youngs, 2004). The initial carriers of the explicit study of religion in IR were special editions surveying and analysing the rise of religion in world politics. For example, in 1991 the journal *Daedalus* produced a special edition on religion and politics[3] which was seen, in part, as a continuation of research began in 1973 into post-traditional societies.[4] These compendia were intended to critique modern theories of economic and political development 'with their too easy dismissal of history and culture', and notably, 'the continued importance of what some chose to see as merely residual values, redolent of another age, represented perhaps most conspicuously in the survival of religion' (Graubard, 1991, p. vi). To draw from the preface of the 1991 *Daedalus* compendium, such studies were seen to have 'challenged the idea that secularism and rationalism were universal goods, only waiting to be realised' (Graubard, 1991, p. vi). Thus 'religion' began to rise as a legitimate subject of analysis partly via the emergence of 'post' theories of society and development, and the broader challenges to secularization underway in social science. How did these special editions contribute to the legitimacy of 'religion' in the discourse of IR? A summary might be that 'religion' entered the discourses of IR through the doorway of development, and progressed toward more 'political' issues around governance and state security. Several articles from 1973 sought to emphasize the role of religious movements and traditions in the context of existing theoretical discourses on post-colonialism, world systems theory and the problems of secularization theory. As such, 'religion' functioned as an object rather than a subject, viewed or transmitted in the context of other more primary debates. For instance, Leach writes of 'Buddhism in the Post-Colonial Order' in Burma and Ceylon (Leach, 1973, pp. 29–52), and Mardin of 'Centre-Periphery Relations in Turkey' (Mardia, 1973, pp. 169–190), whilst others of the challenge to secularization theory by emphasizing the 'persistence' of religious traditions in South-East Asia (Bechert, 1973; Tambiah, 1973) or the political traditions embedded in the cultures of the Maghrib (Hermassi, 1973). For S.N. Einstadt, the focus on post-traditional societies was created 'to facilitate new ways of looking at certain central problems of modernization' (Einstadt, 1973, p. 1) which created a dichotomized relationship between 'traditional and modern societies' (1973, p. 1). It is no coincidence that Clifford Geertz's seminal article on interpreting culture as 'thick description', originally published in the discourses of anthropology (Geertz, 1973, pp. 3–30), was by the early 1970s receiving wide application throughout social science. In this context, and reflected in many of the articles of *Daedalus* 1973, religion was legitimized as an important aspect of the 'culture' debate in social theory.

By the time of the *Daedalus* publication on 'Religion and Politics' in 1991, the representation of religion had changed in three ways. First, the 'culture' debate appears much less evident across these essays, which are instead dealing with an increased recognition that 'religion' in world politics is part of those elements that 'cannot be subsumed under the neat categories developed by social science' (Graubard, 1991, p. viii). Second, articles are genuinely 'political', as distinct from anthropological, with many focusing on the question of the state. Moreover, the states in question are no longer confined to the Third World, but include some limited First World contexts (Beckford, 1991; Demerath, 1991; Linz, 1991). The focus on state contexts across the world makes *Daedalus* 1991 a more explicit representation of religion research in IR discourse than the 1973 edition, though there is an acknowledged causal link between them (Graubard, 1991, pp. v–vi). Third, and connected to the former, between 1973 and 1991 one can detect a more intense interest in political Islam. In 1991 the question of political Islam is addressed around the themes of state security in Egypt (Baker, 1991), issues of governance and stability in

North Africa (Anderson, 1991) and a critique of the 'theocratic' attributes of the Islamic Republic of Iran. These themes fit squarely in the rationale of mainstream IR discourse, and as such, the political function of religion is made to fit, necessarily, into existing analytical frames of the discipline.

The *Daedalus* compendia (1973, 1991) situate religion within frames that privilege state development and the question of culture. This is understandable given that the 'epistemological turn' within IR that challenged the dominance of rational state-centric approaches to world politics was occurring only at the end of this period (Ashley, 1988; S. Smith, 2000, pp. 383–9). Arguably, the movement between 1973 and 1991 on the question of religion and culture reflects the first debate of IR theory 'in which the object of study . . . moved from a preoccupation with the nation-state to transnational processes' (Jarvis, 2002, p. 2). Notably, across numerous essays cited above, state interest appears threatened by religion understood as a transnational or cultural threat to state security. In all of these examples, religion is a secondary concept subordinate to more dominant actors and issues.

### 1.2.2   Religion and the 'Clash of Civilizations'

I shall further describe the secular discourse via two readings in IR. The first reading is seminal in its influence, the second is part of the new attempts to systematize the analysis of religion at the global level.

Samuel Huntington's well-known essay 'The clash of civilizations?' (1993) and subsequent book *The Clash of Civilizations and the Remaking of World Order* (1996) are among the most influential appropriations of religion in IR to date. Almost every contemporary study of religion in world politics contends with its ideas in some way (for example, Johnston, 2003, pp. 19–23; S.M. Thomas, 2005, pp. 30–2; Fox and Sandler, 2006, pp. 115–36; Haynes, 2007a, pp. 4–7). From its inception Huntington's civilizational thesis has also drawn criticism (for example, Hassner, 1997; Rosecrance, 1998; Said, 2001). The contours of the argument are well known and I briefly summarize them from the original article of 1993. First, the end of the Cold War marks a new era in the nature of global conflict: 'the great divisions among humankind and the dominating source of conflict will be cultural' (Huntington, 1993, p. 22). As such, the age of ideologies will give way to an age where civilizational identity defines the movement and shape of world history (1993, p. 23). Huntington writes, 'A civilisation is a cultural entity . . . it is defined both by common objective elements, such as language, history, religion, customs, institutions, and by the subject self-identification of people' (1993, pp. 23–4). Second, although 'the composition and boundaries of civilizations change' (1993, p. 24) up to eight distinct civilizational domains will dominate world politics into the future: 'Western, Confucian, Japanese, Islamic, Hindu, Slavic-Orthodox, Latin American and possibly African civilisation' (1993, p. 25). Third, conflict between these civilizations is likely for the following reasons: differences between civilizations are more fundamental than differences in political ideology and interest (1993, p. 25); increased interactions between peoples of difference enhances those differences (1993, pp. 25–6); economic modernization creates social dislocation that weakens local and national identity, and this is replaced by civilizational identity (1993, p. 26); the dominant West faces a global shift in elite interest in non-Western contexts from 'Westernisation to indigenisation' (1993, pp. 26–7); cultural and religious differences are less susceptible to compromise than political and economic one: 'A person can be half-French and half-Arab and simultaneously even a citizen of two countries. It is more difficult to be half-Catholic and half-Muslim' (1993, p. 27); and the increase in economic regionalism 'will reinforce civilisation-consciousness' (1993, pp. 27–8). Fourth, civilizational conflict will occur at the micro-level between groups 'along the fault lines between civilizations' (1993, pp. 29–35). Two predominant fault lines will shape the future of world politics: between Western and Islamic civilizations (1993, pp. 31–2) with the Islamic world facing confrontations on all of its civilizational borders (1993, p. 33); and, as a derivation of the broader conflict between 'the West and the Rest' (1993, p. 41), an alliance of security interests between Confucian and Islamic civilizations against a Western sphere at the peak of its power (1993, pp. 39, 45–48).

It is not my purpose to attempt yet another contribution to the 'Huntington debate' (see Fox and Sandler, 2006, pp. 115–36). Rather, I wish to briefly explore Huntington's thesis on the question of religion, particularly on whether religion is a primary or secondary concept within the overall argument. The answer to that question is complicated. The first view, as Fox and Sandler have argued, holds that 'religion truly is the basis of [Huntington's] concept of civilisation' (Fox and Sandler, 2006, p. 118). They argue that all of the major civilizations bar one (Africa) 'include some aspect of religion in their definition and some of them appear to be wholly defined by religion' (2006, p. 116). Yet such an observation too easily elides religion into culture. Drawing distinctions between these is important. Huntington adopts Walzer's argument for cultures as 'thick', that is, 'they prescribe institutions and behaviour patterns to guide humans in the paths which are right in a particular society' (Huntington, 1996, p. 318). Such an understanding certainly can account also for religious agency in society, but is not distinctively religious, hence religion functions only as one component of Huntington's civilizational notion. For instance, the Confucian sphere is arguably more cultural than religious in make-up which may explain why IR scholars such as Haynes opt for the broader description of Confucianism as 'a philosophical and religious system' (Haynes, 2007a, p. 15). Huntington's Confucian – or Sinic – civilization is united by the common link of ethics and values held by the peoples of China and its South-East Asian diaspora (Huntington, 1996, p. 45). The attributes of religion are also not central to the important 'Confucian-Islamic connection' which is instead founded on security interests (Huntington, 1993, p. 46, 1996, p. 185).

An alternative view is that whilst religion is a very important identity marker in the clash of civilizations thesis, Huntington does not explore the distinctive content and contribution of religion in any substantial sense. There is no specific appeal to the way civilizations have been shaped by different religious doctrines, no consideration of the intra-religious conflicts that characterize world religions today, including in the Islamic world (Fox and Sandler, 2006, p. 118). These are not omissions from the thesis, rather, they are simply not needed because religion as a mere component of civilizations is the extent of Huntington's religious exploration. A simple parallel to IR realist theory helps explain this further. Unlike liberals who have a primary interest in the kind of political system adopted within states, realists are said to 'black box' the state, thereby remaining ambivalent to the political content of the domestic sphere (Singer, 1961, pp. 81–2). States are a cornerstone to realist international philosophy, but only insofar as they are deemed by realists to be the best mechanism for international stability. In some respects, the state is to realists what religion is to the Huntington thesis. The content of religion is immaterial – what matters is the instrumental function of religion alongside culture and ethnicity to provide an alternative basis for global conflict to those of political ideology and economic interest. Religion *as religion* is relatively insignificant, having little agency beyond its role as a signifier of cultural difference in a post-Cold War global security discourse. On this basis, I suggest that religion is a secondary element in the clash of civilizations thesis and that Huntington's work is thus weighted much more heavily toward being a secular analysis than a sacral one.

### 1.2.3    Religion in the International System[5]

Eric Hanson's recent *Religion and Politics in the International System Today* (2006) is a more nuanced example of religion as a secondary concept of IR. Hanson attempts to construct a 'new paradigm' (2006, p. 17) in the study of IR via the 'central methodological choice, to take religion seriously from the viewpoint of religious practitioners' (2006, p. 8). In so doing, *Religion and Politics* attempts an 'alternative to the compartmentalised, secular Western' approaches of the past (2006, p. 12). The study is situated within the 'technologically-driven' (2006, p. 4) structures of a globalized world, where Hanson argues for the influence of religious actors in 'political, economic, military, and communication'(EMC) systems (2006, pp. 4, 17–69). This four-dimension paradigm, formulated throughout as 'politics + EMC', is then employed in the analysis of five geopolitical regions: 'the West', 'East Asia', 'Middle East and North Africa', 'South and Central Asia' and 'Latin America' (2006, pp. 123, 164). The resulting study offers a complex view of the dynamics of religion at work in the international system. First, the definition of 'religion' (and of globalization) is usefully polysemic, divided in terms of 'religions of the book', 'religions of meditative experience' and 'religions of public life' (2006, pp. 86–8, 92–119). These categories progress IR analysis beyond overly generic readings of religion. Second, Hanson's geopolitical method respects the interaction between tradition and context in the formation of religio-politics. Parallels to Huntington's civilizational thesis are appropriate, however *Religion and Politics* offers an intra-regional rather than inter-regional comparison of religious conflict and peacemaking (2006, pp. 56–8). Hanson also understands religious conflict to be within traditions, not just between them, something neglected in the Huntington thesis. Third, the prescriptions offered in the latter chapters for religion and politics in the next millennium balance issues of the vitality and danger of religion in the international system, and are rooted in a concern for policy by states, international organizations and transnational religious communities (2006, pp. 295–323).

Yet in important ways, *Religion and Politics* also reflects the secular subordination of religion traditional to IR. For instance, the central methodology arguably exists within what Waever originally termed the neo-neo synthesis (Waever, 1996, pp. 163–4). Hanson describes it well as the combination of 'conventional liberal and conservative approaches to international affairs by advocating religious pluralism integrated into all four global systems' (Hanson, 2006, p. 12). The limitation of such an approach is that the values of 'religious practitioners' – especially the world's poor, who are overwhelmingly religious in outlook – are marginalized by the values of mainstream globalization. Moreover, from a critical vantage, *Religion and Politics* assumes a benign character to 'politics + EMC' systems that arguably serve many religious people very poorly. The more fundamental question of how the agency of 'religion' might resist and reconstitute such systems remains unexplored. Second, and not unrelated to the first limitation, *Religion and Politics* reflects the primacy of US foreign policy assumptions rather than the perspective of religious actors broadly understood. For instance, the politico-religious structure in Iran is given short shrift, and is too predictably read through North American security discourse as the mere result of a power vacuum rather than a serious post-colonial, post-secular, development (2006, pp. 215–21, 217). Another example is that Hanson's study of US interventions in Central America doesn't include any incisive analysis of the brutalization of Nicaragua, Guatemala, El-Salvador and the liberation theology movements of resistance that flourished in response (2006, pp. 267–70). Third, Hanson draws on only one of Meslin's 'five conceptions of religion' for his own working definition, adapted as 'a person's willingness to die for his belief' (2006, p. 73).[6] Such a definition equates religion with martyrdom and elides into IR security assumptions about religion as disruption, as something to be contained rather than partnered. Such linkages are certainly valid, however, Meslin's other conceptions, notably religion as 'altruistic service of other people', may have provided the conceptions of religion with more agency. The 'Nine Global Religious-Political Rules' that end the book do promote a broader view but strongly reflect forms of civic-liberalism that have long been part of modern secular appropriations of religion (2006, pp. 73, 320–3).

*Religion and Politics* describes ways religion is integrated into the international system as it is understood within the neo-neo frame of IR, and as it operates within many international policy and diplomatic networks. This is timely, and resonates with broader developments in the politics of globalization such as the Tony Blair Faith Foundation (see Tony Blair Faith Foundation, n.d.). Yet Hanson's argument does not constitute a new paradigm, but rather, adds a faith dimension to extant assumptions and dynamics. *Religion and Politics* is thus a robust contemporary example of the secular discourse on religion in IR.

## 1.3   THE SACRAL DISCOURSE OF IR

According to Martin Krygier the most significant question one can ask in social research, and also the most basic, is 'compared to what?' (Krygier, 2005, p. 291). Accordingly, to what might a predominantly secular understanding of world politics be compared? IR began as a study of the secular modern world of nation-states but has evolved since its inception to include the study of multiple actors and influences (for example, state and non-state actors) that can each be studied at multiple levels of analysis (for example, global, interstate, domestic and individual) (Goldstein, 2003, pp. 3–17). The limitations of the secular discourse of IR are partly balanced by an alternative body of work that engage religion in these broader contexts and discovered new understandings of religion in the international sphere. This corpus belongs to what I call the sacral discourse of IR. It is comprised of a sizeable and growing research agenda that explores the agency of religion beyond the instrumentality of the secular discourse. 'Agency' has a variety of meanings in social science, and is taken here to mean the causal influence of a concept upon the context in which it is used. McAnulla defines agency as 'individual or group abilities (intentional or otherwise) to affect their environment' (McAnulla, 2002, p. 271). The greater the influence of a concept in determining the normative structures around it (for example, the effect of 'state sovereignty' upon the assumption of anarchy within the realist paradigm of IR), the greater its agential capacity. In the same way, the sacral discourse of IR relocates religion from a secondary to a primary position in the analysis of world politics.

### 1.3.1 Religion as a Primary Element in International Affairs

One could argue that we have thus far observed the influence of one religion, Christianity, upon IR. This may, in turn, invite discussions that Christianity holds a different status vis-à-vis the formation of the international system which has been ostensibly controlled by the (Christian) West. Such a view would be more secular than sacral in orientation such as we have observed in Huntington's clash of civilizations thesis (Huntington, 1993). Yet beyond the sacral influences on the origins of IR, the representation of religion as a primary element in IR discourse more generally extends beyond Christian representations. This and others aspects can be seen in two recent compendia on religion and world politics.

The first comes from *Millennium*, the IR journal of the London School of Economics and Politics, published in the year 2000. The essays that consider religion can be divided into two groups. The first grouping I shall identify as *Millennium 2000a* is characterized by high religious agency in shaping the discourse of world politics. Stephen Chan's essay on 'Writing sacral IR' defines sacral as '[n]ot "sacred" but with the capacity to become sacred; founded on ancient rites and beliefs . . . it is a projection of these rites and beliefs into a sphere beyond their antiquity' (Chan, 2000, p. 570). In a broad-ranging essay Chan appropriates Buddhism as a vehicle by which 'each person may sacrally write an IR in a commonality with other writers of sacred text' (2000, p. 570) which conceives of 'the world as dreamt or meditated into existence' whereby 'the self-reflexivity of the universe is on behalf of [and ethic of] goodness' (2000, p. 579). Chan chooses the enlightened figure of the Boddhisattva as exemplar of compassion that transforms its environment (2000, pp. 576–9). In other words, the normative parameters of a religious tradition within Buddhism are employed to determine the scope and parameters of the worlds with which IR engages. This 'religious vantage' is also evident in essays by Esposito and Voll on the theme of Islam and the West from a Muslim purview (Esposito and Voll, 2000, pp. 613–40). Similarly, Anthony Smith presents the case for nationalism to be understood as a form of religion and distils the 'sacred properties of the nation' from a nationalist perspective (A.D. Smith, 2000, pp. 803–10). Bassam Tibi (2000) writes of the agential capacity of a politicised Islam on global politics and Miroslav Volf reflects on the meaning of reconciliation and justice from a Christian perspective (Volf, 2000). The second grouping I shall identify as *Millennium 2000b* and is characterized by the dominance of sacral elements but with an increased engagement with secular structures that impact on religious actors and interests. In this grouping categories external to religious tradition or action are analyzed as gateways to continue bringing religion into IR discourse. These include pluralism (Einstadt, 2000; Lynch, 2000), antiquity versus modernity (Osiander, 2000), culture and community (Thomas, 2000) and the IR subfield of constructivism (Kubalkova, 2000). The agency of religion is significantly high in each of these essays. Similarly, Laustsen and Waever's (2000) essay on IR approaches toward religion and security promotes a reordering of the discipline from a securitization rooted in the secular suspicion of religion, 'To avoid the most violent and ideologised conflicts demands first of all de-securitisation which in the present case means to respect religion as *religion*' (Laustsen and Waever, 2000, p. 739, emphasis in original). While the emphasis on the sacral is diverse in the 2000 *Millennium* compendium no article could be described as secular in orientation.

The second compendium is from a 2003 special edition of the *Journal of the American Academy of Art and Sciences Daeadalus* and extends the useful study in religion and politics from the *Daedalus* compendia from 1973 and 1991 previously considered. The 2003 edition bears the influence of the new post-9/11 genre of writing on religion that is at once concerned to explore the religious roots of those beyond the bounds of the USA and its allies, and also to investigate further 'how a religious self-understanding informs our nation's new imperial impulse' (Carroll, 2003, p. 9). Of the 13 essays from contemporary authors, only one could be described as written from a distinctively secular perspective, that being from the noted atheist and political commentator Christopher Hitchens (2003). Three contributions make important contributions in reframing the secular-sacral balance in the study of world politics. Keddie (2003) distils the existing debate in IR to identify the retreat of secular thinking in addressing the challenges of culture and religion in the contemporary world. The contribution from Marty (2003) is nothing short of seminal and I shall refer to it later in this chapter. Munson (2003) draws a continuity between ancient and modern worlds on the question of fundamentalism neutralizing the religion-secularism distinction to some extent. Further to these, studies on Islam draw much closer to issues of identity as formed by the Muslim faith in contexts such as Turkey (Yavuz, 2003) and the Muslim world more generally (Nasr, 2003). Contributions from Galston (2003), Elshtain (2003) and Bilgrami (2003) have sought to integrate religious agency with existing political frames such as liberalism, democracy and civilization. On the scale of sacral perspectives in IR, the *Daedalus* compendium of 2003 presents a closer engagement with culture from the distinct perspective of religious studies than previous editions.

### 1.3.2   The Metaphysics of World Politics

Ralph Pettman's *Reason, Culture, Religion: The Metaphysics of World Politics* (2004) is a salient example of sacralism that has emerged in recent IR scholarship. In this work Pettman brings the term 'sacral' into IR parlance and weighs directly into the secular modern debate, applied to IR, in innovative ways. For Pettman, the modernist project constitutes 'old' IR and is described thus, 'Modernists articulate world affairs in a range of analytical languages, the most common of which are realist, liberalist, individualist, materialist, and masculinist ones. Being modernist, all such languages are Rationalist, and being Rationalist, they bear the marks of their origin within European Christendom' (2004, p. 157). By contrast, 'new' international relations is represented by communalist alternatives to modernism. Pettman elucidates the nature of communalism against the modernist alternative via a case study on world heritage (2004, pp. 51–67). Whereas the modernist frame emphasizes the materiality, immanence and temporality of heritage objects, the communalist conception emphasizes the transcending continuity (that is, metaphysics) between past and present. Pettman summarizes thus:

> the modernist concept of the human past, as a dead place of tangible products, is radically at odds with communalist conceptions of the human past, as a living process involving intangible practices . . . [understanding] human heritage . . . in non-reified terms. (Pettman, 2004, p. 157)

Importantly for the present book, in exploring the communalist traditions of world politics in depth, Pettman turns to sacral alternatives to the modernist project, understood as 'politico-spiritual traditions' (2004, p. ix) understood from a communalist perspective. For instance, in the area of international security Pettman asks, 'How might anti-Rationalist

ideas of a non-Christian kind be seen as impinging upon this area of international affairs?' (2004, p. 83). In a study of 'Taoist strategics' Pettman
argues that the Taoist tradition has considerable agency in Chinese foreign
policy 'to temper what Chinese state makers think and how they behave'
(2004, pp. 92, 83–92). In a sacral reading of the global market, Pettman
suggests that Buddhist economics offers critical insight and constructive advice to the existing market system that is controlled in the main
by 'white, Western, liberalised males' (2004, pp. 100, 93–102). On the
former, Buddhist traditions critique Western market approaches for 'a
fundamental reliance on a sense of self' whereas the Buddha's emphasis
on the not-self 'has profound economic implications' (2004, pp. 100–1).
Within this understanding, marketeering imperatives would be used 'as
an opportunity to provide tangible proof of life's spiritual purpose, but
also to show marketeers, in practical terms, how to mitigate their greed
and their selfishness, and the sense of "me" and "mine" [instead dem-
onstrating] what it means in market terms to promote true compassion'
(2004, p. 102). Therefore, 'a truly Buddhist economist would not say
that marketeering is bad in itself. Rather, he or she would say that it is
how marketeering is done that matters most' (2004, p. 102). In a similar
fashion, Pettman explores sacral alternatives such as citizenship and civil
society from the Islamic tradition (2004, pp. 103–14), Confucian perspectives on Marxism (2004, pp. 115–24), the deployment of Hindu thought in
constructing notions of world politics (2004, pp. 125–34), and feminism
and environmentalism from neo-pagan and animist traditions (2004,
pp. 135–44, 145–56).

Three aspects of Pettman's work are important for understanding the
broader nature of sacral discourse in world politics. The first is that many
– though not all (see below) – sacral writings can be situated in pluralist, consructivist and communitarian traditions of political thought. For
instance, Kublakova's suggestion of a religion-focused IR subfield called
international political theology (IPT) is shaped by constructivist ideals
(Kublakova, 2000). Pettman's work is stridently post-positivist, and the
reconstitutive impulses that undergird *Reason, Culture, Religion* belong to
the constructivist schools of IR. Second, as shown by both the examples
of China and the market economy, sacral writings in IR are concerned
with both analysis and policy outcomes. The difference between sacral and
secular approaches is the primary function of the sacral tradition to condition and control the analysis and the direction that policy should take.
Third, these same examples are different in important ways, the consideration of 'Taoist strategics' is empirical, using a sacral tradition to analyze
the observable behaviour of a state actor in relation to one of that actor's
foundational traditions; whereas the argument for Buddhist economics is

normative and aspirational, suggesting the potential value of a sacral tradition for a more sustained practice of global economics. Whilst such constructions may not be entirely distinct from more secular approaches, their agents are sacral (that is, are grounded primarily in religion) not secular.

### 1.3.3    Resurgent Religion and Political Community[7]

One seminal contribution to the debate is *The Global Resurgence of Religion and the Transformation of International Relations* by Scott Thomas (2005). Thomas argues that what is needed in interpreting the challenges of religion in world politics 'is not only more facts . . . but better concepts, theories and assumptions' (2005, pp. 11–12). This challenge could arguably be met in two ways: to integrate religion into extant IR structures, and/or to reframe the structures themselves. *Global Resurgence* sheds light on both options. On the former, Thomas takes religion into the heart of IR discourse, arguing that its virtual non-existence as an IR concept is due to the secularity of the discipline (2005, pp. 47–69). These arguments are not unique, and as we have argued above they are potentially more complex than Thomas, Philpott and others suggest. Nevertheless, Thomas situates his argument 'as part of the wider effort to bring ideas, values . . . ideational factors back into the study of international relations' (2005, p. 69). It thus belongs to the constructivist project, similar to Pettman's sacral approach to world affairs, but more interestingly, to the English School of IR which 'took seriously the impact of religious doctrines, cultures and civilizations . . . at a time when they were ignored or marginalised in the mainstream study of the discipline because it was preoccupied with the Cold War' (2005, p. 17). We are thus challenged to rethink the 'newness' of religion in IR, and instead find it the earliest discourses of the field, such as through the writings of Wight (also Thomas, 2001; Hall, 2006) and Neibuhr (Warren, 1997; Craig, 2003). Yet it is the second option, the way of reframing the structures of IR, which more defines *Global Resurgence*. According to Thomas, IR inherited religion as an invention of liberal modernity, summed as 'a body of beliefs', an individualist definition of religion as 'privately held doctrines'. Thomas regards this as a distortion of religion as it really exists, which is more as 'a body of believers', a social definition (S.M. Thomas, 2005, pp. 23–4). Thus, 'it will not be sufficient . . . to simply add religion . . . into our existing concepts or theories' (2005, p. 79). The way forward is instead found in MacIntyre's narrative theory of social action (2005, pp. 85–96) which holds religion to be 'a type of social tradition' that 'cannot be separated from specific social and cultural context' (2005, p. 88). There is a timely benefit to this approach: to speak of religion as 'a source of positive social

capital' (2005, p. 238) opens the analysis of religion in IR to realms beyond
securitization, which tends to collapse religion with fundamentalism,
culture conflicts and war. Thomas subsequently applied this community-
based, virtue-ethics approach to religion to numerous substantive issues in
IR, including security, but also extending to international co-operation,
diplomacy, democracy and civil society, and international development.
In this way, religious communities and cultures become primary sources
upon which alternative conceptions of international society are conceived
(see also Thomas, 2004a).

The work of Pettman and Thomas reflect a growing number of scholars who seek to apply religion as a primary resource in the analysis of
world politics. Religion seems no longer to be the 'missing dimension' of
important IR discourses, but instead takes the role of a primary source
in conceptions of statecraft (Johnston and Sampson, 1997), globalization (Dunning, 2003) and diplomacy (Johnston and Sampson, 1995). In a
body of work on faith-based diplomacy, for example, Rabbi Marc Gopin
can write of the peacemaking qualities of Judaism as revealed in sacred
scripture (Gopin, 2003, pp. 102–23), Steele of Christianity as a reconciling agent in the former Yugoslavia (Steele, 2003, pp. 124–77) and Khaled
Abou El Fadl of conflict resolution as a normative value in Islamic law
(Abou El Fadl, 2003, pp. 178–209). Together, these resources take us
beyond the legitimation of religion as a secondary source, where religion
can often be found on the wrong side of assumptions about securitization
and conflict. They instead function as sacral alternatives contributing to
co-operative outcomes in international affairs. What I have called the
sacral discourse presents religion as object, not merely as subject, and in so
doing has broadened the way religion is being conceived in the discipline.


## 1.4   THE INTEGRATED DISCOURSE OF RELIGION

In an important defence of secularism Rajeev Bhargava observed that
'social facts are not exhausted by whatever people currently believe to
be the case but nor do they stand completely apart from it.' (Bhargava,
1998, p. 487). In other words, it is not a given that the rise of religion
diminishes the claims and achievements of secularism. Yet the texture of
Bhargava's comment could equally work in the other direction: the claims
of twentieth-century secularists that constituted 'current belief' for some
60 or 70 years in the social sciences have not diminished the existence or
influence of religion in the public sphere. Bhargava's comment is incisive
because it suggests an inseparability between beliefs about what is true
from the evidentiary context in which the beliefs are held. I have upheld

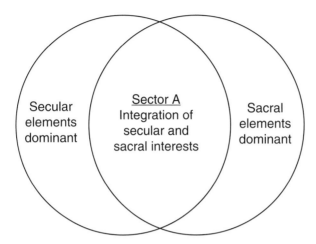

*Figure 1.2    Situating the integrated discourse of religion*

this principle in the present study. By identifying secular and sacral discourses of IR I suggest that each perspective offers valuable but partial insight into the dynamics of religion in IR. Secular sources offer legitimate insights based on the conception of religion as a secondary political element. Sacral sources offer legitimate insights based on the conception of religion as a primary political element. Implicit in this argument is that secular and sacral perspectives cannot be universally sustained. Thus, a third discourse that I have called the integrated discourse on religion in IR exists in the discipline, one that incorporates secular and sacral elements with relative balance. It is not necessarily the 'better' discourse and it is not presented as an ideal type over the others. The distinctive feature of the integrated discourse is the normative assumption that the secular and sacral spheres overlap in the formation of political reality. This is represented in Figure 1.2 where secular and sacral elements are situated in relation to the integrated realm identified as Sector A.

An emerging consensus view in IR on the question of religion is that in many political contexts, and certainly from a global perspective, secular and sacral elements are mutually constitutive. Whereas sacral agency was once considered an exotic element and duly characterized by revolution and disruption, the sacral elements carried by cultural and identity politics are now considered more universally important. At the same time, even in contexts where religion seems to dominate the political landscape, secular factors function as key determinants for political behaviour. When taken together, both secular and sacral dynamics contribute to the international political landscape in important ways, contributing to an integrating process described by Hurd as follows: 'Religion and politics overlap and intersect in complex and multiple formations in different times and locations, composing political settlements that wax and wane in their influence' (Hurd, 2008, p. 134). Such a view can only be sustained by binding secular and sacral political spheres together from an integrated centre and using all of these elements to create a comprehensive framework that accommodates the manifold forms of religion that exist. This is the task we shall undertake in the next chapter.

## NOTES

1. Used in accordance with the origins of the term, analogous with 'the Third Estate in French civil society and emphasizing the revolutionary potential of the countries so classified'. The term is synonymous with 'developing world', 'south' or 'global South' (O'Brien and Williams, 2004, p. 258).
2. First heard by the author applied in an IR context in a conference paper delivered by Ralph Pettman (2002) and subsequently applied in an IR publication considered below (Pettman, 2004).
3. *Daedalus* (1991), Summer, Vol. 120.
4. *Daedalus* (1973), Winter, Vol. 102.
5. The following review originally appeared in Rees (2007). Some details have been re-edited.
6. M. Meslin (1988), *L'experience humaine du divin – Foundaments d'une anthropologie religieuse* (Paris: Cerf).
7. The following review originally appeared in Rees (2007). Some details have been re-edited.

# 2. Modelling religion in international relations

> [I]f the secularization thesis seems increasingly implausible to some of us this is not simply because religion is now playing a vibrant part in the modern world of nations. In a sense what many would anachronistically call 'religion' was always involved in the world of power.
>
> Talal Asad (2003a, p. 200)

This chapter constructs an integrated analytical model of religion in IR. I begin by identifying conceptual approaches that bind the secular and sacral spheres together, thereby turning the multiple discourses of religion into constituent elements of a new structure of IR. This structure is used as a basis for building what I have called the dynamics of religion model. The model enables us to pose a new question for religion research in IR and to construct a new model for differentiating religion in IR contexts. Each aspect is explained in anticipation of the applications of the model that occur in subsequent chapters.

## 2.1 CONSTRUCTING THE RELIGIOUS STRUCTURE OF IR

An important compendium edited by Bhargava titled *Secularism and Its Critics* (1998) opens with several essays written under a banner of 'The Secular Imperative' (Bhargava, 1998a, pp. 29ff.). Implicit in such a phrase is the view that secularism is not only useful, it is also very important. My discussion to date maintains the importance of secularism (over secularization) but unites the secular imperative with another perspective that I have called sacral. Hence, the imperative ground has shifted toward the importance of integrating secular and sacral impulses so as to better deal, conceptually and instrumentally, with the elements of religion as it really exists in the spheres of politics.

### 2.1.1    Binding Secular and Sacral Discourses

As secularism requires core concepts that bind its variants together, so too does the construction of a new analytical model. Many influences have contributed to the model presented here, some are secular and others sacral in nature, whilst others bind the secular and the sacral together. I will briefly identify four binding influences of central importance to the present argument.

### (a)    The 'religio-secular world' (Marty)

The first binding influence is structural, and comes from Martin E. Marty, one of the principal investigators in the Fundamentalism Project for the American Academy of Arts and Social Sciences. Marty reframes the international political space by calling it the 'religio-secular world' (Marty, 2003) of international affairs. By this conception, Marty attempts to find 'a new model for describing the world that we actually inhabit' (2003, p. 42). Marty holds that such a world is 'neither exclusively secular nor exclusively religious, but rather a complex combination of both' (2003, p. 42). He continues,

> The old debates revolve around binary categories, societies were *either* secular *or* religious; worldly *or* other-worldly; materialist *or* spiritual; favouring immanence *or* transcendence, etc . . . [but] most people blur, mesh, meld, and muddle together elements of both the secular and the religious, the worldly and the other-worldly. (2003, p. 42, emphasis in original)

Marty suggests that secular and sacral elements co-exist in any given political context and re-conceives the international sphere as religio-secular. The descriptor presupposes a political structure in which 'religious and secular phenomenon [are] occurring at the same time in individuals, groups, and in societies around the world' (2003, p. 42). It is Marty's concept that first provoked my own thinking about the possibility that a religious structure, unseen but nevertheless at work, was animating religion research in IR. My own appropriation of the term 'religio-secular' was to emphasize the 'secular-sacral' texture of world politics. The latter notion maintains Marty's core assumption but avoids a binary nomenclature that still, in the minds of many, pits the secular against the religious.

### (b)    The 'ambivalence of the sacred' (Appleby)

The second binding influence is ethico-normative in nature, and comes from what R. Scott Appleby (2000) has called 'the ambivalence of the sacred'. What Appleby means by this is that the dual possibilities of life and death 'reside within the holy' (Appleby, 2000, p. 30). An outworking of this ambivalence is that religion brings multiple, often contrasting ethical dynamics into the political sphere such as conflict (2000, pp. 57ff.), on one hand, and peace-making on the other (2000, pp. 121ff.). It is a simple but profound notion that challenges decades of policy making toward religious agency in international affairs. For instance, ambivalence is central to Appleby's interpretation of the motivations behind religious violence:

> If religions have legitimated certain acts of violence, they have also attempted to limit the frequency and scope of those acts. This ambivalent attitude reflects the utility of violence as an instrument of self-defense and enforcement of religious norms on the one hand but also acknowledges its potential for uncontrollable destructiveness on the other. In most religions one finds a deep tension between the use and sublimation of violence and a valorisation of 'holy martyrs' who sacrificed their lives that others might live. (2000, pp. 10–11)

Beyond the analysis of religious violence, Appleby also sees the latent potential of religion as the bringer of peace. Indeed, from a policy perspective he refutes the idea that 'religion, having so often inspired, legitimated, and exacerbated deadly conflicts, cannot be expected to contribute consistently to their peaceful resolution' (2000, p. 7). Such a view breaks open the binary that traditionally understood secularism to be a containment theory against the vices of the sacral. The notion of ambivalence legitimates both secular and sacral ethics in the domain of peace and conflict, and Appleby's case study work attests to religious actors as recognized determinants in conflict prevention as the central goal of 'faith-based diplomacy' (2002, pp. 238–56). Thus, the notion of ambivalence applied to religion in world politics helps deconstruct the secular conceit that assumes religion will be perpetually disruptive and will seed violence. Even when it does seed violence, ambivalence encourages the analyst to consider religious and non-religious sources to find countervailing forces to such violence. The benefit of the principle of ambivalence will be seen later in the book via an analysis of the dynamics of religion in development.

### (c)  The 'mutual serviceability' of IR paradigms (Waever)

The third binding concept is drawn from a broader debate on IR methodology. Ole Waever responds to criticism that the inter-paradigm approach of IR represents the problem of 'incommensurability as a barrier to critique' (Waever, 1996, p. 158). In other words, because the discipline is ordered by different interpretive frameworks, IR paradigms 'could not be tested against each other, since they basically did not speak the same language' (1996, p. 158). There is a present danger for IR research in religion that the languages (and interests) of the secular and sacral 'paradigms' are held to be so different that a 'stand off' exists within the discipline rather than an 'open conversation'. Waever's response to the problem of incommensurability is to consider IR theories in a co-operative relationship, sharing a division of labour that creates a dynamic of 'mutual serviceability' (1996, p. 173). Understood in this way, different theories 'partly explain the same object, but they do not compete for this, and should not be tested against the other' (1996, p. 174). There is considerable value for IR religion research in such an approach. The secular need not collapse into the sacral in order to accommodate the perspectives of religion, but rather, secular and sacral dimensions can mutually service the analytical task. Thus a differentiated approach toward secular and sacral effects in world politics might 'play *with* incommensurability, but against the cognitivist idea of different "lenses" that create different pictures of "the same" (1996, p. 174, emphasis in original). Accordingly, differentiation and integration become equally important: 'the theories can only be linked externally, when one theory reaches out on its own terms for another theory to exploit it, which it can then only do so by grasping the inner logic of this other theory and its material' (1996, p. 174). Mutual serviceability links secular and sacral perspectives whilst maintaining the integrity of each view. What is 'serviced' becomes tested by context and by a comparative analysis that is concerned to situate religion within an integrated secular-sacral framework.

### (d)   The 'modes of secularism' (Taylor)
The fourth binding concept comes not from IR theory but from Taylor's important essay in political philosophy on the 'modes of secularism' (Taylor, 1998). Charles Taylor argues that two oppositional modes of secular thought are partly reconciled by a third mode. The first mode is described as a 'common ground strategy', originally attempted to 'establish a certain ethic of obedience, which while still theistic . . . was based on those doctrines which were common to all' (1996, p. 33). The problem with the common ground strategy, implemented via emphases on concepts such as Natural Law, was the loss of particularities between religious groups and between religious and non-religious groups (1996, p. 33). The reverse effect is then created, 'the ground originally defended as common ground becomes that of one party among others' (1996, p. 35). The second mode of secularism attempted instead to define an independent secular ethic that could be 'abstract[ed] from . . . religious beliefs altogether' (1998, p. 33). In this schema, which for Taylor is reflected in the philosophy of Hobbes, 'the goal is not to make religion less relevant to public life and policy . . . but rather to prevent the state from backing one confession against another'

(1998, p. 35). The problem with the independent ethic is that its original application was into an overwhelmingly Christian milieu, whereas the application to religiously plural societies leads only to 'dissensus' over the application of neutrality understood especially by non-Christians as a mere expression of religious partisanship (1998, p. 36). As a third alternative, Taylor applies an adapted version of Rawls's notion of overlapping consensus:

> The property of overlapping consensus view . . . lifts the requirement of a commonly held foundation . . . aims only at universal acceptance of certain political principles . . . But recognizes from the outset that there cannot be a universally agreed basis for these, independent or religious . . . The overlapping consensus approach recognizes that [a] common political ethic will not suffice by itself; that everyone who adheres to it will have some broader and deeper understanding of the good in which it is embedded. (1996, p. 38)

The third mode of secularism accommodates the politics of identity within a larger concern for universal instrumentality and this, for Taylor, 'is why secularism in some form is a necessity for the democratic life of religiously diverse societies' (1996, p. 46). In the context of the present book, this appeal to instrumentality becomes a rationale for binding the secular and sacral spheres within an analytical framework that can accommodate the variants of both.

The concepts listed above work to bind, or link, the secular and sacral political spheres. This binding effect is represented in Figure 2.1.

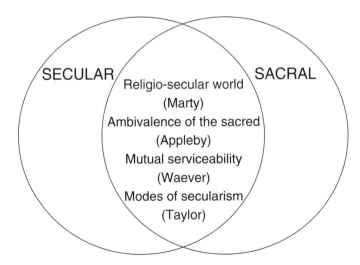

*Figure 2.1    Binding secular and sacral discourses*

Marty's 'religio-secular world' turns the mutually constitutive relations between secular and sacral political spheres into a normative structure of world politics; Appleby's 'ambivalence of the sacred' neutralizes the once dominant assumption that religious political ethics lead to violence by recasting religion as a carrier of peace and violence, disruption and stability; Waever's principle of 'mutual serviceability' offers value to both secular and sacral analytical frames in a shared analytical enterprise; Taylor's application of 'overlapping consensus' between different 'modes of secularism' returns the discourse to universal applications – the secular concern for impartiality – whilst recognizing the communal/identity foundations to ethics – the sacral concern for particularity.

### 2.1.2   New Structure of IR

Binding the secular and sacral spheres creates not only an integrated approach to religion in IR, but also the possibility of a new analytical structure. I have called this the religious structure of world politics. In social theory structure is 'an important source of predictability of behaviour and contributes to the explanation of typicality in social experience' (Parker et al., 2003., p.154). Structure is considered this way because 'structured practices provide units of social analysis for social reproduction and social change' (Cohen, 1996, p.95). The above perspective is influenced by Giddens's four components of structure: (i) procedural rules (how the practice is formed), (ii) moral rules of appropriate enactment, (iii) material (allocative) resources and (iv) resources for authority (Cohen, 1996, p.95). Giddens coined the term 'structuration', which combined the power of structures with a simultaneous recognition of the power of agents who, for Giddens, were much more than 'dopes' to the demands of the structures that surrounded them (Cassell, 1993, p.118). Structuration has subsequently informed a consensus view that 'the action of actors is conditioned, rather than entirely determined, by the positions they occupy' (Parker et al., 2003., p.154). In other words, 'structures do not determine; rather they constrain and facilitate' (Marsh and Furlong, 2002, p.31). A more nuanced definition of structure is provided by Wendt:

> The structure of any social system will contain three elements, material conditions, interest and ideas . . . Without ideas there are no interests, without interests there are no meaningful conditions, without material conditions there is no reality at all. (Wendt, 1999, p.139)

A 'structure' is defined in one leading introductory IR text as 'something that exists independently of the actor (eg social class) but is an important determinant in the nature of the action (eg revolution)' (Baylis et al., 2008, p. 587). Thus in IR we may speak of the global security structure, the structure of international political economy, the gender structure in world politics and the structure of international law. These structures are not 'catch all' constructs designed to explain every behaviour of world politics, but what they do 'catch' bring unique insights into some of the core dynamics of international affairs, notably as frameworks to understand and explain actor behaviour and interests.

To change the metaphor, structures are lenses through which to 'see' certain controlling influences upon actor behaviour in world politics. For example, what we see through the lens of international law is different to what we see through the lens of gender. On the latter, one of the defining achievements of feminist approaches to IR is encapsulated in Cynthia Enloe's now classic refrain 'Where are the women?' (Enloe, 1989, p. 133). The intention behind such a question was to re-conceive notions of international politics other than as a realm 'peopled only by men, mostly elite men' (1989, p. 1). The very act of noticing the presence of women had a critical trajectory by exposing 'how relations between governments depend not only on capital and weaponry, but also on the control of women as symbols, consumers, workers and emotional comforters' (1989, p. xi). Yet because the ways of seeing are not mutually exclusive, the art of IR analysis often involves developing a composite image that incorporates perspectives from multiple lenses.

In the same way, the notion of a religious structure is intended to highlight some of the core political dynamics of world politics via a new set of lenses that are formed by the different conceptions of religion. Wuthnow suggested that interpretations of politics and religion were beginning to change via a 'restructuring process' as scholars were being 'forced' by weight of evidence to reconsider perspectives on culture and social change (Wuthnow, 1991, p. 15). More work was needed, however, on 'religious restructuring' that entailed 'recogni[zing] changing social and political roles that religious communities are playing throughout the contemporary world' (1991, p. 16). The integrative structure of religion in IR seeks to answer this challenge. It does not yet exist in basic IR theory and method. It is the structural implication of Marty's concept of a 'religiosecular world' (Marty, 2003) combined with the emerging consensus that secular and sacral elements are to varying degrees mutually constitutive. It is intended to give order to macro and micro effects of world politics in a way that cannot be fully achieved otherwise. The religious structure offers particularities of analysis that other structures overlook or had no need to prioritize. The religious structure is represented in the simple Figure 2.2.

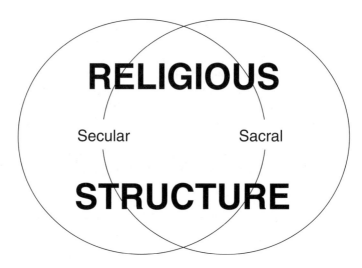

*Figure 2.2    Integrating secular and sacral discourses*

## 2.2   THE DYNAMICS OF RELIGION MODEL

The new structure represented above becomes the foundation for a new analytical model that deepens an understanding of the dynamics of religion at work in the international sphere. I shall now describe the components of this model and build toward its construction by continuing to draw on sources and examples from the discourses of religion in IR.

### 2.2.1   The Spatial Question: 'Where is Religion?'

The first step in maximizing the new structure of IR is to ask a new question about religion in world politics. In a way resonant of recent attempts to incorporate concepts from political geography into IR analysis (Sjoberg, 2008) I suggest that scholars adopt a spatial or situative approach toward the study of religion in IR. I suggest that scholars begin with the question 'Where is religion?' in relation to the secular and sacral interests that shape world politics before asking 'What is religion?' in relation to value-driven debates such as tradition versus modernity or peace versus violence. The reflex toward the latter question is strong and stems from a long-held (and often very reasonable) secularist intention to 'contain' the negative effects of religion in the political domain. However, changing the question keeps open the greater possibility of discovering religious agency afresh. From an IR perspective, such an approach is both practicable and important. Fox and Sandler write,

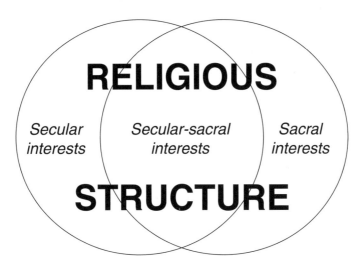

*Figure 2.3     Situating secular and sacral interests in world politics*

> The key focus is not what religion is, but what it does . . . rather than addressing
> the more philosophical issues involved in defining religion, it is easier to stress
> what role religion plays in society. This has the advantage of avoiding difficult
> philosophical and existential issues while focusing on the core issue of the social
> sciences, human behaviour. (Fox and Sandler, 2006, p. 176)

Posing a new question that first situates religion in world affairs allows
the potential to then differentiate religious elements in the international
system. This is represented in Figure 2.3.

The spaces where religious actors and interests could conceivably be
found in world politics are informed by the discourses on religion that
I identified in Chapter 1 and is a constituent element of the religious
structure of IR. Religious actors and interests can be found in different
places, aligned with different interests, and it is important to know why
this is. Peter Gourevitch argues as much in his important essay on the
'interacting variables' that contribute to our understanding of the events
of '9/11' (Gourevitch, 2002). Of interest in the present study is the way
Gourevitch presents religion as a dynamic element that can be situated
in various locations of the issue depending on 'the content of the ideas,
their guide to behaviour, the sociology of belief, and the link to forms
of power' (2002, p. 79). Factors that can situate religion in different
places on different issues include doctrinal responses to political issues
(2002, pp. 74–5), differing relations between religious institutions and
the state (2002, pp. 75–6), and the interaction between religious belief

and alternative political ideologies on offer in specific contexts (2002, pp. 76–7). Each of these elements could be differentiated in secular, sacral and integrated terms, and situated accordingly. It is my contention that we will not know the answer to many of the challenges presented by religion in world politics unless we situate religion before analysing religion in normative terms. As previously suggested, a parallel can be made to Enloe's approach of asking 'Where are the women?' (1989, p. 133) insofar as we are attempting to 'see' religion before co-opting it via preconceived normative assumptions. However, contrasted to Enloe's understanding of the hegemonic nature of the patriarchal structure of IR in relation to study of gender, we do not assume that the invisibility of religion in many analyzes of world affairs automatically implies the hegemonic influence of the secular. Such domination may well exist, but this is best concluded by analysing individual contexts, such as we shall do in subsequent chapters.

### 2.2.2   The Global Dynamics of IR

The new structure and new question help to construct a new model for analysing religion in IR that I have simply named the dynamics of religion model. A summary definition of the value of using models is that they simplify and differentiate complex elements of a given subject that exists in the social world. Applied to the present book, therefore, a model simplifies and differentiates complex elements of religion that exist in the international system. What follows is a progressive series of diagrams that build the dimensions of religion model and highlight the different analytical capacities it holds. In Figure 2.4 the issues and actors of world politics are represented under the term 'global dynamics' in the circle above the religious structure.

The dynamics of religion model is developed by reading the phenomena of IR through the lens of the religious structure of world politics. In a simple adaptation of Figure 2.4, the sphere of global dynamics is lowered into the integrated religious structure to form a Venn diagram. This constitutes the most basic form of the dynamics of religion model and is represented in Figure 2.5.

In applying the dynamics of religion model the Venn structure is employed to offer new insights into the study of religion in IR. The Venn is a common analytical tool, employed, for instance, in Murden's recent study of culture and religion in world affairs (Murden, 2008, p. 429). Yet Michael Jennings and Gerard Clarke incisively warn that such a device may reflect an overly simplistic picture of contemporary religion in the modern world. They write,

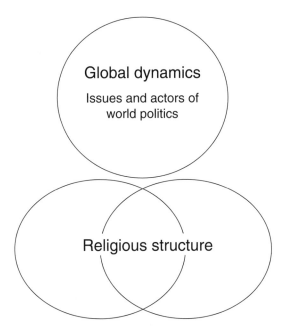

*Figure 2.4    The dimension of global dynamics*

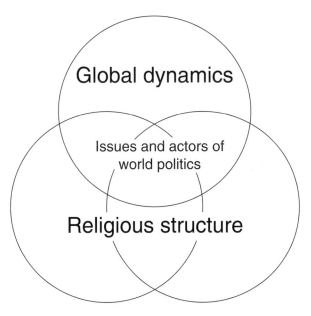

*Figure 2.5    The dynamics of religion model (1)*

> Modern political and social rhetoric has sought to divide the secular and the sacred, present them as entirely separate spheres with separate concerns. The social reality suggests something different, something much more than a Venn diagram of some shared interests. The place of religion in society is complex, dense and difficult to pin down precisely. (Jennings and Clarke, 2008, p. 272)

By contrast, the intention behind my own usage of the Venn is to emphasize the complexity of religion to which Jennings and Clarke rightly attest. There are two ways this is achieved.

First, having created an integrated structure comprised of secular and sacral elements in world politics, the model is intended to differentiate elements within the whole. For instance, the model may highlight elements of shared interest between secular and sacral actors on any given issue of international affairs, but it also aims to reveal important points of divergence between and among these same actors. Wendt defines 'a constituting social structure' as 'the set of relationships with other actors that define a social kind' (Wendt, 1998, p. 113). In these terms, the dynamics of religion model attempts to differentiate interests of a 'secular kind' from interests of a 'sacral kind' whilst recognizing the multiple points where interactions between secular and sacral interests may occur. The same approach can be applied to the dynamics of religion that may exist within the operations of select actors in world politics. Thus, the model is designed to uphold the complexity of religion whilst providing a clearer picture of where this complexity situates interests (and the actors that may coalesce around those interests) throughout the political landscape. This is represented in Figure 2.6.

What characterizes secular political dynamics toward religion in distinction from sacral political dynamics? I shall identify three characteristics of each sphere that help distinguish secular and sacral political dynamics toward religion. These examples feature both the role of religion in the events of world politics and the secular and sacral assumptions employed to interpret those events.

### 2.2.3 Secular Dynamics

Secular dynamics of religion in world politics are characterized by using religion to establish legitimacy at various levels, demographic factors that impact upon religious change and an underlying concern for order. Each characteristic is briefly described below.

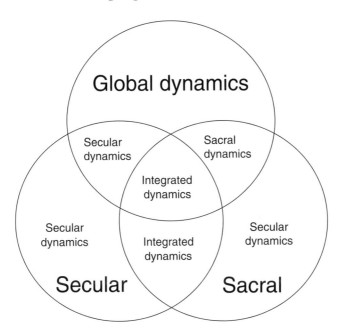

*Figure 2.6    The dynamics of religion model (2)*

**(a)    Political legitimacy and the inclusion of religion**

Having named above the secular discourse in IR as one where religion
plays a secondary role to other more dominant influences, it is not surprising that scholars such as Fox and Sandler argue that one of the main
dynamics of religion in international affairs is the use of religion as a tool
for political legitimacy (Fox and Sandler, 2006, pp. 36–40). They suggest
six issues that ensue from this: (i) religion can be used on a variety of
populations, from domestic constituencies to populations of other states
(2004, p. 43); (ii) religious traditions can be used to support both violent
and peaceful policies (2004, p. 43); (iii) religion can be used to oppose
policy – and even directly oppose those policies that also have co-opted
religious rationales (2004, p. 43); (iv) whilst religious legitimacy is useful
in vindicating policy, religion alone cannot carry the policy debate; (v)
religion is a culture-specific tool: 'For example, invoking Jesus is unlikely
to sway Jews and Muslims, much less Hindus. Thus, appeals to religious
legitimacy are limited by the homogeneity of the audience' (2004, p. 44);
(vi) in addition to 'traditional policy makers . . . Religious elites and other
nongovernment actors can effectively involve religious legitimacy toward
a policy goal' (2004, p. 44). Fox and Sandler suggest a number of reasons
why religious legitimacy is effective (2004, pp. 45–53). The two most salient

of these is that 'other cultural factors such as nationalism and ethnicity have provided legitimacy for political activities' (2004, p. 45) and that 'identity is clearly an influence on international politics and religion is an influence on identity' (2004, p. 45).

### (b)   Social change and the impacts on religion

Some contemporary studies of religious change worldwide remain focused on the importance of secularism. Pippa Norris and Ronald Inglehart, recently conducted a study investigating 'how the experience of existential security drives the process of secularization' (Norris and Inglehart, 2004, p. xiii). The theory was drawn from the World Values Survey (WVS) conducted between 1981 and 2001. The WVS is summarized below:

> These surveys provide data from countries containing more than 85% of the world's population and covering the full range of variation, from societies with per capita incomes as a low as $300 per year to societies with per capita incomes one hundred times that high; and from long-established democracies with market economies to authoritarian states and ex-socialist states. (Norris and Inglehart, 2004, p. xiv)

The authors use WVS data to address two apparently contradictory trends, namely, that advanced industrial societies are becoming more secular, whereas the global population contains more people than ever before with 'traditional religious views' (2004, p. 5). Norris and Inglehart argue that there is no contradiction in these global trends, and that the dynamics of religion and politics worldwide can be explained via three conclusions related to human security and demographic change. First, and in support of the traditional secularization thesis, 'modernization (the process of industrialization, urbanisation, and rising levels of education and wealth) greatly weakens the influence of religious institutions on affluent societies' (2004, p. 25). Second, whilst 'modernization does indeed bring about a de-emphasis on religion within virtually any country that experiences it' (2004, p. 25), due to demographical changes in Third World countries, 'the world as a whole now has more people with traditional religious views than ever before – and they constitute a growing proportion of the world's population' (2004, p. 25). Therefore, 'fertility rates are systematically linked to the strength of religiosity and human development' (2004, p. 29). Third, the authors 'predict' that as a result of 'the expanding gap between the sacred and the secular societies around the globe will have important consequences for world politics, raising the role of religion on the international agenda' marked by a reducing 'peace dividend' and an increasing tendency toward 'ethnic conflict and major wars' (2004, p. 26). The study stands as a secular explanatory framework that prioritizes demographic change as the principal determinant in global religious change.

### (c) Political order and the containment of religion

The third characteristic of a secular politics is the dynamic that stems from the original Westphalian quest to bring order to society such that religions and irreligions can co-exist under a neutral political authority whose ultimate concern remains order itself. This is a well-established area of research only briefly summarized here. The Treaty of Westphalia (1648), one of the cornerstone documents at the origin of the modern state, comes only two years after the death of Grotius and mid-way through the life of Hobbes. It could therefore be argued that at its origins IR assumes a break from the theological to the rationalist traditions in this period, marking Westphalia as the beginning of a politically secular 'European international society' (Jackson and Owens, 2005, pp. 52–55). Westphalia thus 'occupies a seminal position in the constructs of inter-national relations theorists' (Parrott, 2004, p. 153) not the least because 'it required diplomacy of a manifestly different order of sophistication from previous treaties, whose generally bipartite negotiations simply demanded a squaring off of the dynastic and confessional wishes of the rulers' (Parrott, 2004, p. 153; also Guthrie, 2003). The Westphalian nego-tiations produced such political axioms as *rex est imperator in regno suo* (the king is emperor in his own realm) and *cujus regio, ejus religio* (the ruler determines the religion of his realm). For Casanova, this regime oversaw the progressive breakdown of 'sacramental structures of media-tion' (Casanova, 1994, p. 13) between transcendent and temporal realms which were 'replaced by new systems of spatial structuration' (1994, p. 15) and the "passage", transfer, or relocation of persons, things, functions, meanings . . . from their traditional location in the religious sphere to the secular sphere' (1994, p. 13). When this process of structuration takes place, the transcendent space becomes individualized and privatized, and the temporal space becomes specialized around the organizational con-cerns of the secular state (for example, the 'political' realm distinct from the 'spiritual' realm). Whatever the challenges presented by resurgent religion in contemporary world politics, including important re-readings of Westphalia that emphasize the agencies of religion (Philpott, 2000), the quest for order via the containment of religious disruption remains a very dominant (and one might suggest reasonable and desirable) priority of international policy-makers grappling with the issue religion, culture and the politics of identity.

The secular dynamics of religion listed above are unremarkable and are reflected in most, if not all, IR treatments of religion to date. Less obvious are the sacral dynamics of religion that animate much religious activity in the contemporary world. It is to these I know turn.

### 2.2.4  Sacral Dynamics

A sacral conception of politics casts religion as a primary element in political belief and structure. Sacral dynamics occur when, from the perspective of political agents such as individuals and communities, politics is attributed with a primarily religious quality. Moreover, sacral dynamics are shaped by concepts and practices that have a normative trajectory beyond the political moment and the material now. I shall briefly explore three examples of sacral dynamics at work within the religious structure of world politics.

### (a)  The political agency of ritual and tradition

The first sacral dynamic of politics is formed by the practice of religious ritual and tradition. Via such practices, the construction of the political is attributed to have a sacral interior. One example of this comes from the writings of Thomas Merton, trappist monk and political activist. Merton's biography *The Seven Storey Mountain* (1948) was a best-seller and launched a life-long and at times deeply paradoxical career in writing, contemplation and social activism (Baker, 1971; Royal, 1997).[1] Merton's status as a significant religious authority is both particular to his own tradition and universal, each element contributing to Royal's claim that 'Merton is beyond doubt one of the great spiritual masters of our century' (Royal, 1997, p. 38). Merton's influence is evident in recent IR scholarship, with Hanson's study of religion in the international system employing Merton 'to orient the text's approach to spirituality' (Hanson, 2006, pp. 9, 8–10, 72–6). Merton is thus an apt source through which to consider sacral dynamics of the political.

*The Seven Storey Mountain* is the biography of the young Merton's conversion from teaching classics at Columbia University to embracing Catholic spirituality and ultimately the cloister of a Trappist monastery. Paradoxically, the cloister became for Merton a place to ponder and comment upon the pressing social issues of his time such as the Cold War, nuclear arms, civil rights, and Third World rights and development (for example, Merton, 1996, pp. 106–7, 175–6, 185–7). A form of political theology can thus be identified at the foundation of Merton's conversion. At the moment when his entry to the monastery was in its most intense stages, Merton interprets the ritual of the Catholic Mass in the following way:

> The eloquence of this liturgy [reflected] one simple, cogent, tremendous truth: this church, the court of the Queen of Heaven, is the real capital of the country

in which we are living. This is the centre of all the vitality that is in America. This is the cause and reason why the nation is holding together. These men, hidden in the anonymity of their choir and their white cowls, are doing for their land what no army, no congress, no president could ever do as such: they are winning for it the grace and the protection and the friendship of God. (Merton, 1948, p. 325)

We could critically engage with such a passage at many levels. I draw out two simple aspects to illustrate the sacral dynamic of religious ritual creating the political. The first is the de-centring and re-centring of the world that occurs via the liturgy. For so many of the world's religious, political formation does not begin with structures and dictates external to the practice of faith, but rather, finds its genesis in and through such practice. This is not ultimately an issue of origins but of authority. The second aspect drawn from Merton's text is the complex relation between faith and the state. The re-centred world remains the world as Merton knows it ('the country in which we are living') and thus from a sacral perspective the basic political structures remain legitimate. There is an overt linkage in Merton's text between ritual practice and state wellbeing that reflects aspects of what Smith has called the sacred dimension of nationalism (S. Smith, 2000). A linkage but not a fusion whereby sacral autonomy is lost – Merton's sacral formation led often to criticism of state policy on issues such as materialism, and civil rights and the Vietnam war (Royal, 1997, p. 35). This autonomy perhaps illustrates the latent prophetic or politically subversive quality that exists in religious ritual and tradition.

**(b)   The religious interpretation of political events**
The second sacral dynamic I shall highlight occurs when political action is attributed with a transcendent significance. Unlike the first dynamic, which is formed by the nomenclature and actions particular to religious tradition (for example, Catholic liturgy), this second dynamic brings a sacral interpretation to impartial political events that can equally be interpreted according to secular assumptions. In this instance, it is the sacral interpretation of action that acts as the catalyst for political agency. To illustrate this distinction I shall remain in the Catholic tradition and draw from a text of Latin American liberation theology. Once again, the choice is not arbitrary. Wuthnow identified liberation theology movements as a context where political symbolism was located 'in the domain of everyday social practice' (Wuthnow, 1991, p. 15, see also p. 20, fn. 12). I draw on a text from this same period and context.

Comblin's work of political theology titled *The Holy Spirit and Liberation* (1989) draws on decades of pastoral experience in Brazilian peasant communities where the author has lived since 1958. Comblin's writing belongs in the large corpus of texts from the liberation theology tradition (for example, Gutiérrez, 1973; Berryman, 1987; Boff and Boff, 1987; Miguez, 2006; Rowland, 2007). The purpose of his work is distinctly sacral in nature, to show how 'the experience of God in the new Christian communities of Latin America can properly be called experience of the Holy Spirit' (Comblin, 1989, p. xi). As such, Comblin observes the context of development and underdevelopment through a sacral lens. The observation below involves an interpretation of the sources of social change:

> When a little old lady, who has spent her life bent double under the burdens inflicted on her by her situation and all the powers of society, suddenly gets up and goes to the local police station to protest at a sergeant's maltreatment of a peasant, and this because she feels herself a member of a community and this takes away her fear forever, something has happened that science cannot explain. Something has happened to her and she knows full well that this something is stronger than her. Thousands of similar cases could be quoted. (Comblin, 1989, p. 22)

Comblin suggests that this political action has a transcendent quality: 'This is a human strength, but a human strength that comes upon people unprepared for it' (1989, p. 23). He later writes,

> . . . what is extraordinary is that [these actions] are produced by the poor and the oppressed. Neither technicians, nor revolutionary vanguard groups nor political leaders experience the Holy Spirit: what they achieve is within their natural capabilities. But for the poor to achieve such results is something else. (1989, p. 23)

It is not my intention to defend or critique the nature of these claims any more than the Merton example that preceded them. The above passage has been chosen to simply illustrate how a sacral perspective penetrates the process of political interpretation. This is all the more valuable given the charge of liberation theology as simply an uncritical derivation of Marxist thought (see Boff and Boff, 1987, p. 187; Turner, 2007). Rather, we see above a clear delineation within the author's perspective between secular revolutionary agency such as might be assumed within Marxist ideology and the actions that reside, according to a sacral perspective of the transcendence of political action, in ecclesiastical communities of the poor.

### (c)  The political capacity of sacred texts[2]
The third sacral dynamic are sacred texts that function, not simply as sources of religious devotion, but also for political action. I shall venture beyond the Catholic traditions used in the examples of ritual and transcendence above, and illustrate at greater length the ways in which some

of the primary conceptual sources of religion are sacred texts and the interpretive and cultic (ritual) traditions that stem from those texts. Hanson summarizes the issue thus: 'Almost all religions hold certain writings sacred, either as the revealed Word of God, or as the description of the experiences of the Other by revered coreligious. Scripture can also present commentary on that experience privileged by the religious community' (Hanson, 2006, p. 79). Those who practise or observe faith-based politics know instinctively that religious texts do function in this way. For instance, in reference to the Abrahamic religions, Cox and Philpott acknowledge that 'God reveals his vision for how his people are to live together through scriptural texts', and that these texts 'emanate principles that prescribe the nature and purpose of government . . . the duties of citizens . . . the distribution of economic wealth, the treatment of the poor, punishment, war and other matters' (Cox and Philpott, 2003, p. 32). Beyond stand-alone ethical principles, scriptures have long provided what Thomas sums as 'narratives that shape the identity of a community' (Thomas, 2000, p. 823). These narratives are not simply retold for posterity's sake, but rather, to adapt the words of the narrative theologian Hauerwas, have been remembered in a way that has 'formed the soul and determined future direction' of local and international communities of faith (Hauerwas, 1983, p. 77). Whilst Hauerwas, influenced by communitarian thought, would insist that because different faiths tell different stories, they therefore produce particular (that is, unique) community dynamics (Hauerwas, 1983), the faster one asserts this point the sooner one bumps into an important principle of impartiality: through the process of interpretation and tradition building, sacred texts generate community narratives of potential political consequence. It is not until those narratives are experienced and enacted – what Boff calls the 'imperative that praxis addresses' (Boff, 1989, p. .63) – that really existing political commonalities and differences between religious narratives may be understood.

Texts create institutional regimes. Texts constrain and recreate political behaviour. Texts are read as sources of moral authority in the rough realities of international conflict. Texts give content to dialogues regarding human values and rights. Whilst this understanding of texts is a given in respect to the constitutions of nation-states and charters of international law, religious texts have been reduced to function only as sources of ethical principle. It is certainly true that sacred scriptures shape some of the highest (and lowest) principles of human conduct, however we would argue they also help satisfy what Elshtain sees as the need to focus on 'concrete structures and institutions of political power' (Elshtain, 1999, p. 144).

But what sort of structures do scriptures produce? The political theorist and biographer John Keane claims there is a need in modern political theory to break the 'bad monist habit' of constantly referring back to a 'grounding principle' in order to validate a theoretical idea (Keane, 1998, pp. 53–4). He argues, for instance, that the concept of civil society is a 'signifier of plurality' and therefore has a 'polysemic' rather than a singular or fixed quality (1998, p. 53). Keane's 'monist habit' is of particular relevance to political theorists from monotheistic religions such as Judaism, Christianity and Islam. After all, it seems an axiom of a monotheistic worldview that all truth emanates from One God. It would therefore appear a maxim of monist logic to also believe that the scriptures of each monotheistic faith promote a singular coherent view on matters of temporal authority and political life. But they do not. In the same way that Keane understands political theories to be 'signifiers of plurality' monotheistic scriptures contain a diversity of political ideas, not a single political agenda. We wish to illustrate this point from the Islamic tradition.

One might assume, given stereotypes about the inflexibility of Islamic political regimes, notably around applications of *Sharia* Law, that the Qur'anic traditions are more likely to carry a singular political agenda. Not so, according to IR scholar Sohail Hashmi, who criticizes the notion of Islamic political unity in the same way others have attacked the 'civilizational' division of world politics:

> As critics of the 'clash of civilizations' thesis have pointed out, the greatest danger of such an emphasis on civilizations is to make them into holistic, non-porous units. There is nothing, of course, more porous than the boundaries of civilizations. Islamic civilization is no exception . . . It is utterly meaningless today to speak of an Islamic 'tradition' or 'civilization' as a monolithic force operating in international politics. (Hashmi, 2002, p. 149)

Thus, for Hashmi there is an emphasis on the diversity ethics of Islam which can be traced back to differences between the early schools of Islamic jurisprudence, one of which emphasized that 'revelation could be supplemented by reason', the other that 'ethical value was derived entirely from God's command' (2002, pp. 150–1). The former approach (Mu'tazilite) seeks to open Qur'anic interpretation to 'human reason guided by principles of equity and public interest' (2002, p. 152). The latter approach (Ash'arite) emphasizes 'the literal interpretation of the Qur'an and predeterminism' (2002, p. 152). Both ethical approaches 'can be derived from the Qur'an' (2002, p. 152), thereby emphasising the diversity of political ideas and practice that could potentially stem from devout Islamic interpretation.

The importance of Hashmi's perspective is that the political views that are read out of sacred texts are dependent upon traditions of interpretation. Such an inference addresses perhaps the gravest secular fear concerning the role of sacral politics rooted in sacred scripture, namely, that the deployment of religious text will as a matter of course create monolithic inflexible political regimes. This may well be true in some instances, but only by also rejecting open flexible pluralistic traditions that can be derived from the same source.

I conclude this point with a brief example of Islamic conceptions of civil society. Gibbons and Reimer describe the current state of international affairs as one where 'postmodernization and globalization processes are changing the nature of the territorial nation state as well as changing the values of institutions' (Gibbons and Reimer, 1999, p. 115). For scholars and public intellectuals this is producing new visions of civil society. It is not surprising therefore that Keane observes the global trend of 'Muslim actors intent on developing and redefining civil society' (Keane, 1998, p. 28). Keane argues that in some contexts fledgling civil societies 'are best nurtured and protected by renewing religious faith' and that 'these emergent post-secular civil societies not only pose a challenge to political despotism' they also promise the transition toward the rule of law. Keane cites the 'pathbreaking' work of Tunisian Qur'anic scholar Sheikh Rachid al-Ghannouchi in the following way:

> Just as the followers of the Prophet lived the relationship between ad-dini (the religious) and as-siyasi (the political), so Ghannouchi insists that the laws and institutions of a modern political community should nurture and honour the dignity of its citizens . . . He insists that Muslims must also use their human capacity for reason ('aql) and ijtihad [context bound judgements] and work to create, renew and nurture civil society institutions (al-mujtama' al-ahli). (Keane, 1998, pp. 28–31; see also Tamimi, 2001, pp. 135–53)

Not all commentators consider Ghannouchi to be as progressive as Keane suggests. Moroccan scholar Abdou Filali-Ansary contrasts the work of Ghannouchi with Iranian philosopher Abdul Karim Soroush: 'Ghannouchi is a main representative of Islamist attitudes and thought (and faces persecution for that); Soroush is a formidable intellectual opponent of Islamism (for which, he too, faces persecution from his government)' (Filali-Ansary, 1996, p. 77; see also Wright, 1996). Filali-Ansary sees Soroush as the 'true reformer' of the two because his views 'are closer to modern humanism' in the cause of 'open religion' and not simply 'radical innovation'. Filali-Ansary doubts the reformist credentials of Ghannouchi because 'the community [of faith] – not the individual – remains the ultimate reality and objective' of his work. The role of sacred text in each position remains important though, reflecting important secular-sacral distinctions, the primacy of scripture is for Ghannouchi more prominent than for Soroush. Moreover, a politics shaped by religious texts and interpretive traditions need not lose itself, as Filali-Ansary seems to suggest it must, to the universal story of 'modern humanism' – or any other secular structure – in order to function as a constructive democratic influence in international affairs. In a development context, for example, without community text-based approaches – like that of Ghannouchi and many others across most (if not all) religious traditions – there may be little to mediate between reactionary traditionalism (the seedbed of religious fundamentalism) and tradition-less individualism (the seedbed of economic exploitation). The alternative is secularization that 'has entailed severing society's cultural roots; its objective [to achieve] a complete break from the past' (Tamimi, 2001, p. 107). For Ghannouchi, 'secularism brings about the death of man because it views him as a body with a set of material needs, thus eliminating . . . his metaphysical dimension' (Tamimi, 2001, p. 150). This, at least, seems the claim for those who stress religious texts, traditions and communities as primary sources for political life.

### 2.2.5    The Inclusion and Exclusion of Religion

I have thus far employed the Venn diagram to differentiate the dynamics of religion. There is a second intended function of the Venn and this also brings clarity to the research agenda without oversimplifying the complexity of religion in world politics. When applied to specific issues of IR the model is designed to situate religious actors in relation to the dominant political interests associated with the particular global dynamic in question. Where are the actors and agendas of religion included in the dominant interests of world politics and where are they excluded from these interests? Such an approach allows us to 'see' religion in new ways, especially where religious actors and agendas are situated in the central processes of the international system and where they remain outside such processes. In short, the dynamics of religion model probes 'where religion is' in relation to the centres of power at work in world politics. The second function of the model is represented in Figure 2.7.

As previously acknowledged, situating religion in different spaces of the religious structure counters the social-scientific tendency to homogenize religion as belonging in fewer or even single spaces. Another way of challenging the homogenization of religion is by investigating the way religious actors and interests are included and excluded from agendas of power in world politics. As Fox's recent study on government involvement in religion shows religious actors possess and exert very different levels of power depending on the context under investigation (see Fox, 2008, pp. 66–104). What the religious structure provides, in addition, is a differentiation

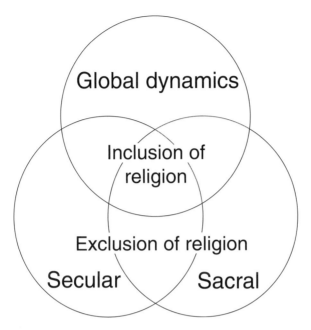

*Figure 2.7    The dynamics of religion model (3)*

among those included or excluded, dependent on whether religion is a primary (sacral) or secondary (secular) influence in actor behaviour.

## 2.3   TOWARD AN APPLICATION OF THE DYNAMICS OF RELIGION MODEL

To summarize, this chapter responds to specific methodological challenges that have emerged from recent IR scholarship in religion. The first challenge is the need to build an analytical structure of 'amicable accommodation' (Madeley, 2003, p. xxii) such that both secular and sacral arguments might find their legitimate place in the discourse of religion and world politics. This is certainly a standing challenge to political science because emphases that lean a priori toward or away from religion will be limited in their view. I have attempted to answer this challenge in two ways. The first is to argue that inscribed across the general discourse of IR there exist three distinct but overlapping discourses of religion. The secular discourse holds religion to be a secondary, or even negligible, dynamic in political formation. The sacral discourse holds religious actors and interests to have a primary role in political formation. Added to this, a third integrated discourse holds secular and sacral political dynamics to be mutually constitutive. The second way I have responded to the challenge of amicable accommodation is to utilize the discourses on religion in the field to construct a new analytical structure equal in function and importance to other structures of IR. The religious structure of world politics amicably accommodates the concomitant effects of secularization and sacralization in international affairs. It is within this structure that we have introduced a new primary question into the study of IR scholarship, namely, 'Where is religion?' Asking such a question allows the analyst to inhabit the religious structure in its entirety, attempting to situate varying interests and actors of world politics according to secular-integrated-sacral criteria. Such an approach can provide wide-ranging insights into the agency of religion in the international realm by transcending binary arguments such as 'secularism versus religion' or 'modernity versus tradition'.

The second suggested challenge in IR religion research is the need to employ the very concept of religion as an organizing force in the international system (Hurd, 2008, p. 1). Models are important tools for making sense of complex social phenomena so that new and sometimes vital insights can be realized. I have argued that this can be most profitably achieved on the subject of religion by constructing a model that offers a breadth and depth of insight into the dynamics of religion in world politics. In regards to breadth, the model allows us to differentiate (via the new structure of IR) the elements of religion across the religious spectrum related to selected dynamics of world politics. In regards to depth, the model allows us to perceive which elements of religion are included in mainstream global agendas and which elements are excluded.

Having constructed the dynamics of religion model so described, the research now moves to an investigation of the secular and sacral impacts of religion upon the conception and practice of international development. The model is applied to the domain of international development at three levels: discourse, institutions and policy. At the level of discourse in Chapter 3 orthodox and critical approaches to development are described and re-evaluated against the secular, integrated and sacral characteristics of religion. This approach enables scholars to more precisely situate religion throughout the development sphere. The reordering effects of religion create new areas of enquiry in religion and development studies. How are differences between secular, integrated and sacral approaches toward religion to be understood in policy terms? How might we employ these understandings to discern the nature and impacts of religion upon development institutions? What elements of religion are included in the global development agenda and what elements remain excluded? The dynamics of religion model is then applied to answer such questions at the institutional and policy level. At the level of institutions Chapter 4 focuses on the engagement with religious development institutions and actors by the World Bank Group (WBG). The WBG is defined primarily as an institutional arena of contestation between competing ideologies of development. The WBG plays a central role in negotiating and setting the global development agenda. The dynamics of religion model is first applied to describe and analyze the way religion entered the policy domain of the WBG, differentiating secular, integrated and sacral interests at work in the policy formation process between the 1980s and the early years of the presidency of James Wolfensohn. This initial modelling acts as a foundation for closer analyzes of the dynamics of religion in the policy formation process. At the level of policy in Chapter 5 the dynamics of religion model is applied to describe and critically analyze partnerships between the WBG and faith institutions that emerged in the period 1998–2005. The dynamics of religion model situates these partnerships differently within the religious structure of world politics, and also in relation to the ideological sphere of the WBG. Chapter 6 features a modest case study and critical evaluation of the WBG partnership with the World Faiths Development Dialogue (WFDD). The dynamics of religion model is employed to analyze the WBG-WFDD initiative against the claims of orthodox and critical development approaches. Chapter 7 completes the exploratory study into the WBG and faith institutions by considering the ways some religious actors are included in the development agenda and others are excluded. The chapter concludes by suggesting that a 'sacral deficit' remains at the policy level despite the increased focus on faith institutions in the development sphere.

## NOTES

1. 'Of all the great modern religious writers, no one harboured within himself a larger cast of dramatis personae than Thoms Merton' (Royal, 1997, p. 34).
2. The following section is an adapted excerpt from an early article by the author (Rees, 2004).

# 3. Religion and the discourse of development

> When I feed the poor they call me a saint. When I ask why the poor have no
> food they call me a communist.
> Dom Helder Camara, Archbishop of Recife, Brazil (1968)

> Religion is like a cow. It kicks, but it also gives milk.
> Ramakrishna (quoted by Arvind Sharma in Tyndale, 2006, p. xiv)

## 3.1 INTRODUCTION

The dynamics of religion model could arguably be applied in multiple
contexts in world politics. In the present chapter the phrase 'dynamics of
religion' refers to the primary and secondary impacts of religion upon different theories that scholars and practitioners have constructed in the field
of international development. The phrase also attests to the role that religious actors and interests play in the dynamics of development that these
scholars and practitioners observe. Each emphasis is a component of what
is meant by the term 'discourse'. The present chapter summarizes two contrasting schools of development theory and practice of development and
reorganizes these approaches using the dynamics of religion model. Such
modelling thus situates religion at the discourse level of development and
anticipates important issues to be explored at the institutional and policy
level in the chapters that follow.

## 3.2 THE DISCOURSE OF DEVELOPMENT

Development is a highly contested term 'concerning how "developing
countries" can improve their living standards and eliminate absolute
poverty' (Kingsbury, 2004, p. 1). Development in practice is constituted
by a broad range of priorities from crisis relief to long-term reconstruction, from environmental sustainability to gender empowerment, from
good governance at the international level to community consultation

at the local level, and many others. In this chapter I will briefly explain why the development sphere has been chosen as the site to operationalize the dynamics of religion model, identify several elements of the discourse of development and situate two contrasting approaches to development within the dynamics of religion model.

### 3.2.1 Choosing Development as a Site of Analysis

Why choose development to test the dynamics of religion in IR? Four introductory reasons are suggested. First, development is directly connected to both secular and sacral assumptions about religion. Development is a practical consequence of the rise of modernization and secularization. Peet argues, 'Development is a founding belief of the modern world. Progress has long since replaced God as the icon of our age' (Peet, 1999, p.1). Rist goes further to suggest that because development 'distinguishes modern societies from those that have gone before' (Rist, 2008, p.13) it has thus become 'an element of modern religion' (Rist, 2008, p.23). These brief statements emphasize the secular subordination of religion by the forces of modernity. By contrast, sacral perspective draws on an increased sense of religious agency in the pursuit of development ideals. Religious actors, whether as faith institutions or religious communities, feature prominently in development contexts. As Tyndale observes,

> The belief that there can be no true development without spiritual advancement, or, as the Hindus put it, that 'all human activities are part of the sacred pattern of the universe' . . . is, in one form or another, still the belief of the majority of people in the world today. (Tyndale, 2002, p.45)

In other words, the sacral dimensions of life are normative for many if not most of the partners to and subjects of development action. Thus, applied to the theory and practice of development, any general discourse that excludes or ignores the question of religion is conceptually and instrumentally inadequate. Whilst the importance of religion in development is rapidly gaining credence (Haynes, 2007b; Clarke and Jennings, 2008a), it still falls outside established development norms. Contemporary introductions on development can, for instance, still neglect religion as a concept altogether (for example, Kingsbury et al., 2004). Hence there is scope to better situate the complex interaction between the secular and sacral dynamics of religion in the discourse of development.

The second reason for choosing development as a means to operationalize the dynamics of religion model is to address a central paradox in development practice and theory: 'the denial of religion at the heart of a modern development, yet at the same time its strong value claims for greater good that many religious organizations share' (Harcourt, 2003, p. 3). Such a tension is reflected across many dimensions of the development field. For example, in the domain of international crisis relief Pfanner notes that religion 'largely remains taboo in humanitarian action', yet also acknowledges that '[m]uch of international humanitarian action consists of intercultural work, in which the religious dimension is an important factor' (Pfanner, 2005, p. 240). This tension is also reflected in the academic study of development. Like other dimensions of IR discourse, religion has been a missing element in the study of development. Clarke attributes two reasons for this neglect: '"secular reductionism" – the neglect of religious variables in favour of other sociological attributes such as class, ethnicity and gender – [and] "materialistic determinism" – the neglect of nonmaterial, especially religious, motivations in explaining individual or institutional behaviour' (Clarke, 2008b, p. 17). The present chapter attempts to move beyond these limitations toward a broader conceptual engagement of benefit to both theory and practice.

Third, development is an appropriate site for applying the dynamics of religion model because some of the early treatments of religion in IR make the linkage between religious agency and the development sphere. This has been previously noted in reference to state development concerns in Third World contexts (for example, Einstadt, 1973; Hermassi, 1973; Leach, 1973). In Wuthnow's important essay from 1991 Latin American liberation theology is thus identified as a subject of study that could help theorists overcome the 'lingering biases' of an over-secularized analysis of world affairs (Wuthnow, 1991, pp. 15, 20 fn. 12). Thus, religion emerges in the discourse of IR from the dynamics of religion that are observed and conceptualized in development contexts.

Fourth, religion has been neglected, until recently, as a primary topic of academic study in development. Ver Beek (2002) conducted an influential survey of the way three leading development journals dealt with the subjects of religion and spirituality. The tabulation of the results (2002, p. 68) is replicated in Table 3.1.

As can be seen in Table 3.1, when placed alongside development priorities of environment, gender and population studies, spirituality and religion are significantly underemphasized. Despite a movement toward holism in development discourse, key sources of ideas on development theory and practice still reflect the marginalization and problematization of religion (McDuie-Ra and Rees, 2010). For Ver Beek this is surprising, given the prominence of religion in the Third World:

For most people of the 'South', spirituality is integral to their understanding of the world and their place in it, and so is central to the decisions they make about their own and their communities' development. Their spirituality affects decisions about who should treat their sick children, when and how they will plant their fields, and whether or not to participate in risky but potentially beneficial social action. Despite the evident centrality of spirituality to such decisions, the subject is conspicuously under-represented in the development discourse. (Ver Beek, 2002, p. 60)

*Table 3.1    Number of articles with references to the listed keywords, by journal*

| Journals 1982–98 | Keywords | | | | |
|---|---|---|---|---|---|
| | Environment | Gender | Population | Spiritual, Spirituality | Religion, Religious |
| *World Development* | 83 | 85 | 89 | 0 | 5 |
| *Journal of Development Studies* | 19 | 46 | 38 | 0 | 1 |
| *Journal of Developing Areas* | 18 | 32 | 43 | 0 | 10 |

*Source:*    Ver Beek (2002, p. 68)

Of significance for the present study, Ver Beek observes that where religion and spirituality do appear in the development sources surveyed, they are limited to a secondary role of 'descriptive categories' and in 'not one of these articles is the relationship between development and religion or spirituality the central theme' (Ver Beek, 2002, pp. 68–9). In other words, even when it is not problematized religion remains subordinate to other more dominant development priorities. Yet, in deference to the cautionary approach needed in the study of religion, Ver Beek's use of 'spirituality' may yet be imprecise – and even a Westernized misnomer – if by spirituality we mean 'spiritual' as distinct from practical. A more nuanced perspective might be to suggest that whilst many Third World people's live in a world of spirits, these spirits impact life at the mundane as much, or even more than, the elevated or transcendent level that 'spirituality' may imply. Many contexts may thus reflect an integration of spirituality, culture and development that is hard to distinguish. The corrective needed may require more than 'adding' religion to development discourse and instead involve differentiating the dynamics of religion situated throughout the development sphere.

### 3.2.2    Elements of the Discourse of Development

The discourse of development is constituted by competing assumptions toward issues such as 'progress', 'economy', 'society', 'growth', 'dependency' and 'globalization'. The elements of the discourse of development can be usefully introduced via the theories, issues and actors central to development concerns. I shall briefly explain each of these components.

According to Roberts development 'can be conceived only within an ideological framework' (Roberts, 1984, p. 7). For example, Staudt (1991) distinguishes development ideologies that prioritize state policy from those that emphasize the empowerment of people independent of state interests. The latter involves 'a process of enlarging people's choices', enhancing 'participatory democratic processes' and providing 'human beings with the opportunity to develop their fullest potential'. The former involves 'a nation's development goals' via 'economic growth' and a sense of 'national self-reliance' (Staudt, 1991, pp. 28–9). Different ideological postures toward development can be seen through the main theoretical paradigms of the discipline of international political economy (IPE) which, at its simplest, can be understood as the study of relations between economic and political affairs (Gilpin, 2003, p. 22). Cohn summarizes these positions in relation to the global divide between Northern and Southern hemispheres and the interests of less developed countries (LDCs):

> Realist [that is, economic nationalist] writers in the North, preoccupied with the issues of power and influence, tend to ignore the economic interests of poorer countries in the South . . . Liberals believe that the growth of interdependence has widespread benefits, and they often argue that North-South linkages provide even more benefits to the South than to the North . . . As historical structuralists, dependency theorists reject the optimism of liberals and . . . [argue that] structural factors related to the global capitalist economy are responsible for constraining LDC development possibilities. (Cohn, 2005, p. 368)

Haque employs a schema identifying 'conservative' 'reformist' and 'radical' theoretical traditions to contrast not dissimilar approaches to those described above (Haque, 1999, p. 163). Beyond the adoption of a three-fold pattern, further distinctions exist between and within these ideological demarcations. One example is the capacity of economic nationalist approaches to adapt to the conditions of globalization and thereby challenge the once-dominant assumptions of economic liberalism (Helleiner, 2002). Another example is the debate within dependency approaches on the merits of adopting an open or closed position on the question of economic globalization and the pursuit of social justice (Kitching, 2001).

Beyond the dependency school lie 'post-development' approaches that critique the legitimacy of development itself (for example, Escobar, 1995).

Differentiating between ideologies of development also occurs via engagements with specific issues. O'Brien and Williams identify three key issues of central importance to studies in economic development in recent decades: how 'national development aspirations and efforts are shaped by international organizations' (O'Brien and Williams, 2004, p. 274); the motivation, effectiveness and conditionality associated with economic aid (2004, pp. 278–82); and the complex historical and political dynamics that undergird the North-South conflict (2004, pp. 282–5). In addition, issues such as environmental impacts and gender participation have shaped development thinking in significant ways over the past three decades (Shiva, 1992; MacDonald, 1998; Jain and Sen, 2005).

The discourse of development also concerns the relative inputs from different actors of world politics operating in a context of globalization. Principal among these are the state, international organizations (Rittberger and Zangl, 2006, pp. 145–78), and those actors associated with 'civil society' understood as a sphere of political activity and social activity separate from the state and the market (Cohen and Arato, 1992, p. 18). Actors within civil society include social movements, community organizations, political parties, trade unions, though the term is increasingly being used to refer simply to non-government organizations (NGOs) (Amoore and Langley, 2004, p. 91).

Together, the theories, issues and actors constitute a discourse of long-standing importance to IR. Though some elements of this discourse may prove more compelling than others, I again apply Waever's principle of mutual serviceability (Waever, 1996) to argue that each component is valuable for a dynamic understanding of development as a whole. Several examples illustrate this idea. O'Brien and Williams argue that a 'complex phenomenon such as development is not attributed to forces arising from one level of analysis', and hence, 'development is neither solely an internal affair, nor driven relentlessly by external pressures' (O'Brien and Williams, 2004, p. 261). For Cohn, different IPE approaches are of benefit in addressing different aspects of the global political economy because 'the same development strategy is not necessarily feasible or desirable for all LDCs [less developed countries]' (Cohn, 2005, p. 398). Whilst remaining within the critical tradition of development theory, Kitching's work on social justice and globalization critiques a priori arguments that collapse capitalism into imperialism (Kitching, 2001, pp. 169–90). For Kitching, if one is concerned with issues of structural inequality and the need for the redistribution of global wealth, it is imperative that capitalism is not understood as 'an economic system that can be endlessly monopolized by one ethnic or cultural group of the world's population, or by one geo-graphical region of the globe' (2001, p. 190). Rather than assuming that globalization universally reinforces a bipolar imperial structure of earlier colonialism, Kitching holds that post-colonial strategies of orthodox state development continued to impoverish some geopolitical regions such as Africa, some states in Central America and the Caribbean, while others in southern Latin America and South-East Asia subsequently advanced to become globally competitive (2001, pp. 185–6). Therefore, in an era of globalization 'the world – the globe – became more complex, more dif-ferentiated in socio-economic structure and in global economic role, and the bi-polar imperialist picture became harder and harder to sustain as a compelling picture of the world' (2001, p. 186).

These assumptions about the dynamic complexity of the global politi-cal economy in relation to development echo earlier understandings of the complexity of religion. The present study assumes that discourses on development in the context of the global political economy are polyse-mous. Thus, the plurality of development approaches reflects the complex-ity of development itself (Haque, 1999, p. 162; Cohn, 2005, p. 398). The study of development and religion together requires structural modelling to order and differentiate the multiple elements that exist in both areas.

### 3.2.3 Development Approaches in the Present Study

This chapter aims to reorder the discourse of development using the dynamics of religion, thereby laying a foundation for further enquiry into religion and development at the institutional and policy levels. To this end, we shall adopt a simplified understanding of the development discourse as comprised of two approaches.

The first understanding may be conventionally called the orthodox approach, incorporating economic nationalist (that is, state development) and neoliberal models of development that emphasize the economically beneficial effects of globalization. In its 'rawest' form the orthodox view of development is an 'economics first' approach (Remenyi, 2004, p. 25) that prioritizes 'GDP per capita and levels of industrialization' (Pease, 2003, p. 178) as a means to progress. Accordingly, poverty is a 'situation suffered by people without money to buy food and satisfy other material needs' (C. Thomas, 2005, p. 650). Orthodox development models reflect what O'Brien and Williams have called a theory of 'internal causation' which begins from the assumption that 'the absence of development in a particu-lar society results from that society's failure to harness its resources in a way relevant to the demands of modern economic growth' (O'Brien and Williams, 2004, pp. 259–60). As such, orthodox development models are 'modernization first' (Remenyi, 2004, p. 25) theories that hold to a linear, evolutionary, perspective on social change (O'Brien and Williams, 2004, p. 260). Advocates for the orthodox model argue that mainstream development approaches have led to higher than average growth rates in the developing world, the upward movement of South-east Asian economies, and significant improvements in global social indicators such as adult literacy, access to safe water and infant mortality rates (C. Thomas, 2005, pp. 651–2). It might also be argued that orthodox approaches have taken seriously and responded to many criticisms (Camdessus, 2001, pp. 363–70; C. Thomas, 2005, pp. 659–60) creating an improved orthodoxy (Dodge and Murray, 2006, pp. 361–72). Yet critics of economic orthodoxy highlight its narrow, technocratically 'thin' approach toward an endeavour that is ostensibly 'thick', namely, the transformation of the material wealth of a society not just an economy. 'One size fits all' development, it is asserted, may only fit the few at the exclusion and/or harm of the many. Peet cites several critiques of orthodox development, the first of which is technical: 'not only do the data [that orthodox models rely upon] vary greatly in reliability from country to country, but the basic accuracy in measuring things like production, income, education, or the use of energy has to be treated with the greatest suspicion' (Peet, 1999, p. 7). This critique holds that the conventions of measurement are 'Western' to the detriment of non-Western contexts, that informal economic activity and gendered work divisions are neglected by such measurements and that 'expertise' from the field is claimed via limited exposure to real-life development contexts and thus an over-reliance, once again, on dubiously gathered data spreadsheets (Peet, 1999, p. 7). In response, the orthodox measure of poverty has broadened to include 'the fulfilment of basic needs, the condition of the natural environment, and the extent to which the marginalised are politically empowered' (Pease, 2003, p. 178). In this view the purpose of development searches beyond economic advancement toward the goal of human wellbeing through an integrated and sustainable process of social, cultural, political and economic transformation (C. Thomas, 2005, p. 650). The global capitalist economy is viewed as an enabling structure. Mandle has argued for the net positive gains of economic development for the poor, attributing as much to the structure of globalization as to specific measures and mechanisms of development: 'Globalization and economic development . . . are desirable to the extent that they result in improved standards of living, and, in particular, reduction in poverty for the people who live in countries experiencing these processes' (Mandle, 2003, pp. 20, 9–23). Within development orthodoxy the relation between market movement and political interest is complex and not always easy to discern. Sen argues that the role markets play 'must depend not only on what they do but on what they are allowed to do', and that vested interests from 'a group of "industrialists" can make sure that their profits are well protected' by ensuring that 'markets are not given adequate room' (Sen, 1999, pp. 120–1). The solution for Sen lies neither in a hyper-globalist loosing of market forces as the principal agent of development, nor a total-ized critique of global capital as innately hegemonic (see Murphy, 2000). Rather, a more adequate response is rooted in the implementation of a 'many-sided approach' to the development challenge 'partly as a result of the difficulties faced as well as the successes achieved by different countries over recent decades' (Sen, 1999, pp. 126–7).

A contrasting understanding of development is conventionally known as the critical approach, incorporating the dependency and post-development critiques of the mainstream development enterprise. Though distinct in many respects, dependency and post-development approaches share the common emphasis of challenging the mainstream development agenda at fundamental levels (Matthews, 2004; Simon, 2007). The criti-cal approach reflects what O'Brien and Williams have called a theory of 'external causation' whereby 'underdevelopment is the result of external forces that constrain a society's efforts to develop' (O'Brien and Williams, 2004, p. 260). Exemplifying such constraints, Peet cites a second 'more profound' critique of orthodox development:

> The argument is increasingly made that GNP/capita, and even more benign statistical devices like the HDI [Human Development Index], have *nothing* to do with the quality of life . . . Statistical tables of GNP/capita are seen as instru-ments of power rather than as neutral methods of measurement, because their very structure . . . implies a hierarchy that must be replicated for people to be said to be living well.' (Peet, 1999, p. 10, emphasis in original)

In the critical development view the constraints of measurement reflect the asymmetrical power relations embodied in global capitalism. From the critical perspective known as the dependency school, the forces of global capitalism – borne of the expansion of European industrialization from the nineteenth century, one of the principle agents of ideological conflict of the twentieth century, and intensified further with the collapse of the controlled economic alternatives of the communist world – create an asymmetry whereby 'development of some countries has resulted in the underdevelopment of others' (O'Brien and Williams, 2004, p. 260). For dependency writers such as Frank, in close conceptual proximity to the 'world-systems' theory of Wallerstein, the divisions of development and underdevelopment reflect global class conflicts similar to those observed and/or constructed by Marx in national contexts of early industrializa-tion (see Wallerstein, 1974, 1979; Frank, 1979). Critical approaches also

extend beyond traditional Marxist applications and focus on the perceived democratic deficit of the global economy. For instance, in the
contexts of advanced global capitalism, the free-flow of money is governed by an autocratic structure of decision making that Martin has
called 'dictatorship with limited liability' (Martin and Schumann, 1997,
pp. 40–67). Beyond the dependency critique of global capitalism – which
in many respects rejects the capitalist structures of global development
but remains economistic in its restructuration of the global toward the
needs of periphery states – lies the post-development school of critical
development theory. Post-developmentalism is rooted in non-rationalist
approaches to the international political economy (Amin and Palan,
2001), and subscribes to a subaltern – radically localized, postmodern
– view of the political sphere. Escobar summarizes the tenets of post-
development thus:

> . . . first, that the proper analytical unit of analysis is modernity/coloniality – in
> sum, there is no modernity without coloniality, with the latter being constitu-
> tive of the former. Second, the fact that the colonial difference is a privileged
> epistemological and political space . . . [W]hat emerges from this alternative
> framework is the need to take seriously the epistemic force of local histories
> and to think theory through the practice of subaltern groups. (Escobar, 2004,
> pp. 217, 207–30; also Guha, 1997, pp. ix–xxii)

The post-development framework characterizes 'development' by the
(patriarchal) domination of peoples and nature, for the benefit of the few
at the expense of the many, using colonial constructions and measures
of poverty, the solution against which is to resist developments' own
epistemological claims to legitimacy (Peet, 1999, p. 123) and break out
of the 'colonial prison' (Arnold, 1994). Whereas dependency is a total-
ized critique of capitalism, post-development is a totalized critique of
development. There are important linkages between dependency and
post-development schools (for a comparative study, see Kapoor, 2002).
One common denominator might be an imperative to resistance for, and
on behalf of, those who remain conditionally or perpetually impoverished
by the 'system', however that system is measured. The critical theorist Cox
has emphasized the role of social forces in determining regimes of power
in the global political economy (Cox, 1986, p. 35). O'Brien and Williams
summarize Cox's perspective on social forces as follows:

> Social forces are groups of people who occupy a particular place in the global
> economy by virtue in their role in the organization of production. Some social
> forces such as the people who own and work in internationally competitive
> industry advocate free trade while other social forces will oppose free trade as a
> threat to their interests'. (O'Brien and Williams, 2004, pp. 31–2)

The realm of social forces is therefore a space of politico-economic contestation defined, in no small part, by the pressures of emancipation against the vested interests of capitalist hegemonic power (Cox, 1986, pp. 236–9). The emancipatory dynamics within this conception of social forces are also carried in Escobar's notion of 'other worlds' beyond coloniality, and the role of 'social movements' and 'place-based politics' is a central part of this (Escobar, 2004, pp. 220–4). As such 'social forces of emancipation' and 'social movements of resistance' are linked by the common theme of emancipation.

In addition to the orthodox and critical development schools, I employ the phrase global development agenda to collectively refer to the dominant issues defined as priorities, problems and solutions in development. Setting the development agenda involves gathering knowledge about conditions in the South, which of these conditions require intervention, the nature of these intervention (reflecting ideological priorities), the policies and processes employed, and partnerships created to implement these policies (McDuie-Ra and Rees, 2010).

## 3.3  THE ELEMENTS OF RELIGION IN DEVELOPMENT DISCOURSE

What difference does the dynamics of religion framework make to an understanding of development discourse? One answer is that religion presents as an equally complex component of the global political economy because the elements of religion spread throughout the development sphere. Applying the dynamics of religion to a study of development, the secular, integrated and sacral manifestations of religion therefore feature within both orthodox and critical approaches. Select elements of religion are summarized in Table 3.2.

### 3.3.1  Secular Religion in Development

The secular elements of religion are those characterized by the subordination of religious actors and interests to other structures and priorities. Both orthodox and critical development approaches to development subordinate religion to other more dominant mechanisms and interests. I shall not explore the more obvious elements of subordination such as the religion-less bureaucratic state or the materialist ontologies of the Marxist-critical tradition. Rather, I have chosen elements of development discourse where religion is more evident yet remains subordinate. Within orthodox development this is represented through state

*Table 3.2    The secular, integrated and sacral elements of religion in*
*orthodox and critical development approaches*

|  | Secular Religion | Integrated Religion | Sacral Religion |
|---|---|---|---|
| Orthodox approaches to development | State patronage of some religions over others<br>Religion as an ethical foundation for globalization | Religion and the turn to authenticity in development<br>Religions as particular agents of capitalist development | Religion-led political development<br>Religion-led economics |
| Critical approaches to development | Religion as faith and ideology<br>Metaphors of development as religion | Religious actors as part of social movements<br>Liberation theologies | Faith communities and organizations contest development priorities |

patronage of some religions over others and the deployment of religion
to promote the ethics of globalization. Within critical ideology it is represented by the critique of state manipulations of religion and by the use
of metaphors of religion to describe development as a kind of market
fundamentalism.

The principal mechanisms to achieve orthodox development objectives
have traditionally been the state and the market, and each remain essential to orthodox development in either economic nationalist or neoliberal
forms (Haque, 1999, pp. 67–8). Consequently, subordinate forms of religion feature within state and market-centric ideologies of development.
Two such forms are state patronage of religion for the sake of political
order, and the instrumental appeal of religious groups in the promotion of
economic globalization.

**(a)    Secular religion and orthodox development**
Because state-centric approaches to development hold to assumptions of
internal causation they necessarily prioritize the stability of the domestic
sphere. Important research by Fox (2008) reveals an interest by state
actors in religion as a means of creating order for its citizens. Fox (2008)
draws from a broad-ranging dataset of 175 state contexts to investigate in
order to discern the level of government involvement in religion (see Fox,
2008, pp. 62–104). One strong pattern to emerge from the quantitative

survey is 'the tendency of most states to give preference to some religions over others' (2008, p. 353). Whilst recognizing that 'each state has a distinct history and unique set of motivations' (2008, p. 353), Fox discerns general motivations behind state policy (2008, pp. 352–6) as follows:

    i)   the protection of domestic culture from outside influence;
    ii)  the protection of citizens from religions that are dangerous;
    iii) the core link between religion and national identity in many contexts;
    iv) a mutually supportive relationship with the state between religious institutions and elites in many contexts;
    v)  support by historical inertia (i.e. accepted tradition)

Only one of the above characteristics – the influence of religious doctrine upon state policy (2008, p. 355) – reflects some degree of primary religious agency. The remainder represent dynamics where religion is the object of state patronage for the greater purpose of maintaining political order.

Religion plays an equally instrumental role in maintaining economic order. Saul (1997) has argued that nineteenth-century industrialization only produced social progress once civil society groups began to agitate against the Dickensian conditions first produced by the new modern cities. Stiglitz (2003b) has argued for a similar role of civil society groups and institutions to produce a new paradigm of development. For some theorists religion plays an important role in this process to produce a more ethical framework for the global market economy (Kung, 2003). Dunning calls the end product 'Responsible global capitalism (RGC) . . . a means of providing a richer, healthier and more meaningful life style for individuals and their families; and of advancing the economic objectives and social transformation of societies' (Dunning, 2003, pp. 11–12). The RGC project includes religious actors as part of 'non-market institutions within which the market is embedded and which, together, characterize a global society' (Dunning, 2003, p. 13). Within this approach, religious perspectives are included to inform the broadening set of development measures such as the Human Development Index (HDI) of the United Nations, thereby becoming embedded in the 'value-adding activities of RGC' (Dunning, 2003, pp. 15, 17). Within the discourse monotheistic religions and some eastern traditions are viewed as an important source of moral standards required to uphold a coherent ethical framework of globalization (Ahmad, 2003; Griffiths, 2003; Sacks, 2003). Of present interest is the way a diverse set of religious traditions is employed as a singular source of moral legitimacy for development orthodoxy at the global level. Although religious particularity features in this discourse, it is the characteristic of impartiality – that is, all religions subordinate to the moral improvement of economic globalization – that makes the RGC project an expression of secular religion as we have defined it.

**(b)  Secular religion and critical development**

Critical development approaches apply a hermeneutic of suspicion toward institutions and dynamics that orthodox development approaches tend to trust implicitly. For instance, in a strong critique of state power, Scott describes the 'pernicious combination' (Scott, 1998, p. 4) of four characteristics of state-led development that often have had tragic consequences upon modern societies. These are the 'administrative ordering of state and society', a 'high-modernist ideology' driven by 'the rational design of social order commensurate with the scientific understanding of natural laws', the use of coercive power in order to fulfil its ideology, and a 'prostrate civil society that lacks the capacity to resist these plans' (1998, pp. 4–5). Within this critical approach to state power, Nandy (2002) perceives the malign subordination of religion via the 'hegemonic language of secularism popularised by Western intellectuals and the middle class' which has 'increasingly become a cover for the complicity of modern intellectuals and the modernising middle classes . . . with new forms of religious violence' (2002, pp. 61–2). Nandy argues that secularism pits one form of religion he calls 'ideology' against another form named 'faith'. For Nandy, religion as ideology takes the form of a 'sub-national, national or cross-national identifier of populations contesting for or protecting non-religious, usually political or socioeconomic, interests' (2002, p. 62). This is contrasted by, and in conflict with, faith as 'religion as a way of life, a tradition which is definitely non-monolithic and operationally plural' (2002, p. 62). Secularism and religion are therefore closely linked, but in differentiating the 'two axis on which . . . contemporary religions can be plotted' (2002, p. 62) the state 'always prefers to deal with religious ideologies rather than with faiths' (2002, p. 62).

Another secular-critical perspective in the discourse of development is the use of religion as a metaphor to critique the perceived 'fundamentalism' of development. Working within a post-development framework Rist defines development as 'the general transformation and destruction of the natural environment and of social relations' for the sake of increasing 'the production of commodities (goods and services) geared, by way of exchange, to effective demand' (Rist, 2008, p. 13). Rist argues that despite its manifold failures development remains unchallenged because the high ethical aspirations of the development enterprise have become a form of secular religiosity (2008, p. 21). The dynamic of religion is understood in this context as 'the belief of a given social group in certain indisputable truths, which determine obligatory behavior in such a way as to strengthen social cohesion' (2008, p. 21). From the perspective of secular ethics, development has become an element of modern religion producing a 'collective certainty' (2008, p. 22) that insulates against its own failure:

> Just as Christians know about the numerous crimes committed in the name of their faith, yet continue to uphold it, so do the 'development' experts increasingly recognise the mistakes without questioning their reasons for soldiering on. Belief is so made that it can easily tolerate contradictions . . . *Development thus appears to be a belief and a series of practices which form a single whole in spite of contradictions between them.* (2008, pp. 22–3, emphasis in original)

Rist distinguishes modernity from religion (2008, p. 21) and is thus using religion as a metaphor to critique another subject, namely, development. This method is employed by others to critique central development institutions such as the World Bank, described by George and Sabelli (1994), for example, as upholding a secular empire of faith in market-led development, motivated by a universal mission to redeem individual men and women to be transformed into the New Economic Man (1994, pp. 248–9).

### 3.3.2   Integrated Religion in Development

Unlike the secular subordination of religion, integrated religion is characterized by a balance of secular and sacral dynamics making it hard (and often unnecessary) to determine which element is the more primary. From an orthodox perspective, integrated religion can be perceived via the turn to 'authenticity' in development, and the role of religions as particular agents of capitalist development. From a critical perspective, integrated religion can be seen in the role of religious actors in social movements that contest the development agenda, and in theologies of liberation that employ critical development assumptions.

### (a)   Integrated religion and orthodox development
Whilst remaining a secondary concept in some 'culture' discourses, as a part of 'second wave' post-colonial development philosophy religion also begins to impact development at state and non-state levels. Thomas suggests three explanations for the rise of religion in the latter half of the twentieth century that is 'occurring in countries with different religious traditions and at different levels of their economic development' (Thomas, 2000, pp. 816–19). The first reason relates to the 'larger crisis of modernity' (2000, pp. 816–17), and is at the heart of the critique of orthodox development practice. The second reason is the 'failure of the modernising, secular state to produce both democracy and development in the Third World' (2000, p. 817). For Thomas, reflecting a consensus view amongst scholars, the first generation of post-colonial elites in the Third World 'believed strong "developmental states" could promote political stability and economic development, and this would be undermined if religion, ethnicity, or caste dominated politics' (2000, p. 817). Subsequently, 'dissatisfaction with the project of the

postcolonial secular state and the conflict between religious nationalism and secular nationalism was one of the most important developments in Third World politics in the 1990s' (2000, p. 817). The third reason is that 'the global resurgence of religion is part of the search for authenticity and development in the Third World' and 'indicates a new direction in the politics of developing countries, an attempt to "indigenise" modernity rather than to "modernise" traditional societies' (2000, pp. 817, 816–19).[1]

In development theory terms, Thomas's second and third reasons relate directly to the Third World and broadening of orthodox development approaches to include an engagement with culture. In this context religion is recognized as an embedded element in society, and as such, may be regarded as a secondary and primary resource in state, community and human development. Post-colonial politics began within a traditional European understanding of the state which sought a supposedly new politics but within colonial state borders and assumptions (Mayall, 1990, pp. 122–5). The movement away from this secular-state model saw the rise of what Bull incisively named 'cultural liberation' (Bull in Thomas, 2000, p. 818). Within the culturalist critique of modernity and development, religion is now of manifest importance to a holistic development agenda. Such an approach still adopts forms and assumptions of the secular modern that are European in origin. The movement toward culture has also meant the emergence of forms of post-secular polity, where the structures remain modern but are given authenticity by the agential power of a dominant religious tradition. Taking examples from the Islamic world, such a view might not be applied to Saudi Arabia (which remains semi-feudal in political structure), only moderately to Malaysia (a pluralist autocracy in a majority Islamic context), but certainly to a context such as Iran. Beyond the Iranian context, scholars such as Volpi reframe Islamism as a potential form of pseudo-democracy alongside republican and liberal models (Volpi, 2004). Volpi invokes Roy's view that 'the issue of the state in the Middle East cannot be properly addressed without reference to the loci of personal allegiances created by solidarity groups (*asabiyya*), networks and communities (particularly religious ones) (2004, p. 1065). Keane argues that Islamism plays an important role in bringing new visions of civil society into being in many parts of the world. For instance, as a counter to the 'compulsory secularism' of the military autocracy in Turkey, Keane highlights the role of

> Muslim actors intent on developing and redefining civil society – pushing toward a post-secular civil society, structured by new codes of ethics and aesthetics and held together and institutionally protected by new post-secularist government policies in such fields as law, education, municipal administration, banking and foreign affairs. (Keane, 1998, p. 28)

For Keane, the concept of 'global civil society' marks an evolution toward a 'new cosmology' (Keane, 2003, p. 40) that employs 'religious civilizations' as a catalyst because they have 'developed world-views and world-girdling institutions that feed the streams of social life that are today global' (2003, pp. 40–43). In another example of secular-sacral integration, Linden suggests that 'the Catholic concept of integral development is constituted by human rights based and directly theologically based discourse, by faith and by reason' (Linden, 2008, p. 2008). These integrated discourses help to situate religion within the new development orthodoxy.

Alongside its place in the 'cultural turn' of development is the observation by some of the role religions have played in capitalist development. It was Max Weber who in 1905 famously connected the Protestant religious tradition with the capitalist work ethic (Weber, 1930). In an essay on the spread of Protestant social and economic ethics throughout the Third World, Berger has recently quipped that 'Max Weber is alive and well, living in Guatemala' (Berger, 2007, p. 239). This ethical framework features 'a very disciplined work ethic' which is 'very important for capitalist development', as well as 'a rational approach to economic activity' and a commitment to 'education' (Berger, 2007, p. 238). As part of a study of evangelical Protestantism throughout Asia, Lumsdaine suggests that the growth of this religion has influenced polity in a similar way:

> . . . the embrace of evangelical Christianity has often enabled poor and marginalised people to have greater prosperity, self-confidence, and civic skills and a more vital associational life and has consequently pushed societies toward more open and democratic processes. (Lumsdaine, 2009, p. 3)

'Such a moral system', argues Berger, 'is functional in moving groups and entire societies into an incipient modern economic development' (Berger, 2007, p. 238). Drawing on 20 years of religion and development research, Berger suggests that the influence of this ethos can be seen not only in the explosion of Protestantism worldwide (2007, p. 239) but also in what he describes as the 'functional equivalents' of Catholicism in Spain (2007, p. 240), Islam in Indonesia (2007, p. 240) and groups such as the Chinese diaspora in South-East Asia that are 'not necessarily religious in any overt way' (2007, pp. 240–241). The research initiatives that Berger represents – describing them as 'an approach to culture and economic development which is neither materialistic nor idealistic' (2007, p. 245) – also suggest that there are limits to this 'Protestantizing' agency of religion. The most important of these is the 'macro-economic and political context' in which religious groups exist (2007, p. 241). As such, religion is both an agent of capitalist influence yet subordinate to economic and political structures. This research represents an integrated form of religion within development orthodoxy.

## (b)  Integrated religion and critical development

The integration of secular and sacral elements of religion is also evident in the critical development tradition. I note briefly the role that religious actors have played in social movements to contest the development agenda over recent decades. For example, Tyndale describes the activities of the Indian spiritual and social movement known as Swadhyaya in development terms. Activities such as *Bhaktipheri* (devotional tour), *Teerthyatra* (pilgrimage), *Yogeshwar Krishi* (divine farming), *Shree Darshanam* (divine communes) have created a particular vision of development 'that claims a place in the public sphere' (Tyndale, 2006, pp. 8, 1–8). In the following chapter we shall explore this role in relation to protest against policies of the World Bank. This is an integrated phenomenon whereby religious actors are secondary to the larger concerns of particular social protest, but also play a primary role in grass-roots community action, something that the World Bank would note with interest.

The liberation theologies and movements that have emerged since the 1960s in the Third World are another expression of integrated religion in the critical development tradition. Not unlike critical approaches more generally, Third World liberation theologies have passed through forms of 'leftist fundamentalism' toward 'a more complex reading' of power and development (Miguez, 2006, p. 125). Rooted in historical, theological and political advocacy for the poor (Bonino, 1975; Boff and Boff, 1987, pp. 1–10; Hoornaert, 1989), Freire's ideology of conscientization (Berryman, 1987, pp. 34–8) and a materialist and indigenous re-reading of religious tradition (Miranda, 1974; Brown, 1984; Clevenot, 1985; Miguez, 2006, pp. 122–5), liberation theologies construct a framework where immanent (liberationist) and transcendent (salvationist) ideals are mutually constitutive, and employed to advocate for those who are 'are totally outside the system' and who suffer the 'idolatry of the market', 'exclusion' and commodification (Miguez, 2006, p. 129). Such peoples are overwhelmingly religious in outlook, and this impacts directly on how development is perceived. For Gutiérrez, it was within a 'radical perspective of liberation' – grounded in the situated faiths and communities of the poor – that development 'finds its true meaning and possibilities of accomplishing something worthwhile' (Gutiérrez, 1973, p. 36). Similar movements have been identified in Korea (Suh, 1991), Malawi (Mitchell, 2002), Senegal (Galvan, 2004), Cambodia (Poethig, 2002) and Thailand (Darlington, 1998) to name a small sample. They represent important expressions of a critical re-reading of culture and a core dimension of the demands for authenticity in development emanating from the South (Haynes, 1994, pp. 18–43; Thomas, 2000). Whilst religious frameworks (and more importantly, communities) are indispensable to liberation theology movements, critical development ideology beyond the particularities of religion are equally important. In his seminal work of radical Catholic theology, Gutiérrez sets the cause of liberation for 'oppressed peoples and social classes' against *desarrolista* or 'developmentalist' policies which 'appear somewhat aseptic, giving a false picture of a tragic and conflictual reality' (Gutiérrez, 1973, p. 36; see also Berryman, 1989, pp. 34–8). For Gutiérrez it is only within the 'radical perspective of liberation' generated from a theological vision of divine justice that development 'finds its true meaning and possibilities of accomplishing something worthwhile' (Gutiérrez, 1973, pp. 36, 21–37). Though the texture of Gutiérrez' argument pits liberation theology against a certain kind of development, it also resonates with other kinds, pitting critical approaches of development against more economistic views. Thus, religion detaches from development orthodoxy but also infuses new elements into critical development approaches (1973, pp. 21–42) thereby reflecting an integration of secular-critical and sacral-critical perspectives.

### 3.3.3   Sacral Religion in Development

In the context of development, sacral religion is defined by the primacy of religious actors and interest to shape the development agenda (within development orthodoxy) or contest development priorities (as part of critical development). The discourse of development has begun to include sacral perspectives. Whether from an orthodox or critical perspective, however, such examples remain contentious. Religion-led politics and economic development challenge many of the maxims of the development agenda that remain secular. Two notable examples of this in a post-9/11 development milieu are Hezbollah's role in political development in Lebanon and, more generally, the place of Islamic traditions in economic development. Similarly, the role of religious communities to provide alternatives beyond the development agenda remains underemphasized in the critical tradition. These examples are explored below.

#### (a)   Sacral religion and orthodox development
A defining test for the practice of 'authenticity' in development is to allow religious groups a leading role in shaping the political landscape. The limits of this challenge would be found when a group that has grass-roots support within a democratic context is associated with a disruptive form of religious activity. These elements can also be observed in Harb's recent

study of Hezbollah as an important faith-based organization (FBO) in the post-war reconstruction of Lebanon (Harb, 2008). Beyond the commonly held view of Hezbollah as a terrorist organization, Harb considers Hezbollah as 'a Lebanese political party which has been in charge of the elaboration and dissemination of development policies for middle and lower-income Shi'i groups for over 25 years' (2008, p. 214). This context adds depth beyond descriptions of the 'moral logic' of Hezbollah's association with terrorism (Kramer, 1998). Authenticity is the starting point. Harb estimates the lower estimates of Hezbollah's social base in which development is practised to be no less than 300,000 (Harb, 2008, p. 220). The author attributes Hezbollah with a high level of agency not merely to work within Lebanon but to determine the very nature of a faith-based society (2008, pp. 222–6):

> Hezbollah's institutions disseminate codes, norms and values that produce a particular type of social and cultural environment, structuring daily life practices, as well as subjective and collective identities. This environment, or Hezbollah's reference group, is referred to as the Islamic sphere (hala islamiyya) or the 'Resistance society' (mujtama' al-muqawama). (Harb, 2008, p. 222)

One might, with good reason, disassociate such a description with an integrated development discourse and the notion of an Islamic sphere the mainline development agenda. However, Harb adds two additional elements that complicate this view. The first is that 'Islamic sphere narratives have increasingly borrowed national references and symbols from Lebanese folklore . . . proposing a hybrid type of national discourse, mixing secularism with religiosity' (2008, p. 223). The second is that 'there is considerable overlap between [Hezbollah's] paradigms of development and those international donors, and they are open to learning and improvement' (2008, p. 234). When these elements combine, we may well situate Hezbollah as a development actor that holds to the primacy of religious identity but incorporates secondary secular state structures as well as the need to learn from 'a type of knowledge that goes beyond [the] current scope and concern of [its own] institutions' (2008, p. 234) in order to fulfil its development mandate. Therefore, Hezbollah are arguably defined as a sacral development institution with significant potential to contribute to the mainstream development agenda.

Equally contentious in strategies for political development is the incorporation of Islamic economic approaches into the global development agenda. In a study on religion and development Haynes observes that 'Islamists claim to offer an improvement on capitalism via a comprehensive Islamic economic system' (Haynes, 2007b, p. 119). The key components of this system are summarized as: 'an Islamic banking system that avoids interest; and Islamic redistribution system based on Qur'anic principles of sharing and equity; and in the marketplace, a set of norms to ensure fairness and honesty' (Haynes, 2007b, p. 119). Haynes argues that the proposition of an Islamic economic system is 'patently unrealistic', yet he also observes extant attempts within the global political economy by states such as Saudi Arabia to promote 'Islamic universities in numerous countries, [sponsor] conferences on the Islamisation of knowledge, and [build] institutes to train Islamic bankers' (2008, p. 120). Indeed, the contentious initiative of Islamic economics is given a mainstream rationale by Ahmad (2003) within the framework of the RGC previously mentioned. He writes,

> The Islamic approach to economic activity focuses on both men and modes of production, but harnesses them into a balanced and harmonious whole . . . Islam is concerned beyond the market, looking to moral principles, values, and commands influencing human motivation, institutions, and processes at all levels . . . All economic activity takes place in the context of culture and society permeated by the pursuit of higher goals in life. (Ahmad, 2003, p. 201)

It is not my purpose to analyze the veracity of each argument. What is important presently is the agency of a sacral tradition to promote a system within the nomenclature and (adapted) assumptions of the global development agenda. Similar (and equally contentious) claims to authenticity and tradition exist in Islam on issues such as freedom and tolerance (Sen, 1999, pp. 238–40) and human rights (Johnson and Symonides, 1998, pp. 52–3).

### (b)   Sacral religion and critical development

Religious traditions long pre-date the rise of development in human history and these traditions animate the imaginations, direct the lives and determine the social structures for hundreds of millions of people today. Yet the reason for the longevity of religions is seen not in their rigid opposition to modernity but to their selective adaptations toward it. The process of selection means that sometimes a religious development actor will reconcile itself to the modernist strictures of the development agenda. Yet in other contexts or on other issues religion will detach itself from the mainstream and even critique the very interests that animate the whole development enterprise. For example, Loy (2003) can write from a Buddhist perspective of the poverty of development and makes the general point that religious institutions need to 'understand that market emphasis on acquisition and consumption [that still drives development] undermine their most important teachings' (Loy, 2003, p. 13). Akin to post-development approaches, some understand the action of religion to be a critique of development itself, whereby deep religious traditions and situated faith communities seem to be in perpetual tension with the secular sphere to the extent that religious maintenance of social cohesion and religious accommodations of social change exist in spaces outside the mainstream development agenda. We shall explore this further in the next chapter when considering the dialogue between the World Bank and religious communities of Africa. For now it is enough to say that religious communities and traditions often embody a prophetic role in relation to development, challenging the instrumental impulses that animate the development agenda on the basis of a more transcendent sense of morality. As Tyndale writes,

> Maybe the most important contribution that the faiths can make at the moment is to highlight the values which are the necessary prerequisite for social harmony, such as justice, compassion and respect for every individual, and demonstrate that, if these are overridden, not even the most basic economic development will be achieved. (Tyndale, 2002, p. 57)

Whilst such a view resonates with core critical development values, the transcendent quality of sacral-critical perspectives mean that religious alternatives are often marginalized in critical discourse (McDuie-Ra and Rees, 2010).

## 3.4   THE DYNAMICS OF RELIGION IN DEVELOPMENT DISCOURSE

I have employed the categories of the dynamics of religion model to open the discourse of development revealing secular, integrated and sacral forms of religion within orthodox and critical approaches. One important aspect not explicitly conveyed by this approach is the interaction between the different dynamics of religion. I therefore reintroduce the Venn diagram structure to highlight the complex and overlapping relations of religion that feature in the discourse. Two dynamics can be observed when we do this: the shift toward integrated approaches to religion and the realignment of development interests and potential areas of dispute.

### 3.4.1   The Shift Toward Integration

I begin by situating the discourses of development within the Venn form of the dynamics of religion model, represented in Figure 3.1. As can be seen in the figure, orthodox development engagements with religion appear

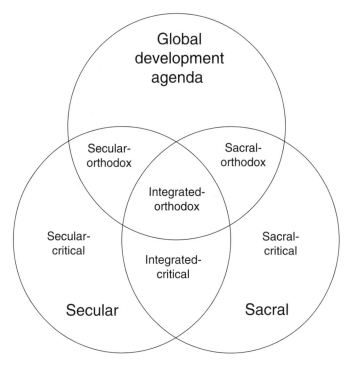

*Figure 3.1    Situating the discourse of development in the dynamics of
            religion model*

inside the sphere of the global development agenda, whilst critical development engagements with religion fall outside this sphere. The model also
differentiates the dynamics of religion according to the three types of religion (secular, integrated, sacral) as opposed to the criteria of development
(orthodox or critical). This religio-centric approach has already yielded
insights into the situated dynamics of religion. When placed in the Venn,
this approach also highlights the space between the secular and sacral
spheres of religion.

    Previous discussions on the evolution of development discourse on reli-
gion, combined with diagrammatic representation of Figure 3.1, attest to
a discernable shift toward an integrated engagement with religion in both
orthodox and critical development discourse. The dynamics of religion
are of secondary importance within orthodox approaches to development
that prioritize state power and economic measures. However, changes
in the orthodox discourse of development have also seen an increased
engagement with religious development organizations, at times creating

an integrated dynamic between secular and sacral interests. Similarly, the dynamics of religion are of secondary importance within critical approaches to development that critique perceived asymmetries of power within mainstream development practice. Yet the agency of religious actors in contesting and reshaping development priorities also reveals a more integrated dynamic of religion within the critical development tradition.

The movement toward an integrated understanding of religion in development discourse can also be seen by comparing two typologies of religious actors in development from 2000 and 2008, respectively. Haynes's important essay on the renaissance of political religion in the Third World (Haynes, 2000) includes a 'typology of religious groups and political interaction' (2000, p. 181) The four types of religion employed by Haynes are described as culturalist, syncretist, fundamentalist and community-oriented. Of interest in the present discussion is that all four types as represented by Haynes arguably fall outside the global development agenda. They each have hostile or indifferent relations with government, and perceive state and society through revolutionary or sectarian goals (2000, pp. 181–6). Overall, Haynes argues that the types of religion fall into one of two categories: 'religion used as a vehicle of opposition [culturalist, fundamentalist and partly syncretist] or as an ideology of community self-interest [community-oriented]' (2000, p. 186). The importance of Haynes's analysis is that he not only differentiates between religious groups, but also links these types to explain why technological development and aspects of modernization left many people with 'a feeling of loss' and how in this context 'religion often assumed a central tenet to political opposition to the state' (2000, pp. 186–7). Using the dynamics of religion model we can further differentiate and unite Haynes's typology as shown in Figure 3.2.

As a differentiation, two religious types (culturalist and community-oriented) can be understood as operating within either sacral or integrated ontologies, with syncretist religion necessarily integrated and fundamentalism necessarily sacral. As a unity, all types remain outside the domain of orthodox development.

A change in the perception and status of religious actors in the discourse of development can be seen when comparing Haynes's typology to that of Clarke in a study of FBOs in development ten years later in 2008. Clarke usefully categorizes FBOs into five types, apex bodies, charitable/development organizations, socio-political organizations, missionary organizations, and illegal or terrorist organizations (Clarke, 2008b, pp. 24–32). These can be situated in the dynamics of religion framework as shown in Figure 3.3.

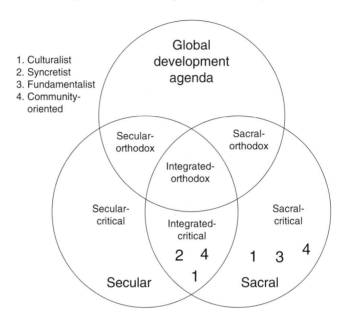

1. Culturalist
2. Syncretist
3. Fundamentalist
4. Community-
   oriented

*Figure 3.2    Situating Haynes's typology of religious groups and political
interaction (2000) in the dynamics of religion model*

Two levels of integration can be observed that distinguish Clarke's
typology from that of Haynes. The first is the integration between sectors
within the global development agenda. I have already suggested religious
actors and interests that exist within the domain of orthodox development. Clarke's descriptors can be used to provide organizational dimensions to this. Second, there is a linkage between integrated-orthodox and
integrated-critical development approaches. Overall, five of the six sectors
of the dynamics of religion model can be emphasized in Clarke's study,
thus reflecting the changed status of religion in development discourse.

A very important question lingers: is the shift toward integration reflective of a genuine secular-sacral balance in the practice of development?
It would be an error to suggest that Clarke's typology is more 'evolved'
than Haynes's. Indeed the comparison between the typologies remains
very important. Haynes's study concentrates on religious groups from the
Third World. Clarke adopts a broader perspective, with numerous types
influenced as much (if not more) by the global North as by the South.
Despite the undoubted broadening of orthodox development discourse
to recognize religious actors, the question remains as to how representative this new understanding is of Third World religious communities

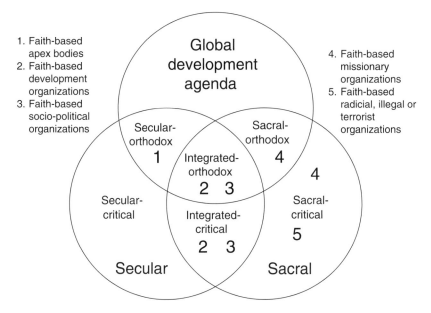

1. Faith-based apex bodies
2. Faith-based development organizations
3. Faith-based socio-political organizations

4. Faith-based missionary organizations
5. Faith-based radicial, illegal or terrorist organizations

*Figure 3.3* *Situating Clarke's typology of faith-based organizations (2008) in the dynamics of religion model*

and interests. This is something Clarke has himself explored in a study of faith-based organizations and the interests of the UK Department of International Development (Clarke, 2007). I shall explore a similar theme in the following chapters regarding integrated partnerships and the World Bank.

### 3.4.2  The Realignment of Development Interests and Disputes

The second dynamic to be observed is that the dynamics of religion model reorders the consensus on development according to the criterion of religious agency. Development approaches hitherto considered oppositional in orientation become realigned according to whether they hold religion to be a secondary, integrated or primary element in development. For instance, orthodox and critical approaches are now linked by the secular subordination of religion in some instances, and by partnerships that attempt to integrate secular and sacral religious dynamics in others. Deep cultural engagements in development that grant primary agency of religion in development remain outside different expressions of this orthodox-critical consensus. An example of the realignment of interests can be seen in the links between secular-orthodox and secular-critical approaches. Haynes's seminal study of religion, politics and analysis of Third World development (Haynes, 1994, pp. 18–43) shows the secular-modern continuity between orthodox and dependency approaches on the question of religion. If modern development begins, as Remenyi suggests, as a 'modernization first' (Remenyi, 2004, p. 25) response to poverty, then orthodox development approaches can be assumed to be secular-linear in their assumptions toward the sacral political sphere. This is summarized by Haynes as follows: 'as societies industrialise, urbanise and are led by secular leaders, religion will increasingly appear as an anachronism, as a remnant from the past, doomed to privatisation and even, ultimately, disappearance' (Haynes, 1994, p. 18). Accordingly, Haynes writes in 1994 that '[o]ver the past 30 years or so' both orthodox development and dependency models of development 'have uniformly and consistently neglected religion when analysing both state-society relations and international relations in the Third World' (1994, p. 19). From the orthodox view, Haynes draws on the works of Rostow[2] and Kautsky[3] to show that 'manifestations of cultural identity, including religion, are merely remnants of a tradition' (1994, p. 23). From the dependency view, Haynes suggests that a study such as Frank's analysis of underdevelopment in Latin America 'ignored the interaction of religion and politics' because it is an 'essentially class-based treatment' (1994, p. 23). Haynes concludes 'both "schools" of analysis, despite their contending and contrasting positions, serve to marginalise the effect of religion and other cultural factors on politics (and vice versa)' (1994, p. 25).

The realignment of interests also raises the prospect of new disputes over religious agency between similar philosophies of development. As can be seen in Figure 3.4, potential disputes within schools of development toward religion (for example, secular orthodox versus more integrated orthodox assumptions) are more numerous than potential disputes between schools of development.

This might be a very important and hitherto undervalued area of study as we move from the level of discourse to a consideration of religion and development at the institutional and policy levels. The discourses of IR and of development have tended to draw lines of dispute between more obvious secular and 'religious' influences. By contrast, the situative approach employed here identifies a myriad of potential disputes, some that may potentially belong to the same operational or ideological spheres of development. For instance, secular-orthodox dynamics (Orthodox A) might be at odds with those of a secular-integrated orientation (Orthodox B), opening up new and precise avenues for enquiry about the dynamics of religion at work within orthodox institutions as well as between these institutions and external dynamics.

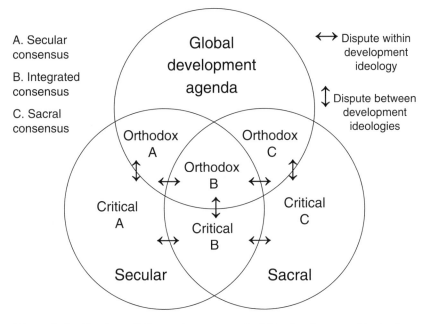

*Figure 3.4    Borders of dispute between and within development ideologies
on the dynamics of religion*

## 3.5   THE PERMEATING DYNAMICS OF RELIGION IN DEVELOPMENT

The dynamics of religion model was constructed to meet two current needs in contemporary religion and IR scholarship. The first was to develop an analytical framework of 'amicable accommodation' (Madeley, 2003, p. xxii) between secular and religious interests. The second was to employ religion as an organizing force (Hurd, 2008, p. 1) in the study of world politics. These needs have become more acute since IR scholars have begun to observe co-existing evidence for both secularization and sacralization (Fox, 2008, p. 7) at work in international affairs. The dynamics of religion model was constructed to meet these challenges. In this chapter I have begun to operationalize the model in the sphere of international development, with attention to examples of the dynamics of religion that can be discerned in the discourse of development. Three summary conclusions can now be made. The first is that a fuller understanding of religion is needed in order to perceive the impacts of religion in development theory and practice. Whilst the secular origins of development are certainly in tension with some sacral forms of religion, the dimensions of religion model highlights the importance of sacral and integrated elements as important and often valuable to development means and ends. The situative approach thus shows that religious dynamics permeate the development sphere throughout. Second, the model has reorganized the interests of development according to the criterion of religious agency. Thus, alongside important demarcations such as 'orthodox' and 'critical' development the chapter has highlighted in specific ways how the distinctions of religion also produce very different engagements within development. Third, the model has identified new borders of potential agreement and dispute as secular, integrated and sacral interests compete for significance in the development sphere. The conceptual foundation is therefore laid to study the dynamics of religion at the institutional level of development. It is to this analysis that we now move.

## NOTES

1.  On secularism and the global cultural shift toward an 'age of authenticity', see Taylor (2007, pp. 473–504).
2.  W. Rostow (1959), *The Stages of Economic Growth. A Non-communist Manifesto* (Cambridge: Cambridge University Press).
3.  J. Kautsky (1972), *The Political Consequences of Modernization* (New York: John Wiley).

# 4.    Religion and the World Bank

Religion is a central part of the international system . . . even if it wished to do
so, the Bank could not entirely sidestep the faith engagement.
World Bank (2006, p. 3)

Development requires a moral vision, not just ethics . . . no moral vision can
shape society without a transcendent reference point.
Vinay Samuel (2001, p. 240)

Having employed religion as an organizing force at the discourse level
of development, I now turn to the institutional level and specifically
to the World Bank Group (WBG). By the phrase 'institutional level
analysis' I mean the contexts and influences within and upon the WBG
to engage with religious actors and interests. The present chapter lays
the foundation for the investigations of Chapters 5 and 6 that takes a
closer examination of WBG religion and development partnerships. The
chapter begins by briefly introducing the significance of the WBG for
the present study and describing its institutional attributes. Using the
secular and sacral criteria of religious agency, I then describe the evolutions of the WBG from its creation after World War II to 2005 (the year
ending the period of case studies examined in this book). Following this,
a more specific modelling of the dynamics of religion is undertaken that
identifies secular, integrated and sacral dynamics that helped bring religion into the policy domain of the WBG. The chapter ends with a brief
discussion of the dynamics of inclusion and exclusion that arise from the
WBG's opening to religion, and that necessitate further investigation at
the policy level.

## 4.1.    THE WORLD BANK GROUP (WBG)

We now briefly introduce the significance of the WBG and the basic
characteristics of its institutional structure.

### 4.1.1   The Significance of the WBG for the Present Study

I have chosen the WBG as a site for analysis because in recent years it has broadened its development approach to include civil society actors and has created an explicit space for engaging with religious actors in development. It has been argued that knowledge underpins the setting of the development agenda and is concentrated in international financial institutions (IFIs), particularly the World Bank and regional development banks, as well as influential bilateral aid donors. Since the shift away from state-led development toward market-led development in the 1970s the power of IFIs has increased as they control knowledge to set development priorities and the material capacity to implement them (Bøås and McNeill, 2004, pp. 3–6). This has been a complex process involving multiple actors and the set of ideas emerging from this process remains heavily contested. However, one clear and significant outcome of this process is that IFIs have opened a space for other actors to negotiate and set the development agenda (Guttal, 2006, p. 27). The opening of the development space has led to a greater role for civil society in setting, negotiating and implementing development priorities (Carbone and Lister, 2006, p. 7). I am principally concerned to analyze this 'opening' process at the WBG in the context of the religious structure of world politics.

There are multiple ways to conceive the World Bank as an object of analysis. Having previously established the boundaries of secularism, religion and development it would be an error to approach an actor as significant and contested as the WBG with any less attention. My intention in this first section is to draw an implicit continuity between the WBG and these earlier subjects. The connection is made via the following assumption, the WBG is a dynamic arena where the norms of closed and open ideologies of development are contested. Like the dynamic interconnections between different notions of secularism, between different elements of religion at work in political society, and between the overlapping tensions that exist between different schools of development, the policy domain of the WBG is formed by a mutually constitutive interplay between divergent actors and interests across the multiple institutions that make it up. This can be seen from the perspective of the WBG's founding, historical evolution and the dynamics that have continued to shape its role as one of the premier development institutions in the world today.

### 4.1.2   The Institution of the WBG

At the close of the World War II and the beginning of the modern development era, the World Bank and the International Monetary Fund (IMF) were established to stabilize international currencies and facilitate post-war reconstruction (Woods, 2001). Along with the General Agreement on Tariffs and Trade (GATT) these institutions were also created to align free-market economies and deal with problems that had arisen in the international economy in the 1930s (O'Brien and Williams, 2004, p. 118). The value of each international organization (IO) to the international system is contested (for example, Carvalho, 2000). Analytical perspectives of the WBG vary from conceptions of an (often malign) hegemonic power (Murphy, 2000, pp. 789–80) to an (often ineffective) development bureaucracy (Einhorn, 2001; Woods, 2001; Stiglitz, 2003a) to a pluralistic institution of ongoing importance and (often unrealized) potential to better development practice (St Clair, 2006).

The WBG consists of five distinct but interrelated parts, the International Bank for Reconstruction and Development (IBRD), the International Finance Corporation (IFC), the International Development Association (IDA), the Multilateral Investment Guarantee Agency (MIGA) and the Centre for the Settlement of Investment Disputes. Each of these constituent parts performs distinct functions and, more importantly, can be potentially understood according to varying procedural values. For instance, Pease understands the IBRD to be the 'conservative base' of the WBG functioning as a traditional lender, whereas the IDA provides 'soft loans' to 'the poorest of the poor' states that are 'otherwise marginalised in the global economy' (Pease, 2003, pp. 181–2). Rittberger and Zangl differentiate the World Bank – originally the IBRD only – from the IDA, where the IDA is more of a fund administrator than a bank (Rittberger and Zangl, 2006, pp. 50–1). Whilst the IDA acts as a mechanism for guiding poor states up into the more conservative regime of the IBRD, the complexity of structural and political issues that the IDA must deal with create the potential for a broader development agenda to be operationalized. Accordingly, the IDA might appear more like the United Nations Development Programme (UNDP) (Rittberger and Zangl, 2006, p. 51) and the IBRD more like the IMF. Thus, the WBG is at once a single organization and what may be legitimately called an intergovernmental organization (IGO) cluster. The present book shall at times abbreviate the proper noun World Bank, where it is appropriate, as WBG. On no occasion shall I use the shortened form 'the Bank', even though it is a common usage in secondary literature and also the World Bank's own abbreviation. My preference for WBG in the present book is a way to continually assert the World Bank as both a plural and a unitary entity.

There are several reasons why the World Bank is the subject of considerable attention. First, it is the largest multilateral development institution in the global political economy (GPE) with a constituency that is equally global. As noted by Nobel Prize winner and founder of the Grameen Bank in Bangladesh Mohammad Yunus, 'the World Bank's influence is global and total' (cited in Benjamin, 2007, p. xi). Most WBG loans are part of larger packages that involve regional development banks and United Nations (UN) agencies (such as the UNDP). In 2008, the WBG committed US$38.2 billion in loans, grants, equity investments and guarantees to its members and private businesses in member countries (World Bank, 2008, p. 2) Its focus is to fund investment in infrastructure, reduce poverty and help countries adjust their economies to the demands of the GPE. The most significant international organizations to affect disparities in global economic development belong to the WBG (Rittberger and Zangl, 2006, p. 50).

Second, the WBG wields a relative though not insignificant autonomy from the constituent states that govern it. In financial terms, the World Bank is creditworthy on private capital markets and can conduct its core operations without the constant ratification of states (Rittberger and Zangl, 2006, p. 173). The World Bank is also an independent agency within the UN system (Pease, 2003, p. 22). Importantly, the World Bank is an autonomous actor in the international system functioning at times independent of state interests. Such a view reflects assumptions attributable to the constructivist and liberal institutionalist schools of IR. The relations between IOs and states are analyzed by Park as follows:

> States bestow a variety of tasks and functions upon IOs, and IOs are often viewed as agents of powerful states' interests. While IOs may reflect unequal power relations between states through their structure and function, they may also operate as actors in their own right. (Park, 2005b, p. 112)

What is the impact of such an assumption on our view of the WBG? In 1999 Barnett and Finnemore appealed to seven major studies that 'consistently [identified] an independent culture and agendas for action' (Barnett and Finnemore, 1999, p. 705) to conclude that IOs such as the World Bank are diffusers of norms – understood as collectively held views or standards of behaviour (Finnemore, 1996b) – that simultaneously serve, inform and create the interests of states. Building on this literature, Park argues that IOs are both diffusers and consumers of norms (the latter socialized by state and non-state actors) (Park, 2006) and applies this to studies of different organs of the WBG (Park, 2004, 2005a, 2005b). The diffusion of religious norms within and by the WBG is an underdeveloped area of analysis in this important process.

Third, influenced by growing demands for authenticity in the developing world, the shifting discourse that has created the broadening of development orthodoxy, to geopolitical changes in world affairs, and the sustained criticism of its project record, the WBG has undergone numerous missional changes that have increased the scrutiny of its operation (Krasner, 1985; Einhorn, 2001; Woods, 2005). Forman and Segaar (2006) have suggested the existence of 'changing dynamics of mutilateralism' in the global political economy created by the conditions of 'accelerated globalization'. Such a view represents a very different context in which to understand the operations of the World Bank today. The contemporary dynamic to WBG operations is different from its original intent, particularly as it relates to the shifts in the discourse of development previously observed. This shall become relevant for understanding the World Bank's openness to, and engagement with, the actors and interests of religion.

## 4.2 THE EVOLUTIONS OF THE WBG IN RELIGIOUS PERSPECTIVE

As Pincus and Winters note, 'the World Bank as we know it bears little resemblance to the institution envisaged at the Bretton Woods conference in 1944' (Pincus and Winters, 2002, pp. 2, 1–25). Rittberger and Zangl summarize the evolution of the World Bank's development from its creation to the present through four phases (Rittberger and Zangl, 2006, pp. 175–6). The four-phase evolution allows us to contain our study of the WBG within reasonable limits. Within this application the present emphasis will make the dynamics of religion the main focus. I employ secular and sacral distinctions acknowledging the integration between these dynamics later in the chapter. A tabulation of this analysis including factors that will be explored throughout the chapter appears in Table 4.1.

I shall now briefly describe the secular and sacral dynamics of religion at work within the four phases of the WBG operations.

### 4.2.1 The Subordination of Religion: Modernization to Poverty Eradication

Given my earlier focus on the negligible role of public and political religion in the modern period, it is unremarkable to suggest that the first two phases of the WBGs evolution were characterized by the strong subordination of religion. The question 'Where is religion?' in the policy domain of the WBG in this period is answered in the negative. The absence of religion reflects its strong subordination to two dominant influences that were uncontested in the three decades after 1945. These were secularization and the dominance of economistic development orthodoxy, both central to the worldview of

*Table 4.1    The World Bank and religion: secular and sacral dynamics*
            *(1946–2005)*

| World Bank Phases | Secular Dynamics: Religion and Development | Sacral Dynamics: Religion and Development |
|---|---|---|
| **Phase 1** Modernization (1946–68) | Strong subordination of religious actors and interests | No internal dialogue on religion |
| **Phase 2** Poverty Eradication (1968–79) | Strong subordination of religious actors and interests | No internal dialogue on religion |
| **Phase 3** structural adjustment programmes (SAPs) (1979–94) | **1985–87** NGO advocacy successfully obstructs the 7th funding replenishment of the IDA **1986** HRH Prince Philip chairs a dialogue on religion and the environment in Assisi, Italy | **1981 +** Friday Morning Group begins. The FMG is an informal forum where WB employees discuss the impact of 'values', including religious values. **1981 +** Religious concern and emerging resistance **1985–87** Dialogue with select NGOs begins on environment and development including 'Poverty/Church groups' |
| **Phase 4** Comprehensive Development Framework (CDF) (1995–2005) | **1995** Wolfensohn advocates working with religious actors **1996** Alliance of Religions and Conservation (ACR) at Windsor Castle advocates for 'a more systematic and structured dialogue' between 'representatives of different religious organisations and multilateral development institutions, especially the World Bank'. **1990s** IO policy development on religion (ILO, WHO) | **1995 +** Development Dialogue on Values and Ethics established to enable faith and development partnerships **1996** Jubilee 2000 faith-based campaign to reduce Third World debt **1998** Launch of the World Faiths Development Dialogue **1999** Voices of the Poor – religious institutions gain increased credibility **1998–2005** WBG Faith and development partnerships |

twentieth-century modernity. I shall very briefly describe priorities of the WBG at this time before moving to the third and fourth phases.

The first phase (1946–68) of the WBG was characterized by modernization and focused on monumental state development projects (Kapur et al., 1997, pp. 85–137). During this period, 'the standard view of an underdeveloped country saw it as one with a predominantly large population characterized by the absence of modern values' (O'Brien and Williams, 2004, p. 268). As previously noted, in the 1950s and 1960s the view that 'modernization necessarily leads to a decline of religion, both in society and in the minds of individuals' (Berger, 1999, p. 2) was an uncontested axiom of the West. Remenyi observes, with notable exceptions, development theorists in the period

> . . . regarded the improvement of people's livelihoods as little more than by-products of the building blocks of modernization, i.e., i) economic returns to successful accumulation of capital, and ii) economic growth fuelled by productivity improvements arising from the transfer of technology from technologically and economically advanced areas to technologically and economically backward areas. (Remenyi, 2004, pp. 25–6)

According to this orthodox logic, the advantage for developing countries lies in their ability to 'pick and choose from a vast range of ready-made and tested technological developments and new industries "off the shelf"' (Remenyi, 2004, p. 25). Simultaneously, the global development agenda was established within a theory of economic dualism whereby modern dynamic political economies were contrasted to the traditional stagnant society of the Third World (O'Brien and Williams, 2004, p. 268). The subordination of religion, generally considered as belonging to a premodern cultural layer, was an automatic consequence of this view in development. As such, there appears to be no emphasis on religion within the WBG agenda.

Whilst the WBG would begin to move toward a broader philosophy in the late 1960s, religion was no less subordinate. One general reason for this may be that post-colonial demands being formulated by Third World coalitions such as the Non-Aligned Movement and Group of 77, and formalized in the United Nations Conference on Trade and Development (UNCTAD) were driven by secular-critical ideological positions. For instance, in 1974 the proposed New International Economic Order marked an ideological clash between critical development approaches of the South and orthodox-liberal approaches that favoured Western modernization models (Cohn, 2005, pp. 105–6). The driving forces for change in this context were secular-critical ideologies that argued exclusively within a materialist ontology of justice. As I argued in Chapter 3, whilst the religious dimension of these movements (for example, liberation theologies) was evident, it was often not recognized as such.

In this context, the second phase of WBG operations (1968–79) under the presidency of Robert McNamara marked a significant shift toward a basic needs approach combined with an economistic emphasis on growth and distribution (Rittberger and Zangl, 2006, pp. 175–6). Poverty eradication and a focus on 'poverty projects' became the central objectives of the World Bank at this time (Kapur et al., 1997, pp. 331, 269–330). During this phase, in important contexts such as Africa, the WBG became a 'leading aid coordinator, analyst, and source of technical assistance' rather than a direct deliverer of aid (Kapur et al., 1997, p. 710). It should therefore be noted that significant and dynamic debate characterize this period when understood from the perspective of broader WBG operations. However, it is equally true that this dynamic process subordinated religion to a negligible status at the institutional level of the WBG. There was much movement within the secular sphere of development, but few openings existed for sacral influence.

### 4.2.2   Subordination and Resistance: The Shift to Structural Adjustment

In the third phase of the WBG's evolution (1979–94), religion remained a subordinate element to secular development orthodoxy, however the sacral agency of religious actors did begin to play a role in contesting and broadening the orthodox agenda. The third phase of the World Bank's development is characterized by a strategy of structural adjustment programmes (SAPs) (Rittberger and Zangl, 2006, p. 176). First articulated in 1979 (Kapur et al., 1997, pp. 506, 505–11), structural adjustment operated when the WBG and the IMF 'linked the allocation of loans initially to macroeconomic conditions and later even to political conditions' (Rittberger and Zangl, 2006, p. 175) favourable to neoliberal assumptions and interests. In development terms, this phase can be seen as the dominance of market-led economistic development orthodoxy, and gave birth to the phrase 'Washington Consensus' in international politics (Gore, 2000). However the poverty theme also 'reappeared in 1987 and permeated policy debates' (Kapur et al., 1997, p. 331) and this may have assisted the transition into a new phase beyond a SAPs approach.

The third phase is marked by increased and at times intense conflict between the WBG and an array of dissenting actors in the international system, and not without some justification. Although described as the 'most powerful of the public institutions of global governance' Murphy (2000, p. 791) argued that the WBG, along with the IMF and World Trade

Organization (WTO), was beholden to the interests of states and corpora-
tions most benefiting from 'unregulated economic globalization' (2000,
p. 799). Fomerand, in turn, saw 'a continuing marginality' of institutions
such as the UN in international affairs principally because it 'remains
subservient to that of the Bank, the IMF, and the newer World Trade
Organization' (Fomerand, 2002, p. 399). Thus, from above and from
below, the World Bank was perceived by many as having malign interests, seeking patronage from hegemons and bestowing structural injustice
upon lesser actors. The World Bank was held by its critics as representing
only one side of the North-South conflict via mechanisms such as SAPs.
Structural adjustment promoted economic growth 'by imposing a very
particular model of development and a narrow set of economic instru-
ments' (Pender, 2001, p. 399). However, the role of the state in Asian
economic growth, 'the failure of adjustment to deliver high and sustained
levels of growth' in the LDCs and the Mexican crisis of 1994–95, 'all
called into question fundamental tenets of the World Bank's approach to
development' (Pender, 2001, p. 402).

The 1980s was therefore a period of intense protest toward World Bank
policy. Since the shift away from state-led development toward market-
led development in the 1970s the power of IFIs increased as they began
to control both knowledge to set development priorities and the material
capacity to implement them (Bøås and McNeill, 2004, pp. 3–4). The development agenda espoused by IFIs came under heavy criticism in the 1980s
and 1990s and the response of IFIs has been referred to as a 'new kind of
synthesis' (Stiglitz, 2003b; Öniş and Şenses, 2005, p. 273;) that has opened
a space for other actors to negotiate and set the development agenda
(Guttal, 2006, p. 27).[1] Religious actors played a role in this process, both
contesting the development agenda set by the WBG. Marshall observes
aspects of this critique from the vantage of religious actors in development:

> Conflicts around dam building and displacement of indigenous people, in
> particular, resonated deeply with many faith institutions, as did the mounting
> indebtedness of many poor countries, and perceived links between economic
> growth and environmental damage. (Marshall and Van Saanen, 2007, pp. 2–3)

Mihevc (1995) describes the increased agency of religious actors in
Africa responding to the conditions generated by the ideology of SAPs.
In the mid-1980s the All African Conference of Churches (AACC)
commissioned a long-term study to examine the root causes of drought
and famine in the continent. The report observed that 'The economic
mechanisms of exploitation and oppression once set in motion are difficult to reverse and this is the problem that all Africa is facing' (quoted

in Mihevc, 1995, p. 227). Such observation led to the Luanda Declaration of 1989, formulated by a network of economists, theologians, social scientists and grass-roots community activists to decry SAP ideology (Mihevc, 1995, p. 227). Thus, Mihevc observes a significant change in the broad-based agency of the churches of Africa from the 1980s onwards, becoming 'far more outspoken in criticising the national elites who . . . actively participated in a model of development that have led to greater impoverishment and the repression of basic human rights' (1995, p. 229). He continues,

> The grace period indicative of the 1960s and 1970s where churches . . . subordinated issues like democracy and human rights to the more pressing problem of development has given way to a spate of harsh indictments of the political elites who have profited from this model of development [that is, SAPs] at the expense of the poor. (1995, p. 229)

The changed posture described above did not go unnoticed by the WBG, and as we shall explore in the next chapter, would shape the interactions between the WBG and ecumenical Christian institutions.

In summary, the third phase of WBG operations can be understood as the continuing secular subordination of religion via the economistic philosophy of the SAP regime. Simultaneously, the third phase is also characterized by sacral elements of resistance as religious actors emerged both in coalitions opposed to SAPs and as distinct respondents to SAPs.

### 4.2.3 From Subordination and Protest to the Integration of Religion: The Comprehensive Development Framework

The turbulence of the phase of structural adjustment led to transformations of development orthodoxy (Stiglitz, 2003b). This new period (1995–2005) saw the emergence of religious groups from the status of secondary players in development advocacy against SAPs to development partners within a new development framework.

The transition beyond structural adjustment policy-lending was partly internal, via a rededication to poverty reduction and internal reviews such as the Wapenhans Report of 1992. Yet other reports held to a firm ideological commitment to the SAP regime. 'The Bank's 1994 Adjustment in Africa report concluded that the fruits of adjustment had not yet been borne in Africa [because of] the inadequate and half-hearted adoption of reforms' (Kapur et al., 1997, p. 797). Significantly, policy change was also the result of advocacy for change by civil society actors such as development NGOs (Rittberger and Zangl, 2006, p. 175). Thus, the fourth phase is marked by a range of broader initiatives, most significantly formulated in the Comprehensive Development Framework (CDF) introduced in 1999 during the presidency of James D. Wolfensohn (1995–2005). According to Pincus and Winters, the WBG 'internalised the logic of its critics to a surprising degree' (Pincus and Winters, 2002, pp. 10–15) and with this came the transition to a broader development agenda.

Under WBG President James Wolfensohn the CDF was established as a response to the failures of structural adjustment, predicated on the concept of partnership between the WBG and the borrowing government, with the former playing 'the repositioned institutional role of "Knowledge Bank"' (Pincus and Winters, 2002, pp. 175–6). In essence, the World Bank 'simultaneously combines the activities of financial intermediary, development research institution, consulting company and intergovernmental agency' (Pincus and Winters, 2002, p. 10).[2] Alongside this, and in a radical shift from the top-down agenda of structural adjustment, was the WBG's adoption of Sen's bottom-up 'human poverty' approach emphasizing a liberal democratic concept of 'capabilities', defined as 'the overall freedoms people have to live the kind of lives they have reason to value' (Sen, 1999, p. 10). The emphasis on human capabilities also placed a high priority on increasing the WBG commitment to democratization in development, and to partnership with civil society actors such as trade unions, small business and, of course, religious communities.

The impact upon WBG relations with religious actors was immediate. I continue the example drawn from the African churches to illustrate the kind of expectations and approaches held by religious actors toward the CDF. In March 2000 a conference was jointly organized by the WBG and the Council of Anglican Provinces of Africa. Held in Nairobi, the conference on Alleviating Poverty in Africa was designed to explore closer collaboration between the participants 'especially at the grass-roots level' in anticipation of future meetings 'involving the full range of faith communities in Africa and other important actors, such as governments and the private sector" (Belshaw et al., 2001, p. viii). The exchanges identify issues important for both partners of the African dialogue, which can be summarized below.

### (a) The context of coming together[3]
According to Vinay Samuel, a participant at the Nairobi conference, the principal issue behind the WBG's motive to build 'coalitions for change' (Samuel, 2001, p. 237) is the need to work beyond state-only endeavours because 'some governments are part of the problem' and 'some issues cannot be resolved by governments acting in a top-down manner', which only leads to powerlessness and the 'marketisation' of cultures (2001, pp. 237–9). To realize that 'finance and economics are not the only issues' in development is an implicit acknowledgement of the World Bank's

CDF-driven process toward a holistic model of development, and also something that has impacted upon faith institutions that 'are now realizing that finance and economics are areas they must deal with' (2001, pp. 237–9). From the World Bank's perspective, the 'priority of better governance . . . implies decentralising economic and political power, moving beyond "participation" to community driven development, and treating people as subjects rather than as objects of development' (Madavo, 2001, pp. 53, 51–6). When combined with the priority of 'releasing and using the capabilities already latent in society' (2001, p. 53), the adoption of a comprehensive approach to development will immediately prioritize a high level of engagement with religious actors in many contexts (2001, pp. 55–6). Such a view emanating from the WBG resonates with holistic development thinking on the importance of cultural authenticity, an issue of immediate relevance to religious actors in development contexts. Thomas asserts that successful development 'can only occur if social and economic change corresponds with the moral basis of society' (Thomas, 2004a, p. 136). At the intersection where faith and economics meet, comprehensive development must draw on the resources of religious communities because they are 'crucial repositories of social development' (2004a, p. 138). Thomas states,

> A church, temple, or mosque congregation is more than just a group of people tied to a place of worship – 'bums on pews', as they say in Britain. The social connections that faith communities provide are often only of secondary importance in understanding their importance as reservoirs of social capital. It is the *kind* of communities that they are, or are struggling to become, that are of primary importance in their ability to facilitate bonding [inward looking] and bridging [outward looking] social capital. (2004a, p. 138, emphasis in original)

The WBG shift to a comprehensive ethos of development situated religious actors to a central place among civil society actors in pursuit of grass-roots participation and change.

### (b)   'What do religious actors bring?'
For Samuel, the input of religious actors was crucial for avoiding development practice that may focus on poverty but lose perspective on the poor, 'This is a salutary lesson for development agencies. We may lose sight of the subjects – the poor. We may lose our passionate commitment to them. That is where the Church can feature so prominently. If you want to know where the poor are, ask where the Church is' (Samuel, 2001, p. 239). Through its presence, the Church therefore 'provides dignity to the poor' characterized by 'individual responsibility, community solidarity, and willingness to sacrifice for the common good' (2001, p. 240). To engender such a dignity involves development actors being locally relevant

– something that NGO 'brief-case people' cannot be over time – and to situate their work within a transcendent moral story. In the same way, within specific faith and development initiatives the World Bank faces the challenge of operating according to moral vision over ethics, and to the legitimacy of religious actors as present among the poor in a way that secular development agencies and governments may not be. The WBG's own extensive *Voices of the Poor* survey, which we shall explore in more detail below, discovered poor people trust religious organizations and that religious authorities were held in high esteem (Narayan, 2001, pp. 39–48).

### (c) 'What can the World Bank bring?'

Samuel observes that the world's largest development agency brings to religious organizations 'enormous resources, professionalism, an understanding of markets, and finances' (Samuel, 2001, p. 242). One consequence is that the World Bank brings a professionalism of reporting that challenges the practice of religious actors and makes them more accountable to donors. Yet the WBG also 'brings its own vulnerability and its interest in refashioning itself so that it can serve developing countries more effectively' (Samuel, 2001, p. 242). These elements combine to reinforce the perception of the WBG as dynamic, and from the perspective of at least some religious actors such as Samuel, open to change and transformation in the implementation of development partnerships. To adopt Christian religious parlance in keeping with the current example of prospective partnerships with African churches, the World Bank could also bring a deal of penitence for past mistakes to new partnerships with religious actors. Mihevc parallels the religious zeal for SAPs in the 1980s with missionaries of previous generations (Mihevc 1995, pp. 10–19; also George and Sabelli, 1994). Thus, the burdens of the past seem to be a shared challenge for religion and the WBG. For instance, the African Church must face a legacy of both missionary imperialism and the concomitant role as pacifier, on religious grounds, of populations against their own political interests (Mihevc, 1995, pp. 226–32).

These elements lead to perhaps the most important instrumental role attributed to the WBG by Samuel, namely, that of an advocate for religious actors in their relations with states, 'Could the World Bank lean on governments and ask them to work with the Church? [To say to governments] If you want to work with the World Bank, work with the Church also.' (Samuel, 2001, p. 242) The advocacy role so described is important and complex. Not only does it equate with the conventional challenge of representing the weak in the face of the powerful. In terms of the present study, it also embodies an expectation that the WBG will represent the interests of sacral agents in their relation to secular state actors. It is a crucial litmus test on the issue of partnership that takes seriously the secular-sacral dynamics of religion. Could the WBG meet this expectation? Early indications through the third and fourth phases of WBG operations were positive and led to the creation of a religion and development programme at the WBG. Whilst the example I have used is that of dialogue between the WBG and Christian leaders, the ensuing engagements by the WBG were broadly based across multiple faiths. I turn to the broader story of its creation from the perspective of the relevant dynamics that surrounded and penetrate the World Bank. Beginning in the early 1980s several factors lay the ground for the creation of a specific WBG focus on religion in the late 1990s. These elements deserve closer analysis, and we shall do so by once again applying the dynamics of religion framework.

## 4.3   THE DYNAMICS OF RELIGION AT THE INSTITUTIONAL LEVEL OF THE WBG

Aside from the general impetus created by the CDF, how did religion enter the institutional domain of the WBG? I shall attempt to answer this question by identifying dynamics that emerged over two decades and lay the foundation for the creation of specific faith and development partnerships involving the WBG. These partnerships will be analyzed in Chapter 5. Research into the effects of religion upon the policy domains of IOs is just beginning, the resources are scarce, and the connections between factors often vague and hard to codify. As Katherine Marshall, formerly of the WBG, observed:

> . . . while a fairly clear evolution of thinking about development and global thinking can be chartered for the World Bank and other secular organizations since 1945, which stands as an important turning point for modern concepts of development and foreign aid, tracing a parallel path in the vast and variegated world of faith institutions is far more difficult. There are many very different philosophies and approaches and the whole presents a dynamic and intertwined picture. (Marshall and Van Saanen, 2007, pp. 2–3)

Therefore, what follows aims to capture factors deemed representative of core effects upon the World Bank's policy formation on the question of religion. As the literature on such a question grows so also might the cluster of factors identified.[4] The following dynamics are categorized according to the criteria of the secular, integrated and sacral dynamics of religion.

### 4.3.1 Secular Dynamics of Religion

I begin by categorizing two dynamics that helped to bring religion into the development discourse of the WBG as secular. As in previous applications, secular factors are understood to hold religion as a secondary element in the development process. These dynamics are the policy approaches of comparative IOs toward religion and the motivations of WBG President Wolfensohn (1995–2005).

#### (a)  Policy developments on religion in comparative IOs

We have argued that the WBG operates in a milieu of complex interdependence with other actors in the global political economy. NGO advocacy against WBG policy, of which we will say more below, attests to the effect that external actors do influence the WBG's ideological posture and practice to some extent. Scholars have observed the effect of socialization processes upon IO behaviour. As a recent study on the WBG and culture summarizes,

> . . . the World Bank ought to be understood as a cultural as well as an economic institution . . . economics and economic systems are culturally constituted frameworks, both productive of and reproduced by complex networks of social relations. (Benjamin, 2007, p. xii)

To this extent, the WBG's faith and development thinking is part of a broader collective process of engagement by IOs on the question of religion. For example, Thomas observes that at the same time the WBG was beginning to face the issue of religion in its policy framing, the WHO 'started to redefine health, wellbeing and quality of life to include spiritual health' (Thomas, 2004, p. 25). Similar engagements with religion were also being made by the International Labour Organization (ILO) (Peccoud, 2004) and the Inter-American Development Bank (Wolfensohn, 2004, pp. 21–2). These examples portray an IO sector responding to the instrumental pressures of religion in contemporary world politics and potentially the legitimacy dividends that such engagements could yield. It is the socialization process between IOs that is to be emphasized here rather than the primary agency of religious actors. As such, it is a secular factor where religion plays an important secondary role in the policy development process.

#### (b)  WBG President James Wolfensohn

It is hard to imagine a faith and development programme at the World Bank without the influence of key leaders and relational networks among them. However, by far the most significant personal influence upon the increased agency of religion at the World Bank goes to its

Australian-born Jewish President, James D. Wolfensohn. Throughout the volumes of World Bank documents that bear his name, religion is not a prominent theme. His biographer mentions little of religion, nor of Wolfensohn as a gatekeeper for faith and development (Mallaby, 2004; on Jubilee 2000, see pp. 251–2). Nevertheless, it remains the case that 'the systematic attempt to engage the worlds of religion' is directly attributable to him (Marshall and Van Saanen, 2007, pp. 5–6). It is Marshall, who worked for several years as a counsellor to the President and was heavily involved in the WBG religion initiative, who explicitly identified a religious motivation to Wolfensohn's pursuit of faith partnerships (Marshall, 2006, p. 4). However, Marshall is equally clear that beyond religious conviction, three other factors of an instrumental nature were guiding Wolfensohn forward:

> A negative one was that we were hearing a lot of criticism from faith institutions about the Bank . . . This was one reason to engage, whether to explain ourselves better or to understand better why there was this opposition . . . The second reason was that Jim saw religious or faith organizations as the largest distribution system in the world . . . The third was that he was very impressed by specific data about the role of faith organizations in education and health. (Marshall, 2006, p. 5)

On the weight of argument, therefore, the agency of ideas and interests affecting Wolfensohn on religion was secular instrumental more than it was sacral.

### 4.3.2    Integrated Dynamics of Religion

I shall now classify two dynamics that influenced the WBG on religion as integrated. An integrated dynamic is constituted by a balance of secular and sacral effects such that it is hard to discern which is the more primary element. The three dynamics are NGO advocacy on the environment and the extensive WBG study titled *Voices of the Poor*.

#### (a)    NGO advocacy on WBG environmental policy
Pallas identifies the issue of the environment as the first explicit linkage made between the WBG and religious actors (Pallas, 2005, p. 678). Based on concerns with SAPs a broad-based coalition of NGOs successfully acted in 1985–86 to block the seventh replenishment of the IDA (Kapur et al., 1997). Pallas writes,

> In 1987 the Bank created the Environmental Department . . . Here, for the first time, we find faith groups mentioned specifically; the Bank listed 'Poverty/

Church Groups' as a single category in its liaison strategies . . . Bread for the World, a Christian NGO based in Washington DC, was involved in these early lobbying efforts. World Vision was also approached by the Bank in 1987. (Pallas, 2005, p. 678)

In this way religion becomes part of the larger external dynamics between the WBG and non-state actors. It is a 'secular' process as we have defined the term because the inclusion of religion is a secondary, indeed minor (Pallas, 2005, p. 678), effect to the more dominant pressures exerted on the WBG by NGO lobbies in the larger sense. However, we also see the increased agency of religion within the secular structures of the new synthesis via another process of the environmental advocacy. In 1986 the NGO World Wide Fund for Nature (WWF) facilitated a dialogue on religion and the environment in Assisi, Italy. The meeting involved representatives of five major world faiths – Buddhism, Christianity, Hinduism, Judaism and Islam. This was the beginning of a dialogical process that led in 1995 to the creation of a new religion and development NGO (Palmer and Finlay, 2003, p. xv). In 1997, at a conference at Windsor Castle, UK, the newly formed NGO called the Alliance of Religions and Conservation (ARC) had developed the idea of 'a more systematic and structured dialogue' between 'representatives of different religious organizations and multilateral development institutions, especially the World Bank' (Alliance of Religions and Conservation, n.d.). The ARC initiative is shaped by wider contexts, such as the contacts made by religious groups in 1987, and involving wider actors, the WWF and British Broadcasting Corporation, beyond the bounds of religion (Palmer and Finlay, 2003, p. xv). Andrew Steer was the director of the Environmental Department, established in 1987. According to Pallas, Steer was a Christian who used his faith connections to help nurture the WBG's relations with the ARC and forge ties with the Archbishop of Canterbury (Pallas, 2005). Pallas adds that this network became important for working on a groundbreaking meeting of faith and development leaders in 1998, 'Steer became country director for Vietnam and passed the project to Alex Rondos of the Bank's NGO unit and John Mitchell who was then involved in [Heavily Indebted Poor Countries] and happened to be a church mate of Steer's' (Pallas, 2005, p. 680). It was as part of this circle of influence that the first explicit linkage between the WBG and religious actors in development was made. The combined influence of the NGO protest and the emergence of ARC constitutes an integrated dynamic that balances secular and sacral influences that helped open the WBG to religion.

**(b)  *'Voices of the Poor'***
The second integrated dynamic on the issue of religion came via the
WBG's extensive survey *Voices of the Poor* conducted to inform the *World
Development Report* (WDR) *2000/1*. The study collectively surveys over
sixty thousand poor women and men so that the WDR 'could benefit from
their voices, their experiences, and their recommendations' (Narayan,
2001, p. 39). The study's convenor summarized 'persistent patterns of findings that emerged' across the global survey to include the holistic nature of
wellbeing, an increase in the sense of insecurity, the prevalence of gender
inequality and domestic violence, and the ineffective and corrupt nature
of state institutions (2001, pp. 40–5). Significantly, contrasting the low
status of the state, Narayan observes that 'churches and mosques, as well
as sacred trees, rivers, and mountains, were mentioned time and again as
important and valued by poor men and women' (2001, p. 45). However,
reflecting what Thomas elsewhere refers to as the 'dark side' of social
capital provided by religious communities (Thomas, 2004a, p. 139), the
poor also identified the churches with creating disunity among the community, non-participatory decision making (especially the exclusion of
women), some corruption (but much more favourable than the state) and
focused on institutional survival rather than transformation (Narayan,
2001, p. 45). In a bureaucratic context where political knowledge is accu-
mulated via reports and surveys, *Voices of the Poor* (Narayan et al., 2000)
provided a report-based rationale for the World Bank to increase efforts
to develop partnerships with religious actors in development. The sacral
agency of religion was thus embedded within the texture of the WBG's
own secular knowledge expertise.

### 4.3.3   Sacral Dynamics of Religion

I shall now suggest two sacral factors that helped to bring religion into the
development discourse of the WBG. As in previous applications, sacral
factors hold religious actors and interests to be a primary force in political dynamics. The dynamics are an informal forum on ethics held among
WBG staff, and the Jubilee 2000 debt advocacy campaign.

**(a)   The Friday Morning Group**
The first sacral factor is situated in the individual religious motivations
of WBG staff that led to a small group with a disproportionate influence.
Institutions can be understood in operational, historical and also personal
ways. The latter approach might include characterizations of an organization's members, such as cultural background, education and also religious
belief. According to Marshall and Van Saanen,

a small but not insignificant number of Bank staff members have some training in theology, and many more are members of faith communities or are inspired and motivated by the values that have drawn them to development work. (Marshall and Van Saanen, 2007, p. 5)

In 1981 some of these staff members based at the WBG headquarters in Washington, DC began to meet every Friday morning at 8 o'clock to, in the words of its founder David Beckmann, 'gather for coffee and discussion about the role of values at the World Bank and, more generally, in the world's development' (Beckmann, 1991). So it was that the Values for Development Group, more popularly known as the Friday Morning Group (FMG) began (see Friday Morning Group, n.d.).[5] The term 'values' holds central place in the FMG title, perhaps as a more inclusive term than religio-specific nouns allow, leaving open the discussion of values and ethics beyond religion. Yet the FMG was at its origin, and remains, fundamentally concerned with the question of religion in the broadest sense. Beckmann described the forum thus:

The group's members are nearly all Bank staff, including both secretaries and vice presidents. Women and men from all over the World, they represent a variety of religious and cultural traditions. The composition of the group varies from week to week, but it might include a Catholic from Cameroon, a Jew from the United States, a Palestinian, an evangelical Protestant from Australia, several Hindus and those who distrust all religion. (Beckmann et al., 1991, p. ix)

What role might such a group have played in steering the WBG toward religion? First, the FMG became a place where the topic of religion could be explicitly interwoven with World Bank policy discourse, and this had an implicitly broadening effect on policy discourse. It is no coincidence that the same David Beckmann, who in 1981 helped found a holistic forum like the FMG, also warned the institution in 1983 'the Bank's activities have become markedly less focused on reducing poverty' (Kapur et al., 1997, p. 349). Such internal discourses were to become important for the holistic developments that ensued in subsequent years. Beckmann, for instance, would go on to lead Bread for the World, one of the Christian NGOs who linked with the WBG's new Environmental Department in 1987. Second, it could be argued that the FMG provided the concept (and nomenclature) of 'values' that would, subsequently, help create an institutional space for engaging religion called 'the DDVE on Ethics and Values' (see below). The concept of 'values' may have thus allowed both informal and formal discourses on religion to flourish without being collapsed into, or lost inside, more generic discussions of 'culture' in development. At the FMG, 'values' translated into topics such as 'Hindu philosophy in action'

(Argawala, 1991), development and Christian hope (Beckmann, 1991), relations between faith and science (Burmester, 1991) and Islamic views of a just society (Serageldin, 1991). Third, the longstanding presence of the FMG provided the idea of religion-as-values with a longevity beyond any particular evolution of the WBG. Ownership of the FMG by the institution to this day constitutes, de facto, a small but not insignificant ownership of the importance of religion as part of its historical and ideological identity. Each of these factors alludes to the agency of religion to shape aspects of WBG culture and policy, thereby encouraging the view that the FMG embodies a sacral dynamic that helped bring religion into the WBG.

### (b)   Jubilee 2000 and debt advocacy

One of the most important religious actors to emerge in the development sphere in the past decade has been the Jubilee 2000 movement. The concept of Jubilee originates in the biblical concept of debt forgiveness laid out in ancient Hebrew Law, and is specifically referred text in the biblical text of Leviticus 25. Jonathan Sacks describes the Jubilee principle from its original meaning into the contemporary context. I cite it at length as an example of a sacral concept of development rooted in both Jewish and Christian religious traditions.

The Bible is acutely aware that the workings of the free market can create, over time, inequalities so great as to amount to dependency and which can only be removed by periodic redistribution. Hence the sabbatical year in which those who had sold themselves into slavery through poverty were released, and all debts cancelled. In the jubilee year, ancestral land returned to its original owners. The idea was from time to time to restore a level playing field and give those who had been forced to sell either their labour or their holdings of land the chance to begin again. This was the biblical legislation behind the successful campaign, Jubilee 2000, to provide international debt relief to developing countries and underlies Chancellor of the Exchequer Gordon Brown's proposal for a 'modern Marshall Plan' for the developing world. (Sacks, 2003, pp. 223–4)

Whatever the hermeneutical merits and pitfalls of transferring a principle of political economy from a Near Eastern nomadic context to the contemporary global order, in terms of advocacy and action the concept of Jubilee became a prime influence behind one of the most significant global advocacy movements of recent decades. In the post-Cold War period Third World debt became one of the leading points of contestation between and among civil society actors, states and IFIs. Debt remains critically high in sub-Saharan Africa, for instance, and the African Churches have advocated for change on this and the effects of structural adjustment since the 1980s (Mihevc, 1995, pp. 225–72). Building on this foundation Jubilee – both the concept and the advocacy movement of the same name – seemed to act with gravitational force to pull this energy into a larger global protest phenomenon.

> Drawing on the moral imperative inherent in Christianity and Judaism as well as other world religions, the campaign brought together unlikely partners, including liberal inner city Democrats and conservative Republicans in the United States, and trade unions and development agencies such as OXFAM, Christian Aid, and Catholic Agency for Overseas Development in the United Kingdom. Jubilee campaigners in the North incorporated the experience of trade unionists from Mozambique, priests from Zambia, and economists from Ecuador, while campaigners in the South benefited from the unique expertise of their Northern partners. Although solidarity did not always guarantee agreement, North and South discovered common objectives. These unprecedented partnerships resulted in a global social movement that altered popular and official views of debt relief and enabled civil society to participate in development decisions. (Marshall and Keough, 2004, p. 44)

The power of the Jubilee movement was not lost on the incoming World Bank President of the mid-1990s. Marshall and Keough write, 'When James Wolfensohn became president of the World Bank in 1995, one of his earliest acts was to pose demanding and far-reaching questions about the approach to debt and highly indebted countries . . . Thus the Jubilee 2000-inspired movement . . . helped to encourage and accelerate alternative mechanisms to relieve the debt of the world's poorest countries' (Marshall and Keough, 2004, p. 40). The resulting strategies included the Heavily Indebted Poor Countries initiative (HICP) and Poverty Reduction Strategy Papers (PSRPs), both designed to manage debt reduction in the context of sustainable and structural development.

Busby has also argued that Jubilee 2000 was successful because it galvanized a broad spectrum of moral actors who built a mainstream global coalition accessible to 'policy gatekeepers' in the international system:

> [Jubilee 2000] earned the endorsement of leaders of diverse ideological and professional orientations – the Pope, Bono, Jeffrey Sachs, and Pat Robertson. The campaign earned the support of strong political allies in the UK and US governments, making it harder for other creditors – such as Japan, France and Germany – to oppose debt relief . . . the religious appeal of Jubilee gave debt relief a plausible cultural match at the societal level in a number of countries . . . The religious case for debt relief had direct appeal to important individual lawmakers and also created some measure of political mobilisation that pressured skeptics. Aside from activists and leaders like Pat Robertson, prominent Congressional Republicans – Spencer Bachus and Jesse Helms in particular – found the religious message compelling. (Busby, 2007, pp. 248, 265, 267–8)

Just as interesting as the connections generated by Jubilee were the tensions it created with the WBG as the campaign progressed. Wolfensohn had misgivings about a second round of debt relief, which created conflict with a coalition of actors including Oxfam, Jubilee and state governments such as Uganda (Mallaby, 2004, p. 44). Moreover, the Jubilee push to debt cancellation was not met, and the prescriptions for its advancement were deemed too slow. Thus, whilst the 'Jubilee organizers generally came to recognise that the World Bank . . . had become more inclusive', dissatisfied with the HIPC-PRSP initiatives, the successor movement to Jubilee 2000 'continues in its critique of the World Bank and works to mobilize popular support in favour of alternative solutions' (Marshall and Keough, 2004, p. 44). Thus Jubilee 2000 became a key learning ground for the simultaneous connections and disconnections that sacral development partnerships could bring.

## 4.4   MODELLING RELIGION AT THE WBG

To remind the reader, this book attempts to move the study of religion in IR toward a new analytical question of 'Where is religion?' at work in international affairs. It is only until we situate religion in the international system that we can begin to assess what religion is in a normative sense and what influence it has to shape political dynamics. Answers to the situative question are facilitated by the construction of the religious structure of world politics. This structure allows us to see where the primary, secondary and integrated elements of religion are situated in the dynamics of IR. When applied to analyze specific issues and actors in world politics (global dynamics) two insights become possible. First, the elements of religion can be differentiated and assessed against the issue of the primary and secondary capacity of religion to constitute the given dynamic. Second, the elements of religion can be assessed against whether they are internal or external to the domain or influence of the dynamic chosen. I argue that policy development toward religion in IR cannot adequately progress unless these specific insights are attained. I shall now attempt to draw such insights from the WBG engagement with religion.

### 4.4.1   Integrating the WBG into the Religious Structure of World Politics

The dynamics of religion that helped bring religious actors and interests into the WBG discourse on development are differentiated in Figure 4.1.

Two observations ensue from the above representation. First, secular,

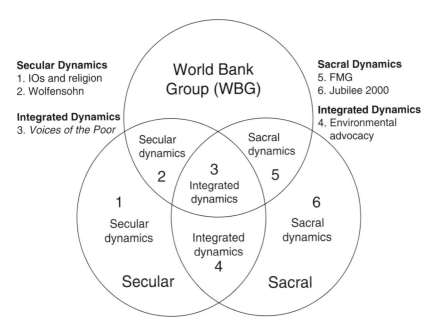

*Figure 4.1    The dynamics of religion influencing the WBG: secular, integrated and sacral elements*

integrated and sacral factors outside the WBG domain play a role in influencing the WBG on religion: the socialization process among other predominantly secular IOs (1), the intregated influences at work in the environmental advocacy movements (4) and the sacral concept of Jubilee (6). Whilst Jubilee 2000 involved action on the equally secular issue of debt reduction for the Third World, without the sacral *concept* of Jubilee drawn from religious tradition the impetus behind this specific campaign action would not have existed. Second, secular, integrated and sacral factors also play a role inside the WBG domain, President Wolfensohn engaged faith actors and interests mainly from an instrumental motivation (2), secular and sacral factors integrate within the policy domain of the WBG via *Voices of the Poor* (3) and the FMG (5) was created from the vestiges of religious belief in the lives of WBG staff.

We can therefore observe that the dynamics which animated the WBG's initial engagement with religion are spread across all sectors of the religious structure. This is significant because it suggests that the locus of religion as it was introduced to the WBG is not to be found in particular sectors over others, but rather, the beginnings of religion at the WBG were broadly based. Potentially each element could coalesce around an

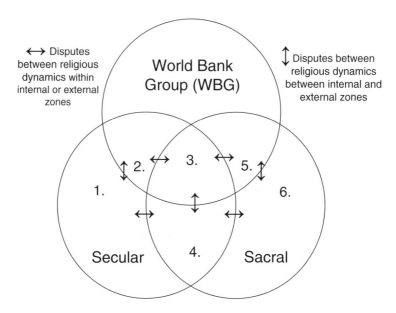

*Figure 4.2    Borders of potential dispute between dynamics of religion at the WBG*

ethos of partnership that recognized the value of secular, integrated and sacral dynamics of development. However, each element could also pull the development agenda of the WBG in competing directions, thus having a disintegrating effect on the faith and development initiative as a whole. As such, the engagement with religion at the WBG could be characterized by potential ideological disputes between secular, integrated and sacral interests. This is represented in Figure 4.2.

### 4.4.2    Toward a Policy-level Analysis of WBG Partnerships

As stated at the start of this chapter, the WBG is representative of the global development agenda. The central debates on the evolutions of the international development agenda revolve around whether IFIs such as the WBG have indeed broadened their approach particularly in response to the pressures applied by civil society actors to do so, including religious actors. Kapur distils this debate between two views, one that holds the WBG to be a vestige of elite power and the interest of global financial markets, and a pluralist view that holds the WBG to be a domain of multiple open and competing groups (Kapur, 2002, p. 54). This chapter suggests the latter definition applies to the WBG in relation to religious actors. As we have now considered, religious actors form an important and broadly based part of the story of the WBG since the early 1980s founded on an increasing engagement with sacral as well as secular elements of religion. However we need to probe further before knowing to what extent the openness of the WBG toward religious actors translates into integrated partnerships of a secular-sacral nature.

This investigation can be done from an internal and external perspective. Internally, the analysis would seek to determine whether WBG faith and development partnerships consolidate the secular and sacral dynamics of religion around an increasingly integrated centre. Integration would require more than an instrumental approach by secular interests seeking to maximize the practical value of working with such a large constituency of the Third World. Similarly, it would require more of religious communities than merely seeking the funds and expertise on offer from the WBG. Only an integrated approach to partnership between secular and sacral interests will cause the centre to hold and not disintegrate. Externally, the analysis would seek to determine to what extent the WBG can bridge, not simply a secular-religious divide, but also an ideological divide between itself and religious actors that are embedded in the critical traditions of development. If, as I have argued in Chapter 3, religious development activity is strongly represented outside the development agenda, there is a high priority to constructively engage religious actors on issues of ideological difference.

The transition from SAPs to the CDF has led some to believe in 'a new World Bank for a new century' (Picciotto, 2003). If Malraux was right to suggest that 'the twenty-first century will be religious or it will not be at all' (Johnston and Cox, 2003, p.11), it is important to analyze the WBG engagement with religious groups. Have partnerships with religious civil society actors occurred in substance as well as in form? To answer this question requires us to move from an institutional analysis to a policy-level analysis of specific partnerships with faith institutions and communities.

## NOTES

1. For a summary, see McDuie-Ra and Rees (2010, pp.20–36).
2. Quoting C. Gilbert, A. Powell and D. Vines (1999), 'Positioning the World Bank', *Economic Journal*, 109, p.612.
3. The subheading for this section is drawn from Vinay Samuel's article 'The World Bank and the churches, reflections at the outset of a new partnership' (Samuel, 2001).
4. See McDuie-Ra and Rees (2010) for a prior contribution to this research by the author.
5. Observation of the FMG was conducted by the author at the WBG, Washington, DC, 11 February 2005.

# 5. Analyzing World Bank faith and development partnerships

> Development is not something which is done for people, or even with people,
> by involving them in projects designed by someone else.
> Michael Taylor (2005, p. 133)

> Archbishop Martin's definition of development – as a realisation of everyone's
> God-given potential – resonates, and it is what many of us
> at the World Bank believe.
> Jean-Louis Sarbib (Marshall and Keough, 2005, p. 112)

Having considered the dynamics of religion at the discourse and institutional levels, the dynamics of religion model is applied to describe and critically analyze policy partnerships between the WBG and faith institutions that emerged in the period 1998–2005. This time frame stems directly from the meetings on faith and development that occurred at the beginning of Wolfensohn's presidency and culminates in the final year of his tenure. The study initially compares WBG partnerships with three faith institutions – the *Fes* Festival of Sacred Music, the World Council of Churches (WCC) and the Community of Sant'Egidio.

## 5.1 ENGAGING RELIGION AND DEVELOPMENT AT THE POLICY LEVEL

In the previous chapter I examined secular, integrated and sacral dynamics of religion that opened the institutional spaces of the WBG to a possible policy engagement with religious actors. An important observation to draw from these factors is the emergence, not simply of religious actors in the spaces of development (for they have long-existed in such spaces) but of a faith-based development sector (Clarke and Jennings, 2008a) that prominent IFIs including the WBG could no longer ignore. As a WBG assessment acknowledged, '. . . religion is a central part of the international system . . . even if it wished to do so, the Bank could not entirely sidestep the faith engagement' (World Bank, 2006, p. 3). The department within the WBG designed to further the engagement was a specialized unit called the Development Dialogue on Values and Ethics (DDVE). According to the website of May 2007, the DDVE remains 'primarily responsible for engaging with faith institutions around development issues and working with other institutions and leaders who are addressing the complex ethical issues around globalization' (DDVE, n.d.). The WBG engagement with faith communities and development organizations was encapsulated in three key areas:

1) Building bridges – stronger, bolder partnerships
2) Exploring a more 'comprehensive,' 'holistic,' and 'integrated' vision of development
3) Transforming dialogue into practice and action (DDVE, n.d.)

Taken on its own, the above programme might simply appear as a manifestation of Wolfensohn's entrepreneurial leadership, who was criticized by some as a 'charismatic, passionate president [who] makes spectacular personal gestures and supports worthy but peripheral institutional commitments' (Rich, 2002, p. 53). However, in the context of both the importance of religion in the discourse of development (Chapter 3) and the broadly based foundations for the WBG's institutional engagement with religion (Chapter 4) the emergence of the DDVE is an instrumental extension of the momentum created by these earlier developments. There are larger stories of transformation to tell at the WBG than the story of religion, such as the norm contestations surrounding gender and the environment (for example, Wade, 1997; Gutner, 2003). However, by situating the WBG within the religious structure of world politics we can see that the faiths and development agenda was more embedded in both secular, integrated and sacral dynamics than might have otherwise been imagined. The DDVE was thus the culmination point for these earlier dynamics and a bridge to the next. Originally a unit within the External Affairs Vice-Presidency (DDVE, n.d.) the DDVE is now part of the Human Development Network Vice-Presidency (DDVE, n.d.).

Yet at this point the momentum stalls. Once religion moved beyond the institutional level and into the policy domain of the WBG, the initiative to engage religion within the WBG's core policy development agenda was neither celebrated nor without significant and arguably insurmountable obstacles. Whilst the DDVE was established to operationalize WBG partnerships with religious actors, it remained institutionally insecure. For example, in late 2000 the Executive Board of the WBG voted to reject Wolfensohn's proposal to establish a small 'Directorate on Faith' by a margin of 24 votes to zero. Various explanations of this vote have been offered, Tyndale (2003, p. 25) suggests anxiety about a 'link between religious groups and political conflicts in many parts of the world'; Clarke (2007, p. 82) posits 'concern about the erosion of church-state boundaries in the USA and its potential spill-over into US policy on international development'; informal discussions conducted by the author at the DDVE (11 February 2005) summarized the attitude of the Board via the question 'Who would we work with?'. This suggests an instrumental rationale behind the vote that were counter to those that encouraged faith and development links at the WBG, namely, that WBG state stakeholders were concerned that religious lines of authority are often unclear (see also Wolfensohn, 2004). I shall return to this important event placing it in a secular-sacral perspective later in the chapter. Another example of the troubled beginning of religion is that public reporting of the WBG's religion initiative was muted in its enthusiasm (*The Economist*, 2006, p. 62). A third example can be found in Sebastian Mallaby's valedictory account of Wolfensohn's time as WBG President which does not mention the religion and development programme explicitly at all (Mallaby, 2004). Adding further perspective is the fact that the faiths and development programme survived as a specialized unit within the External Affairs Vice-Presidency and was funded by the discretionary President's Contingency Fund (World Bank, 2006, p. 1). The DDVE may have had the intimate support of its President, however it was virtually ignored at the executive levels of the WBG (World Bank, 2006, pp. 1, 4). In the post-Wolfensohn era, its inclusion in the Human Development Anchor is also described as philosophically and instrumentally unsuccessful (World Bank, 2006, p. 4).

Although Marshall and Van Saanen (2007, pp. 7–8) argue that 'due to their breadth and diversity' the WBG's myriad connections with religious actors lie beyond the scope of formal evaluation, Clarke and Jennings make the salient point that while 'the place of religion in society is complex, dense and difficult to pin down' it is nevertheless very real (2008a, p. 272). This latter observation invites further analysis of the dynamics of religion at work in the WBG's faiths and development agenda. What is to explain such negative outcomes for the DDVE, especially given the significant momentum described in the previous chapter that helped create the WBG engagement with religion in the first place? How are we to understand the dynamics of religion at play in faith and development policies? How were these policies embodied at the level of development partnerships? Does the differentiation of faith and development partnerships engaged by the DDVE offer important insights, and if so, what are they? The present chapter answers these questions by considering three partnerships of the DDVE and lays the foundation for a closer examination of a fourth unique partnership in Chapter 6.

## 5.2   MODELLING THREE PARTNERSHIPS IN FAITH AND DEVELOPMENT

The three partnerships described below are very different, and in the first instance not easily comparable. One could aptly be described as an annual inter-cultural seminar, another as a negotiation over ideological differences between like-organizations, and the third as a linkage between an international religious development NGO and a multilateral development agency. Our primary focus is to classify and analyze each initiative according to the religious dynamics that surrounded and animated them.

### 5.2.1   The *Fes* Colloquium

Between 2001 and 2006 the WBG jointly facilitated a forum on ethics, spirituality and globalization as part of an acclaimed annual sacred music festival held in Morocco. These fora provided an invaluable opportunity for the WBG to engage in dialogue at a cultural level among a diverse range of actors and interests to which it was not previously exposed.

#### (a)   *Fes*: culture, religion and the politics of globalization

The *Fes* Festival of World Sacred Music began in 1995 in the city of Fes, Morocco. The festival has the objective of bridging cultural divides through music and art representative from all over the world. Moroccan scholar Faouzi Skali, himself a member of the European Commission's Groupe de Sages, established the event with the underlying theme of 'giving soul to globalization' (Marshall and Keough, 2004, pp. 49–56). The *Fes* Festival is embedded in an internationalist culture. In a way not dissimilar to the openings of dialogue provided to the WBG by the ARC (see Chapter 4), such a context opened the way for the WBG to enter into an intentional conversation on culture, religion and the ethics of globalization.

Between 2001 and 2006, the *Fes* Festival hosted the *Fes* Colloquium, a forum jointly sponsored by the WBG and designed to 'face directly the controversies, divisions and passions that the topic of globalization had evoked in different parts of the world' (Marshall and Van Saanen, 2007, p. 222). The WBG described the dialogue from its own perspective as 'a key partner for the annual *Fes* Colloquium since 2002 due to its substantive engagement 'without conditions'' (DDVE, n.d.). Implicit in the notion of facilitation 'without conditions' is an acknowledgement of the contested nature of globalization and portrays the WBG as having a benign intent lest its motives for involvement in the symposium be predetermined by participants and observers to the dialogue in a negative fashion. In other words, *Fes* provided a safe forum for the WBG to engage in cultural debate. Whilst the first colloquium in 2001 has been described as a modest affair, the fault lines around the nature and purpose of globalization were clearly established among participants (Marshall and Keough, 2004, pp. 51–2). For the next five years, the WBG, along with the European Commission (EC) and the Aga Khan Foundation, sponsored an expanding and increasingly cohesive dialogue (Marshall, 2005, p. 24).

The *Fes* Colloquium has a cosmopolitan ethos where religious figures are numbered among 'thinkers, policy makers and critics' (Marshall, 2005, p. 16). Thus, whilst dialogue topics have included 'changing roles for and expectations of religion', over the life of the symposium broader themes such as 'the challenges of identity and their links to historical and living culture, the underlying theme of equity, the ethical responsibility of the media . . . and the role of political leadership in focusing attention on global social justice' have also been prominent (Marshall, 2005, p. 16). Participants are as broadly based as the topics addressed. These have included Sulak Sivaraska (Thai Buddhist leader), Luis Lopez-Llera (Mexican activist), Swami Agnivesh (bonded labour activist in India), Peter Eigen (chairman, Transparency International), Domonique Strauss-Kahn (former French finance minister), Fatema Mernissi (Moroccan feminist writer and activist) and Idrissa Seck (Prime Minister of Senegal) (Marshall and Keough, 2004, pp. 51–5).

The first three colloquia saw the dialogue gradually move from an informal to an institutionalized gathering, drawing larger crowds and participant groups. From 2003 to 2006 further emphasis was placed on moving the dialogue toward actions, though no formal *Fes* declarations were made. Actions have been seeded via the Colloquium back into the behaviour of its constituent members, including 'music festivals and associated dialogue on several continents, development projects in Morocco and *Fes*, the movement towards an "interdependence day"' (Marshall and Van Saanen, 2007, p. 227). More concretely, the Colloquium led to plans for the creation of the Al Akhawayn University's Institute of Cultural Diplomacy, which aspires to develop leadership for peace, especially in the Islamic world (Al Akhawayn University, n.d.).

What is the utility of the *Fes* Colloquium for the WBG's religion and development initiative? Are these motivations primarily secular, sacral or constituted by the integration of both? I shall consider four possible factors from the perspective of these questions. First, the festival was 'inspired by the furor around the first Gulf War' (Marshall, 2005, p. 1). After the events of 9/11 profiled perceived 'civilizational' differences in world politics, the stakeholders of the WBG may have aligned themselves with the founding rationale from *Fes* and thought it prudent to engage with a mainstream forum on the increasingly vexed issues of hegemony, globalization and culture. Such a motivation is more secular than sacral, driven by an instrumental demand to enter an important dialogue on identity politics that had become relevant to all politics worldwide. Second, in a post-Seattle milieu of anti-globalization protest, the *Fes* Colloquium helped the WBG to situate itself between the World Economic Forum at Davos (in Switzerland) and the World Social Forum at Porto Alegre (in Brazil), presenting itself as a conciliator rather than a combatant (Marshall and Keough, 2004, p.49). Such an approach is arguably integrated in its ethos, though the drivers of these larger debates hold religion at the periphery. The WBG's rationale remains instrumental, and situated within the realm of comparative IO behaviours alluded to in Chapter 4. Third, as we also suggested in the previous chapter, one of the WBG's internal mechanisms for an increased engagement with religious actors was the conceptual shift toward the CDF, with a new emphasis on partnership and dialogue, especially with civil society and 'cultural' actors in development. As such, the *Fes* Colloquium is one example of the CDF made manifest. Moreover, as an initiative of the DDVE, the *Fes* Colloquium was part of the External Affairs programme of the World Bank and thus a mechanism for the WBG to promote its interests and its name via a cultural sphere instead of an economic one. As the CDF was constructed as a tool for integration between economic and cultural approaches to development, though mainly secular in orientation, there remains room for sacral elements to enter the discourse. *Fes* is thus one expression of this. Fourth, a core feature of the communication process in the *Fes* Colloquium has been the attempt to construct a 'thoughtful and engaged dialogue' with a focus on symbolism and music, as much as on words (Marshall and Keough, 2004, pp.54–5). This culture of relative informality, creating a focus on 'listening and transformation' (Marshall and Van Saanen, 2007, p.222) presented a familiar format for WBG involved in the informal and conversational protocols of the WBG's own Friday Morning Group, which was structured around brief presentations from life experience, silence and an open discussion (Beckmann et al., 1991, pp.ix–x). If such a forum were conducted with an open ideological posture, the latent potential for sacral agency to further integrate into the WBG development agenda would be realized.

### (b)   WBG-*Fes* Colloquium: engaging religion in a secular context

Taking these elements into account, can we arrive at a more definitive assessment of the *Fes* Colloquium on the question of religious agency? I suggest the answer depends on what we compare it to. Looking out from *Fes* in a secular direction we see forums on globalization that exist in ideological opposition to each other, namely, the World Economic Forum (WEF) and the World Social Forum (WSF). Both events have incorporated religion into their agendas. The WEF has in recent years included dialogues on comparative belief systems and the economic order (World Economic Forum, 2008a), relations between the West and Islam (World Economic Forum, 2008b) and faith and modernization (World Economic Forum, 2008c). The WSF has included discussion of religion in its workshop structure, and participants included a high, notably Christian, presence of religious actors involved in 'campaigning on everything from justice for street-children to HIV/AIDS projects and rights for women' (Beattie, 2007, p. 2). Looking out toward the sacral domains of world politics we find gatherings such as the Parliament of the Worlds Religions (n.d.) and the World Spirit Forum (n.d.). These forums remain formed by the modern world – the use of parliamentary structures, for instance – yet they privilege the traditions of religion over other agendas and as such are considered post-secular, part of the new sacral politics (see Parliament of the Worlds Religions, 1993) that have so impacted the policy domains of IOs. Yet the universalist culture of so many IO religious networks is also contrasted to the situated and particular expressions of religion that are part of localized cultures.

So where does the *Fes* Colloquium lie in relation to these comparisons? The sacral dimension might at first seem to exist in closer proximity to *Fes* than the secular. Without religion, understood in its context as a defined and tradition-bound sense of the sacred that gives the festival its focus in music and art, the *Fes* Festival would certainly not exist. Yet the *Fes* Colloquium, with its broad agenda to interface between spirituality, culture and globalization, reflects that closer nexus between religion and internationalism that privileges the secular over the sacral. As an extension of the principle of ambivalence that holds religion to be a resource for peace-building as much as a root for violence, the positive internationalization of religion via movements such as *Fes* help to create a kind of multilateral religionism that fits easily into a globalized – even neoliberalized – conception of the world. It is a prime example of the discourse of the new development orthodoxy described in Chapter 4. As such, *Fes* accommodates a kind of religion that is secondary to the overarching emphasis on cultural rights and responsibilities, and to the achievement of a certain kind of cosmopolitan internationalism. The *Fes* Colloquium borders the integration of secular and sacred, but is more reflective of the utility of religion that belongs more within the secular sphere. From the WBG's perspective *Fes* reflected many of the progressive assumptions embedded in the CDF, and as such provided another opening for civil society actors to enter the new synthesis in global development that the CDF and the Millennium Development Goals (MDGs) are a central part of. I therefore conclude that the *Fes* Colloquium is an expression of secular religion as we have previously defined the term. There is a basic continuity between the *Fes* Colloquium and the RGC project in relation to the global development agenda, incorporating the ethical and cultural dimensions of religion into a pre-determined economic discourse on globalization.

### 5.2.2   The World Council of Churches

If the *Fes* Colloquium highlighted to the WBG that religious and cultural dialogue could be productively accommodated, the second partnership would prove more difficult. The World Council of Churches (WCC) might be interpreted as a sibling institution to the WBG. The partnership between them, rather than opening the development space to new and innovative engagements, would highlight an age-old sibling rivalry.

### (a)   WCC: ideology and faith

The World Bank was created in 1947 to help meet the development challenges of post-war Europe and beyond. The WCC was formally established in 1948 under a not dissimilar mandate, this time toward the reconstruction and development of a religious internationalism, or ecumenism, practised in the context of *oikoumene* meaning 'the whole inhabited earth' (World Council of Churches, n.d.). The World Bank was originally limited to dealing with capitalist countries and now in a post-1989 context extends its reach to a mixture of ideological political-economies. The WCC was initially limited to working with and among Protestant churches, and now incorporates the Orthodox Church worldwide, and since the liberalizing effect of the Second Vatican Council (1968) the Catholic Church 'sends representatives to all major WCC conferences as well as to its Central Committee meetings and the assemblies' (World Council of Churches, n.d.). The beginnings of the Cold War in the West marked a moment of Protestant influence in the shaping of IR. In the USA, Protestant theologians such as Reinhold Niebuhr and a host of others became public intellectuals who 'helped to shape and change America's political culture so it was willing to accept the hegemonic responsibilities of global change' (S.M. Thomas, 2005, p. 161). As Thomas argues,

> . . . at least during the early years of the Cold War, Christian ecumenism, multilateralism, and internationalism should be seen as interlinked political

and cultural narratives that led to the founding of the United Nations, the Bretton Woods system, and the World Council of Churches at the same time. (S.M. Thomas, 2005, pp. 161, 155–66)

Protestantism in Europe, with the fledgling WCC at its central international bureaucracy, faced the immediate and difficult question of post-Holocaust confession by the German Churches and their reincorporation into a worldwide Christian communion (Burleigh, 2006, pp. 304–6). The framework of a post-Holocaust theology, in turn, gave rise to the political theology movement, established in reaction to the perceived pacifying influence of Lutheran 'two-kingdoms theology' upon German Christians during the War (Moltmann, 1999, p. 49). Thus, the new political theology presupposed 'the public testimony of faith and political discipleship of Christ' (Moltmann, 1999, p. 49). This platform has led parts of the WCC in different ideological directions to the realism espoused by Niebuhr in the USA. Situated in a context of ideological division, European political theology began in the late 1960s to facilitate dialogues described by Moltmann as 'unforgettable encounters between reform Marxists and reform theologians, between revolutionary inclined Christians and religiously inquiring Marxists' (Moltmann, 1999, p. 50). A parallel process was also happening in the Catholic context of Latin America via the emergence of liberation theology (Berryman, 1987). The WCC was thus at the centre of conflicting ideological agendas, including a growing programme exploring critically oriented feminist and ecology theologies which, over time, led to a lessening influence of the mainline US Churches – who were also suffering a membership decline at the expense of the non-WCC aligned Pentecostal and evangelical Churches – toward becoming more global in outlook and 'European' in its bureaucratic ideology. Today the WCC remains based in Geneva and has an internationalist culture perhaps not unlike the ideological cultures one might find within other IOs such as UNCTAD and the ILO. These cultures reflect political ideologies which have, in recent years, been at odds with perceptions of US hegemonic influence.

At one level, therefore, there is nothing 'exotic' about the WCC in relation to the WBG. It is an international bureaucracy and network, whose core constituents arguably exercise a larger total influence upon world affairs than the WBG. At another level, the ideological formations described above allude to differences in the normative assumptions that have governed the institutions since their inception. Together, these elements provide a necessary background for understanding the dynamics of the WBG-WCC dialogue, established via the DDVE, in February 2003.

The dialogue with the WBG was part of a larger series of engagements between the WCC and other IOs such as the IMF and the ILO (Marshall and Keough, 2004, pp. 75–86; Peccoud, 2004). The specific dialogues of 2003 were precipitated by public WCC criticism – described as 'a blistering critique' – of a joint UN, IMF and WBG report on global development (Marshall and Van Saanen, 2007, p. 198). In an often tense process that extended over several years, the ground was laid for the official dialogue of 2003. The WBG described the WCC dialogues in the following way:

> [The dialogue] examined a series of issues around *institutional governance* and *accountability*, participation of *civil society* in development processes, the respective roles of the *public and private sector* in poverty alleviation, and the challenges of *globalization.* Through this dialogue with WCC, the World Bank and the IMF have been encouraged to re-examine their respective *concepts* of development approached and evolving institutional mandates. (DDVE, 2005, emphasis added)

When read in the context of the comparative ideological development of each institution, the texture of the above statement alludes to numerous points of potential disagreement (emphasized in italics) over the fundamentals of development. The cleavage between relative ideological concepts is clearly seen in descriptions of the first encounter in a WCC press release dated 22 October 2004.

> Recalling the World Council of Churches' (WCC) foundational mandate to make 'the church in every place *a voice for those who have no voice*' as well as its firm commitment to justice, rooted in the *'ecumenical perception of God's preferential option for the poor,'* WCC general secretary Samuel Kobia affirmed encounters with the Bretton Woods institutions as a 'critical engagement in the search for viable pathways towards *global justice*, so that all people can have their *fair share in the common wealth* of all. (World Council of Churches, 2004a, emphasis added)

We can see the embedded nature of assumptions (emphasized in italics) emanating from the WCC that are rooted in political and liberation theology traditions. In development terms, such traditions are more aligned to the critical school theories of advocacy for the global periphery against those actors, including the WBG, that control the global development agenda. As we have previously noted, such forms of critique are important for understanding religious agency in the developing world.

Given the influence of emancipatory assumptions at work in the WCC's conception of development, it is unsurprising that the WCC-WBG dialogues (February 2003 and October 2004) were characterized by several fundamental differences. The first were differences in 'vocabulary and assumptions' (Marshall and Van Saanen, 2007, p. 199). The second was precipitated by the 'strongly held and generally negative WCC perceptions that IMF and Bank policies, operations, and governance are firmly set within the neoliberal ideological framework of "the Washington Consensus"', against which the WCC was called to promote a 'spirituality of resistance' (Marshall and Van Saanen, 2007, pp. 199–200). The dialogues culminated in a high-level meeting in Geneva in October 2004 without developing a programmatic agenda, but having succeeded in opening up a dialogue that was hitherto closed via the formulation of a joint statement of commitments, organized around the UN established MDGs, by the IMF, the WBG and the WCC. In addition, plans were drawn from the conducting of 'country-level case studies that could help to inform the Poverty Reduction Strategy Paper (PRSP) process' of the WBG. At the final Geneva meeting Wolfensohn mentioned his personal commitment to building bridges with faith institutions as a central motivating factor. Beyond this general commitment, the President also noted his dismay at the WCC report *Lead Us Not Into Temptation* (World Council of Churches, 2001) that in his estimation 'presented such an untrue picture of the World Bank's mission, work and staff' (Marshall and Van Saanen, 2007, p. 207). In practical terms perhaps the significance – both historically and in relation to the size of the WCC's constituent base – of such an engagement was too important to ignore. The high-level nature of the WBG-WCC dialogue shows the importance of religious actors within the growing space for civil society in IO policy domains.

### (b)   WBG-WCC: contesting religion in an ideological dialogue

How can we measure the agency of religion in the WBG-WCC dialogue? The description of the WCC as a sibling institution is contrasted by the parallel portrayal of the WCC as an ideological other to the WBG. Similar to our study of the *Fes* Colloquium, comparisons to other actors serve to deepen this view. As suggested, the WCC operates within an ideological framework that could be favourably compared to other IOs such as UNCTAD and the ILO. Unlike the preliminary nature of negotiations with the WBG, UNCTAD has active partnerships with two arms of the WCC, the Association of World Council of Churches related to Development Organizations in Europe (APRODEV) and the Commission of the Churches on International Affairs (CCIA) (UNCTAD, 2003, p. 2). The APRODEV mandate reflects a critical ideology similar to the general WCC mandate we have discussed above, to 'influence decision-making in the European Union institutions related to North-South issues in order to promote fairness and justice and the eradication of poverty' (APRODEV, n.d.). APRODEV has also expressed a common critical interpretation of the WBG:

At various occasions, Non-Governmental Organizations (NGOs) have pointed out that the integration of Southern countries into the world economy cannot be considered to be a goal in itself. During the last 50 years or so, Southern countries integrated into the world economy, often following arm-twisting by the IMF and the World Bank and through the implementation of Structural Adjustment Programmes which, typically, aimed at liberalisation, de-regulation and privatisation of Southern economies. (APRODEV, 2001, p. 5)

UNCTAD, though in partnership with the WBG through the UN system, has its origins in the advocacy for Third World states and the formation of the Group of 77 which existed in tension with much of the agenda of the Bretton Woods institutions. Surviving the ideological changes to the world economy that came with the end of the Cold War, UNCTAD remains committed to 'addressing the imbalances of globalization and the need to overcome the supply constraints of developing countries, so as to ensure development gains and poverty reduction' (UNCTAD, n.d.). The WCC and UNCTAD therefore find their operative rationales in the same ideological constellation.

The ILO has had a similar ideological history to UNCTAD. It recently 'welcomed growing links with the World Bank' following current WBG President Robert Zoellick speaking to a 'lively interactive discussion' on the subject of 'an inclusive and sustainable globalization' at the 301st session of the ILO's Governing Body (International Labour Organization, 2008). The emphasis on this new development signifies a longer history of ideological tension, and the dynamic nature of IO relations going forward. In February 2002 the ILO and the WCC convened an interfaith dialogue to 'shed light on how their ideas, values and precepts support the principles of the [ILO's] Decent Work Agenda' (Marshall and Keough, 2004, p. 78). The WCC and the ILO are ideologically aligned in the view that the economic disruptions of globalization make the relation between work and decency (conditions, dignity, relations to life) tenuous. For the ILO, decent work is so important it constitutes a 'development paradigm' (International Institute for Labour Studies, n.d.). The WCC has helped add the moral and ethical traditions of religion to this central ILO agenda (Peccoud, 2004).

From these brief summaries, we can see marked contrast between WCC relations with the WBG to that of UNCTAD and the ILO. What does this mean for our understanding of the agency of religion in the WBG programme toward the WCC? The first inference is a de-linkage with the WBG. If, as we have suggested above, that the ideology of development promoted by the WCC is formed by the post-1945 tradition of European political theology and the liberation theology movements of the Third World, then the kind of religious agency at work at the WCC is one that critiques a neoliberal approach to political economy and the new synthesis in global development. The second inference is that the ideological texture of the WCC's message is resonant with the ILO and UNCTAD, which, though ideologically divergent with traditional WBG policy on development, are similarly structured and share common organizational inter-linkages with it. Putting these two inferences together, de-linkage and inter-linkage, we may conclude that the WCC embodies a balance toward secular and religious influences in its operation, formed by communities and traditions of faith that are, in turn, common with secular traditions critical of global capitalism. Thus, the WCC embodies an integrated dynamic of religion, and one that can be situated in the critical development tradition beyond the boundary of the global development agenda. The ideological dispute that this creates thus characterizes the WBG-WCC partnership.

### 5.2.3   The Community of Sant'Egidio

The Community of Sant'Egidio, a lay Catholic organization founded in Rome in 1968 on a platform of service to the poor and the working for peace, is a noted actor in the area of conflict mediation (Appleby, 2000, pp. 288–92; Haynes, 2007b, pp. 91–4). The WBG entered into negotiation toward partnership with Sant'Egidio to assist in another war, namely, against the spread of HIV/AIDS in Africa. What ensued highlights both the possibilities and obstacles in faith and development partnerships.

#### (a)   The Community of Sant'Egidio: partnership and difference
Sant'Egidio's efforts in political mediation extend to contexts as diverse as Algeria, Burundi and Guatemala. Two prominent examples of this work are Sant'Egidio's central role in the successful resolution in 1992 of the civil war in Mozambique (Haynes, 2008, p. 92), and its role as a central mediator in the unsuccessful peace negotiations between Serb, Albanian and Kosovar leaders prior to the international war between NATO forces and Serbia in 1999 (Appleby, 2000, pp. 290–1). Based on these kinds of efforts and achievements, Appleby describes Sant'Egidio as an 'exemplary' institution evidencing 'the ability of religious NGOs to collaborate fruitfully with secular government and non-governmental organizations' (2000, p. 290). It was in dealing with the issue of Kosovar refugees that Sant'Egidio and the WBG first worked together (Community of Sant'Egidio, 2003). Progressing the faith and development partnership the two organizations 'signed a Memorandum of Understanding on 1st August 2003 outlining areas of common concern and potential cooperation, sharing information and continuing efforts to work together to

enhance their impact and effectiveness' (DDVE, n.d.). The most immediate area of common concern was the treatment of HIV/AIDS in Africa. Since 2002 Sant'Egidio's DREAM programme has been focused on HIV/AIDS treatment and prevention programmes in Mozambique (Liotta et al., 2005).[1] Using Sant'Egidio's established roots in Mozambique, the two organizations established a 'pilot effort' in the treatment of HIV/AIDS described in the following terms:

> Sant'Egidio through on-the-ground services and . . . advocacy, including yearly DREAM conferences bringing together international development agencies with African health ministers and DREAM practitioners, and the Bank through its work in helping countries build sustainable HIV/AIDS strategies. (Marshall and Van Saanen, 2007, p. 60)

In sum, Sant'Egidio joined the Treatment Acceleration Program (TAP) funded by the IDA as part of its operation of ten day hospitals in Mozambique. Significant, from a WBG perspective, is the way Sant'Egidio's service delivery occurs 'entirely within the framework of the Mozambican health system . . . reflecting the fact that the government of Mozambique is the primary partner' (Marshall and Van Saanen, 2007, p. 59). This integration of state-sponsored development delivered by a grass-roots faith-based provider provided an excellent model for faith and development partnerships within the new orthodox framework.

By 2006, however, the WBG also acknowledged the need to better understand the 'system' of Catholic medical care, especially given that 'Catholic medical institutions play critical roles in a large number of countries and have experience that is a critical part of the story of development' (Marshall, 2006). Sant'Egidio's role in Mozambique is a clear example of this. In the context of this commitment there were acknowledged 'areas of real disagreement' between Catholic health assumptions and 'the secular development world', notably 'the role of women and women's reproductive health rights' (Marshall, 2006). Involvement in Sant'Egidio's DREAM programme provided the WBG with an opportunity to begin addressing these issues, and particularly to influence an established Catholic development culture – formed around Sant'Egidio's reputable day hospitals – with the WBG's own core institutional mandate. Aptly described as a transnational expertise institution (St Clair, 2006) the WBG is in its own perception most adept to make a contribution within the nomenclature and practice of capacity building through 'training, external support, and sharing among institutions' (Marshall and Van Saanen, 2007, p. 62) and the development of 'budgets, long-term plans, sector approaches, education systems etc' (Marshall, 2006). Key to the WBG partnership strategy with faith institutions was the need to assist faith-based actors 'understand and navigate IDA-funded Multi-country AIDS Projects (or MAP Projects, a core part of the World Bank's HIV/AIDS response)' (Marshall and Van Saanen, 2007, p. 60). For instance, the WBG DDVE team held two workshops, the first in Addis Ababa in 2003, the second in Accra in 2004 to further these objectives. Undoubtedly based on the Sant'Egidio partnership, the World Bank also undertook 'preliminary mapping' in 2006 of the role of faith leaders and institutions in Mozambique's HIV/AIDS strategy (Marshall and Van Saanen, 2007). The DREAM partnership was one way the WBG could apply its capacity building influence upon an existing programme delivered by a non-government provider. Significantly, the MAP negotiations between the Mozambican government, the WBG and Sant'Egidio were described as a 'protracted dialogue' that 'ultimately proved unworkable' (Keough and Marshall, 2006, p. 2).

The WBG was more a follower than an instigator in this endeavour, in the present case following the lead of UNAIDS and faith institutions themselves. In addition, a broader movement of FBOs engaged with HIV/AIDS exists quite apart from World Bank influence (PACANet, 2005). These efforts might be described as small beginnings in the WBG aspiration to promote 'coordination and harmonisation' (Marshall, 2006) of its own agenda – a direct reflection of the global development agenda and the new synthesis of economic and cultural determinants – with that of a prominent religious actor in the development space. It also is evidence of the ideological and operational obstacles the WBG must yet negotiate to further its partnership strategy with religious actors engaged in grass-roots development.

### (b)   WBG-Sant'Egidio: partnership and difference in secular-sacral development

Unlike the ideological differences that prevent significant partnership with the WCC, the WBG has engaged in shared endeavours with the Community of Sant'Egidio. One notable partnership was through the TAP, described as 'an innovative three-year multi-country project, aimed specifically at testing and scaling up different models of non-government delivery systems for holistic treatment programs' (Keough and Marshall, 2006, p. 2). Yet partnership in the TAP is contrasted with a breakdown in negotiations over Sant'Egidio's participation in the MAP, which is the main WBG strategic plan for addressing HIV/AIDS (World Bank, n.d. a). The TAP is concerned with treatment, and in this Sant'Egidio's day hospital system of care provided a well-regarded context for high-level patient care. However the MAP project is preventative, and thus deals with issues of contraception and women's reproductive health rights that are considered issues of 'deep discussion and disagreement' (Marshall, 2004, p. 13) between the WBG and Catholic FBOs such as Sant'Egidio. Whilst the MAP project is a strategic part of the WBG attempt to engage with religious actors in combating HIV/AIDS (Marshall, 2004, p. 10), Sant'Egidio's resistance to preventative strategies at the heart of the MAP also highlights how, from a WBG perspective, the role of religious actors in the issue is ambivalent:

> Religion is 'part of the problem' in the HIV/AIDS pandemic, contributing to denial, stunting open discussion, impeding some programs, but also that it is 'part of the solution', essential for precisely this open public discussion and a critical part of the community response which is vital to successful efforts to combat HIV/AIDS. (Marshall, 2004, pp. 6–7)

This is a telling distinction and helps us understand the dual agency of religion at work in the WBG-Sant'Egidio partnership. On the issue of patient care, via the TAP framework, the WBG is in partnership with Sant'Egidio. Here a sacral resource (such as the traditional and values system of Catholic health care) integrates with a secular development provider (WBG) to help build capacity in the fight against HIV/AIDS. Yet this same sacral resource also creates capacity constraints via a tradition and values framework opposed to preventative strategies around contraception and women's health rights that are accepted as normative by the WBG. In putting these two elements together, we may legitimately conclude that the WBG-Sant'Egidio represents an integrated approach toward religion via the TAP. This is also a trilateral programme (along with the WHO and UNECA) not of the WBG's own instigation (UNECA, 2005). The MAP strategy, more uniquely linked to the WBG, highlights how Sant'Egidio's sacral orientation falls outside the WBG sphere of influence.

### 5.2.4  The Dynamics of Religion in Three Faith and Development Partnerships

The three faith and development partnerships instigated by the DDVE of the WBG can be situated in the dynamics of religion model (Figure 5.1).

By differentiating the WBG partners according to the criterion of religious agency, the faith and development partnerships can be analyzed as follows.

WBG-*Fes*: A harmonious partnership within the operational sphere of the WBG. An engagement with religious actors, however the agency of religion is secondary to two other dynamics, the primacy of 'globalization' in the discourse of the *Fes* Colloquium, and the engagement with broader conceptions of 'culture' that extend beyond a focus on religious

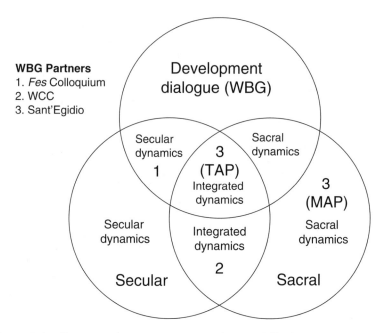

*Figure 5.1   Situating three WBG partnerships with faith institutions*

traditions. Partnerships with religious actors are smoothly incorporated into the secular rubric of WBG development regimes such as the CDF. A public relations dialogue largely structured by secular assumptions within a broadly based conception of orthodox development.

WBG-WCC: A conflictual partnership within and outside the sphere of WBG operations. Within the DDVE religious agency plays a secondary role to the conflicting ideological narratives that gave rise to the WBG and the WCC. These ideologies also create oppositional dynamics on the priorities of global development. Outside the DDVE, critical development approaches combine with political and liberationist theologies to form an integrated secular-sacral ideology at the WCC. This integration reinforces an oppositional dynamic with the WBG.

WBG-Sant'Egidio: A partnership involving dual dynamics. The first dynamic represents an integrated secular-sacral approach to HIV/AIDS patient care that builds capacity through the TAP. It occurs within the operational sphere of the DDVE and the ideological framework of its faith-based partner. By contrast, the second dynamic de-links the partners on the issue of prevention via the primacy of sacral (Roman Catholic) ideologies that oppose contraception-based family planning and infection containment strategies central to the WBG MAP. On this issue, the agency of Sant'Egidio exists outside the operational sphere of the WBG. The partnership via the TAP is concessional, or perhaps a bridge building arrangement, with the hope of overcoming the MAP-related difference.

The differentiated approach modelled here enables us to see that partnerships between religious actors and IFIs such as the WBG require some level of integration between secular and sacral ideologies toward agreed development goals. As can be seen from the brief study of the three DDVE 'partnerships' between the WBG and religious actors in development, integration poses a significant challenge for all actors involved. The paradoxical insight is that partnership cannot be purely instrumental in their goals, but must engage at the level of ideology or else they will be limited in scope and effect. By its very nature integration must occur by accommodation from both directions – from the secular toward the sacral and in the reverse direction. Partnership cannot mean the sacral administration of secular assumptions whereby religious groups act as mere conduits for WBG programmes. The inherent agency of sacral elements of development will place inherent limitations upon such an approach. Nor can partnership equate to secular resources being used for sacral ends whereby religious groups gain access to WBG funds and knowledge expertise without being challenged by the conditions and assumptions that such provisions carry. By the standard of our first application of the dynamics of religion model, only one aspect of one engagement with religious actors by the DDVE – namely, the Sant'Egidio-WBG TAP – can be defined as an integrated partnership.

The modelling also highlights the religious conflicts that proved to be obstacles to integrated partnership with both the WCC and the Community of Sant'Egidio. These are represented in Figure 5.2.

Two particular insights are gained in this regard. First, a religious structure of development highlights the limits to WBG influence, and the nature of some of those limits. For instance, the WCC is a formidable interlocutor with the WBG operating outside the policy domain of the WBG, a dynamic reinforced by both the WCC's secular ideological allegiances with other IOs (UNCTAD, ILO) and the sacral principles of critical religion (rooted in political and liberation theological traditions). Combined, these elements create an integrated religious ideology of emancipation in fundamental conflict with the development orthodoxy of the WBG. By contrast, the Community of Sant'Egidio's contrary position to the WBG on preventative strategies on HIV/AIDS is not integrated into an oppositional secular ideology. Rather, Sant'Egidio's position is situated within an established sacral tradition of health care. In this latter example, the WBG is portrayed with admirable flexibility (for example, seeing the TAP as opportunity not failure) precisely because Sant'Egidio

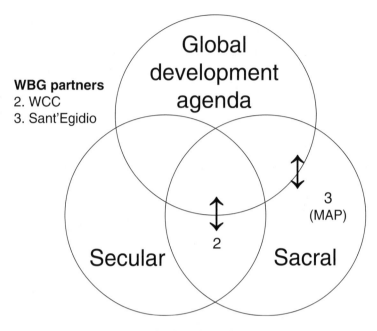

*Figure 5.2    Disputes in WBG faith and development partnerships*

is of a magnitude more important to HIV/AIDS development strategy than its opposition to a core aspect of the WBG's central strategic framework. That dialogue is pursued by the WBG with actors like the WCC and Sant'Egidio across such challenging, and very different, lines of dispute is testament to the status of religious actors it is engaged with and how much of their operational framework falls outside the WBG's sphere of influence. These dynamics also illustrate the extent to which religious actors in development 'sort out for themselves what can be jettisoned from inside and absorbed from outside' their own ideologies of operation 'without jeopardising the integrity of their communities and the physical, spiritual, social and political well-being of their people' (Tyndale, 2002, p.47), as well as the religious traditions of development through which people are valued. Religious actors must therefore be analyzed in ways that extend beyond mere instrumentality to include analyzes of their interior ideological motivations.

The three faith and development partnerships that I have considered above offer an introductory insight into the challenges and opportunities facing the WBG in its engagement with religious actors. By modelling the faith and development partnerships against the dynamics of religion model the study highlights the diverse dynamics at play between and among all actors when situated within a religious structure of analysis. The modelling above stresses the importance of these dynamics for more analytical attuned research and policy formation in the area of development and religion. As valuable as these initiatives are for understanding the dynamics of religion in international development, another partnership initiated by the WBG DDVE is more unique and offers more insights. It will be studied in the next chapter.

## NOTE

1. The DREAM programme was extended to Malawi, Tanzania, Kenya, Guinea, Guinea-Bissau, Nigeria, Angola and the Democratic Republic of Congo (Community of Sant'Egidio, n.d.).

# 6. The World Faiths Development Dialogue (1998–2005)

> Religion is no panacea, but aspects of it can complement as well as motivate development. It can also obstruct and undermine. The avenues by which religion influences development activities in different faiths and religions are haunting in their complexity . . . Religious people and institutions may be agents of advocacy, funding, innovation, empowerment, social movements and service delivery. Equally, religious people and institutions can incite violence, model hierarchy, oppose empowerment (women should stay at home); deflect advocacy (we care about the next life); absorb funding (build a new hall of worship); and cast aspersions on service delivery (they are trying to convert you). A further complication, the gusto of development experts who resonate with religion is enthusiastically matched by the repugnance of those who revile it.
>
> Sabina Alkire (2006, p. 502)

The fourth partnership in our analysis warrants a more detailed examination, and to this extent constitutes a modest case study. It could be argued that WBG initiatives involving *Fes*, the WCC and Sant'Egidio were conceived as less than partnerships, holding the status of dialogue (in the case of the WCC) and forum (in the case of *Fes*). One could also suggest that to some extent each initiative operated within conditions not of the making of either participant. Whilst these reasons do not inhibit our insight into the obstacles faced by the WBG in engaging religious actors, a fourth initiative reflects both the aspiration of partnership and the opportunity of a new venture. The initiative involved the WBG and the World Faiths Development Dialogue (WFDD).

## 6.1 THE IMPORTANCE OF THE WORLD FAITHS DEVELOPMENT DIALOGUE

The result of high-level consultation between secular and sacred actors and interests, the WFDD offers a unique insight into the formation of ideas and initiatives at work within the WBG on the issue of religion. In this study I aim to further situate the WBG engagement within a secular-sacral framework of development; to assess policy implications for the

WBG faiths and development initiative going forward, and to anticipate broader inferences that situate religious actors within contending conceptions of development.

The story to be told is complex. The WFDD began in February 1998 amidst high expectation yet was placed in temporary 'hibernation' in July 2005 seven years later (World Bank, 2006, p. 1). Today the WFDD exists by name as a faith-based organization in Washington, and maintains its historic ties with the WBG. At the time of writing it had resumed operations as a research initiative linked to the Berkeley Center for Religion, Peace and World Affairs (n.d.) at Georgetown University. As it is too early to assess the new organized form of the WFDD, the years 1998–2005 of the first organizational phase also mark the time frame of the present study. The story of the WBG-WFDD in this period can be told in three phases, integration, contestation and disintegration. As with earlier applications of the categories of the dynamics of religion model, the details of each phase shall be considered against the criteria of secular, integrated and sacral agency of religion. A chronology of the history of the WFDD appears in the table of Appendix A.

### 6.1.1   Phase One: Integration (February 1998–November 2000)

The WFDD was created to be a bridge institution between the worlds of faith and development (WFDD, n.d. b). At its inception the WFDD was considered to be unique, belonging neither to the IFI nor faith-based development sectors, but facilitating linkages and deepening partnerships between them (Marshall, 2001, p. 353). The WFDD began modestly, yet also had the patronage of leaders from development, religious and political contexts at the highest level. The WFDD also began as an explicitly interfaith organization, yet one that was situated in the religious advocacy networks of the UK from which earlier faith-based development activity such as Jubilee 2000 and the ARC had been generated. The first phase of the organization (February 1998 until late 2000) was characterized by a high expectation from all stakeholders that the WFDD would act as a catalyst for new institutional and programmatic expressions of faith and development partnerships. This is significant because unlike previous initiatives that worked toward the ideal of integration, the WBG-WFDD venture began from an integrated understanding. In describing the phase of integration I shall highlight four activities, two Faith Leaders meetings that set the principles for WFDD operations; the facilitation of a high-level dialogue between faith-based actors in development and the WBG on the draft version of the *World Development Report* (WDR) *2000/1*; the publication and success of the WFDD booklet 'Poverty and

Development: an Interfaith Perspective'; and the establishment of WFDD interfaith working groups in Guatemala, Ethiopia and Tanzania.

One direct consequence of the dynamics of religion considered in Chapter 4, especially the imperative for IFIs such as the WBG to enter into a dialogue with religious actors, occurred in February 1998. The location was Lambeth Palace, seat of the Archbishop of Canterbury, the occasion was a symposium titled 'World Faiths and Development' and was co-chaired by WBG President Wolfensohn and Lord Carey of Clifton, Archbishop of Canterbury (WFDD, 2001, p. 7). Participants in the meeting represented nine major religious traditions – Baha'i, Buddhism, Christianity, Hinduism, Jainism, Judaism, Islam, Sikhism and Taoism (WFDD, 2001, p. 7). The purpose of the meeting was 'to help promote a dialogue on poverty and development, both among different faith traditions and between them and [multilateral] development agencies, such as the World Bank' (WFDD, n.d. b). The Lambeth meeting 'inspired the notion of a continuing dialogue to address the many unanswered questions and insights that emerged during the encounter' (World Bank, 2002, p. 17). The WFDD was created to facilitate this continuance, described as a 'small and informal initiative', a pilot programme 'to test the future potential for dialogue and action' (WFDD, 2001, p. 7). By June 1998, the WFDD was working out of a small office in Oxford, UK, and run by only a handful of mostly part-time staff and volunteers. Wendy Tyndale, a development theorist and practitioner of longstanding based in Oxford was appointed as the first WFDD Director in July 1998. The WFDD was funded by a mix of public and private foundations and endowments, including from the Wolfensohn Family, but mainly from a significant start-up contribution of £156980 (July 1998–March 1999) by the Swiss Agency for Development and Cooperation (WFDD, 2001, p. 33). Such an arrangement reflected the expressed intention that the WFDD be autonomous from the WBG.

The WFDD began with three general operational objectives, 'thinking together' – making a contribution to the thinking of the World Bank; 'engagement groups' – research initiatives on how the World Bank and the faiths are addressing the four areas of development identified at Lambeth; and 'training' – pilot seminars on 'how development projects can be carried out within the framework of faith-based values and without the danger of local people losing their cultural identity' (WFDD-B1, November 1998, pp. 1–4). Four areas of engagement for development thinking and practice were decided upon, hunger and food security, the delivery of social services, post-conflict reconstruction and culture as an element of development (WFDD-B1, 1998, p. 4). Poverty would be the central issue binding these objectives together (World Bank, n.d. b).

Between October 1998 and November 1999 concerted energy was channelled into the issue of 'thinking together', focused on a consultation on the draft *World Development Report* (WDR) *2000/1*, a key report on poverty. The first WFDD debate on this issue was held on 21 October 1998. Whatever the language about the WFDD as a modest initiative, this meeting highlights the high-level access it immediately gained. The WDR 2001 dialogue was hosted by Prince Phillip at Buckingham Palace, headlined by the WDR 2001 team led by Senior Vice-President Joseph Stiglitz, chaired by the Archbishop of Canterbury, and attended by senior members of the Blair government. Theologians and religious leaders from traditions such as Christianity, Sikhism and Buddhism made active contributions. There was consensus among participants that macroeconomic orthodox models of development were limited and in some ways deficient (WFDD-OP1, 1998, p. 6). Yet, in a reflection of tension cited in the previous chapter, conceptual differences between the WBG and religious actors were also emphasized, notably on whether globalization was more fundamentally a benign or malign force (WFDD-OP1, 1998, pp. 6–8). Religious actors here represented integrated and sacral approaches to development in opposition to secular approaches. For instance, culture (of which religion was a core element) was 'not merely to be seen as an instrument to be harnessed to obtain good results for development projects' (WFDD-OP1, 1998, p. 8). Further WDR dialogues were facilitated in Rome (December 1998), Johannesburg (January 1999),[1] as well as smaller conferences in Brussels, Sri Lanka and India. The meetings were attended by WDR representatives, members of religious communities and development organizations, and the WFDD facilitators.[2] In June 1999 the WFDD comment on the draft of the *World Development Report 2000/1 Attacking Poverty* was handed down at the WBG in Washington, DC.

The WFDD review was ultimately characterized by an integrated dynamic of religion, but was shaped as much by a critical development ideology as by an orthodox one. Titled 'A New Direction for World Development?' the WFDD comment presented a critical reading of WDR including a call to reappraise the pro-Northern, pro-multi-national corporation (MNC) assumptions embedded in the WDR (WFDD-OP3, 1999, p. 6), and an affirmation of 'the positive contribution of the poor – their resourcefulness, spiritual groundedness and their awareness of the importance of community and personal relations' (WFDD-OP3, 1999, p. 11). Whilst accepting that the WBG's vision of development 'would almost certainly be different from a religious one' (WFDD-OP3, 1999, p. 6), the WFDD also found hope in progressing its agenda via two WBG mechanisms. The first was the *Voices of the Poor* survey for its embrace of the 'cultural framework' of the poor themselves (WFDD-OP3, 1999, p. 5).

The other was the CDF, affirmed as presenting 'a real opportunity for civil society (including religious groups) to share their experience and voice their opinion' (WFDD-OP3, 1999, p. 9). The WFDD consultation made an expressed commitment to 'make sure that members of the religious communities participate in these processes' (WFDD-OP3, 1999, p. 5).

The second Faith Leaders meeting occurred on 11 November 1999 at the WBG headquarters in Washington, D.C. Building on the momentum of earlier WFDD activities, especially the WDR consultation process, the Washington meeting was described as setting 'a bolder agenda' with 'broader participation, particularly among development institutions (the IMF, in particular, was actively represented)' (Marshall, 2001, p. 351). The momentum toward an increased mandate for the WFDD was implicit in the final statement by the co-chairs (Wolfensohn and Lord Carey) which acknowledged 'the enthusiasm that the Dialogue has engendered in countries such as India, Ethiopia and Tanzania and pointed to expected results in areas such as health and food security' (World Bank, 1999b). Noteworthy in the Statement was an assumption not previously stressed about 'the particular link of the WFDD to the World Bank *and the IMF*' (World Bank, 1999b, emphasis added), and an explicit declaration that the CDF was 'an instrument in the Dialogue . . . an ideal opening for religions to participate in vital decision-making processes' (World Bank, 1999b). Also linked to the WFDD's expansion at this time were two other WBG mechanisms, namely, the HIPC initiative which had become so closely associated with the advocacy surrounding Jubilee 2000 and the linked usage of PRSPs (WFDD-B4, 1999, pp. 1–2).

In November 1999 the WFDD published a small booklet titled 'Poverty and Development, an Inter-Faith Perspective' (WFDD, 1999c). It was an abbreviated and updated version of the WDR response, emphasizing the integrated dynamic of religion at the core of the WBG-WFDD initiative. The central thesis focused on a multidimensional understanding of poverty, including multi-faith perspectives on themes such as community, cultural diversity, work, the environment and moral education. By July 2000, 'Poverty and Development' was translated into Spanish, French, Hindi, Portuguese, Swedish and Amharic (WFDD-B6, 2000, p. 2). The circulation of this publication reflected the broad scope of initiatives under Tyndale's coordination in the highly productive first phase of the WFDD. The agency of religion is here realized as a latent force released into the domain of development in the production of resources and networks. Another example is the establishment of interfaith working groups to explore the WFDD mandate in Guatemala, Ethiopia and Tanzania. These dialogues were the first grass-roots engagements 'to explore common interests and competing priorities among various faith traditions and

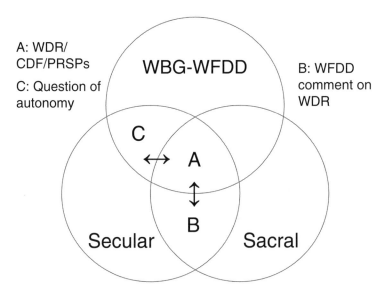

*Figure 6.1    The dynamics of religion in the integration phase of the WBG-WFDD partnership*

development partners' (Marshall and Keough, 2004, p. 87). The purpose of these groups was to establish inter-faith working bodies in development contexts that were previously characterized more by religious differences and conflict, thus providing a broader social base to target the themes of social service and hunger (Tanzania), food security (Ethiopia) and poverty reduction (Guatemala) (WFDD, 2000, pp. 16–18).

Where is religion in the first phase of the WBG-WFDD venture? The immediate answer is to say that religion is situated in the integrated dimension of the religion development agenda. The clearest embodiment of this is perhaps found in the WBG willingness to openly consult with religious leaders, the willingness of WFDD constituents to work within the frameworks of the CDF and PRSPs, and the engagement of religious communities. This is represented by position **A** in Figure 6.1.

Yet despite evidence of integration, two other dynamics are also evident in the integration phase and represented in Figure 6.1. The first, represented as position B, is the implicit ideological tension carried in the WFDD comment on the WDR. It is best summarized by one of the final statements of the WFDD report:

> The *WDR* . . . runs the risk of being understood to restrict the meaning of human well-being to the material, as though inequality and social exclusion

might only be considered undesirable because of their negative effects on economic growth . . . The recognition of [the] vital link between the practical and spiritual aspects of life would necessarily imply a basic reconceptualisation of the goals and methodologies of current development activities. (WFDD-OP3, 1999, p. 11)

In other words, it is the clear view of religious actors involved in the review that the WDR is too economistic and not embedded deeply enough in the human resources of culture of which religion is a part. Whilst such a comment is part of a report that is as positive as it is critical, it is evidence that the prospect for ideological dispute between different visions of development integration existed early in the WFDD-WBG venture.

The second dynamic, represented as position C in Figure 6.1, was the core issue of the autonomy of the WFDD. Katherine Marshall, Director of the WBG DDVE and one of the Trustees of the WFDD in this period, has defined 'dialogue' within the terms of the WFDD as a means to 'bridge the gulf of understanding separating development and faith institutions, with poverty as the central focus' (Marshall, 2001, p. 352). Canon Richard Marsh of Westminster Cathedral, and another Trustee of the WFDD, defines 'partnership' as a process by which both participants are transformed (Marshall and Marsh, 2003). From the above consideration of the commencement phase of the WFDD, it could be argued that the WBG acted as facilitator and accommodator of faith groups, and by implication invested considerable energy to meet religious actors in a DDVE. Yet the journey toward transformation still had significant distance still to travel. By the end of the commencement phase, the WFDD initiative was being defined in and through the CDF and MDG frameworks, the HIPC and PRSP processes, and had become as much a partner to the IMF as the WBG. In this development future demands would be placed upon religious actors to transform their operations to conform to the requirements demanded by these structures. Such mechanisms reflect a secular-orthodox development agenda that potentially threatened the secular-integrated dynamic of religion that was emerging.

How autonomous was the WFDD in the commencement phase of its operation? At the funding level the WFDD and WBG were, in the main, separate. The largest contributors between July 1998 and December 2000 were the Swiss Agency for Development and Cooperation and the British government's Department for International Development (WFDD, 2000, p. 33). One notes the absence of sacral donors as a counterbalance to the traditional secular donation base that existed. At the operational level, and connected to our prior noting of WBG mechanisms at the centre of the partnership, there can be little doubting the influence of the WBG over the WFDD. That said, the 'voice' of the WFDD emanating from the

WDR response and other initiatives was indeed autonomous, marked by the advocacy for holistic models beyond the WBG's own modus operandi and prioritizing religious traditions as a way of reading holistic values into the spaces of development.

In summary, we could suggest that whilst an ethos of integration was established in the WFDD-WBG initiative, potential dispute on the issues of ideology and autonomy were being sown. Yet a most surprising and more significant dispute was to unfold, not between partner entities, but within them.

### 6.1.2  Phase Two: Contestation (November 2000–May 2005)

If the early phase of the WFDD ended with a sense of expectation, the beginning of the next phase represented disappointment and delay. Two determining factors can explain this; core elements of the WBG were muted in their enthusiasm for the faith and development partnerships, and the WFDD entered a period of leadership uncertainty. Resolving each impasse produced a dynamic of separation between the two entities, and would hinder the co-operative potential imagined in the earlier stages. Despite these obstacles, core WFDD programmes continued revealing both continuity and discontinuity between religious actors in development and the ideological assumptions of the WBG. In describing what we shall call a phase of contestation we shall identify four activities: the unanimous veto by the WBG Executive Directors of Wolfensohn's plans to expand the faith and development programme (late 2000); the unexpected withdrawal of a new WFDD CEO (January 2001), the appointment of Michael Taylor as WFDD Director (February 2002) and the WFDD move to the University of Birmingham; the WFDD's facilitation of the PRSP process among religious actors; and the Memorandum of Understanding (MOU) signed between the WBG and the WFDD (October 2002).

Prior to and during the period in question the WBG was undergoing considerable change, and occasional rupture, at its highest levels. In late 1999 former chief economist Stiglitz resigned from the WBG, a culmination of his growing concern at WBG-IMF short-term lending policies toward highly indebted countries (Uchitelle, 1999). Stiglitz's resignation was important in two broader ways. First, as the ultimate insider in such a powerful institution, the drama around Stiglitz at the WBG further galvanized the newly forming anti-globalization movement that had so effectively disrupted world trade talks in Seattle in the same year. Second, Stiglitz's public and increasingly strident criticisms of the IMF were exacerbated by perceptions that Wolfensohn had willfully allowed his chief economist free reign because he may have agreed with much of what Stiglitz was saying (Mallaby, 2004, p. 268). Then, in May 2000 chief researcher Ravi Kanbur resigned from the WDR (Global Policy Forum, 2000), the end result of an increasing disquiet at the US Treasury, the IMF and among the heads of the WBG itself. The worries emanating from these high-level networks concerned the broader consultative development agenda that the WBG was embarking upon and, more specifically, that 'Kanbur's exposition of voicelessness would distract the Bank from the basic challenge of getting economic policy right in poor countries' (Mallaby, 2004, p. 269).

These elements combined to provide some of the missing pieces to why, in late 2000, the WBG Executive Board vetoed Wolfensohn's proposal for a small 'Directorate on Faith' – a planned scaling up of religion and development parallel to the expansion of the WFDD – by 24 votes to zero (Tyndale, 2003, p. 25; Clarke, 2007, pp. 81–2). From the vantage of the WFDD, the veto is an extension of the concern about the broader consultative and instrumental agenda for the WBG. When Kanbur resigned the WFDD expressed 'regret' and noted that 'the WFDD had been in close contact' with him and 'appreciated his open mind' (WFDD-B6, 2000, p. 2). Wolfensohn was regarded in a similar way and his rejection by the Executive Directors was interpreted as a not dissimilar obstacle to that posed to Kanbur. From within the WBG-IMF, the veto was an exercise of control management over issues that had created such public controversy in the 18 months before. As such, the veto did not have a concern about religion at its core. Rather, the directorate on faith proposal was perceived by key stakeholders to be the outer edge of an already worrying expansion of what would subsequently be called the 'World Bank's mission creep' (Einhorn, 2001).

Yet the question of religious agency remains central to our interpretation of the decision. Interpreted through the dynamics of religion model, the veto represents a classic strategy of Westphalian control where state stakeholders contain the energies of culture and religion for reasons of operational stability. As a consequence, the veto halted the progress of the ideals of dialogue and partnership at the heart of the WFDD-WBG partnership. There can be no doubting Wolfensohn's own perspective on the finality of what he viewed to be regressive attitudes of the WBG Board toward such ideals:

> . . . there will not be a grant program specifically for faith-based development institutions. And the reason for that, I might tell you, is because our Board, including the United States, and other members of the Board, have vigorously opposed the mixing of faith and the work that we do. They say that the faith-based organizations – it's the old story of church and state. You don't want to mix the running of the country with any sort of infection from the faiths . . .

So I would love to have a faith-based organization in place, but I'm a voice of one, maybe two, and the reason is that national governments do not give homes to faith-based organizations typically in their own administrative set-ups, and they're just not prepared to let us do it. (Wolfensohn, 2004, pp. 21–2)

If the veto marked a seminal blow to the ideals of the WFDD-WBG partnership, it also changed the function of the WFDD in relation to the WBG's faith engagement. Whereas at the end of 1999 both entities were upscaling their faith and development agendas in a parallel fashion, after the veto the WFDD became the de facto entity of the WBG, as a means to engage the issue of religion at arm's length:

That was the reason that we did the World Faiths Development Dialogue, and separately funded through external fundraising, the Office of the WFDD, which now is in Birmingham, UK, and where we are undertaking work along the lines of [an office for faith-based development]. (Wolfensohn, 2004, p. 21)

Therefore, after the veto the WFDD existed as an extension of Wolfensohn's personal enthusiasm for engaging religious actors, mediated by a small unit – the DDVE – within the external affairs structure of the WBG. Perhaps more significantly, the DDVE-WFDD partnership became one of the conduits for Wolfensohn to implement his larger agenda of ideological change via the CDF launched in January 1999. This represents another secular dynamic of religion at work, religion had become a secondary bit-piece in a larger dynamic of contestation within the WBG itself. The central dispute surrounding the WFDD initiative was now between a secular-orthodox and an integrated-orthodox approach to religion. I have represented this as VETO in Figure 6.2.

There were contests impacting the WFDD also. The optimistic plans for upscaling planned at the end of 1999 meant the appointment of an Executive Director to replace the celebrated co-ordination of Wendy Tyndale. In January 2000 the WFDD announced the appointment of David Bryer as its new Executive Director. Described as 'an Orthodox Christian, who has studied Muslim theology and has had a lot of contact with the Muslim faith', Bryer was at the time of his appointment to the WFDD the director of Oxfam in Britain (WFDD-B8, 2000, p. 1). Under Bryer, the plans for expansion of the WFDD included a relocation to London and an expansion of the WFDD team of up to 12 (WFDD-B8, 2000, p. 1). The move to London would maximize Bryer's existing links with Oxfam, who had worked effectively with faith-based advocates on debt relief through Jubilee 2000. Suddenly, prior to taking up the position, Bryer withdrew from the appointment, a decision that also placed all other plans for expansion on hold. It is difficult to discern the reasons

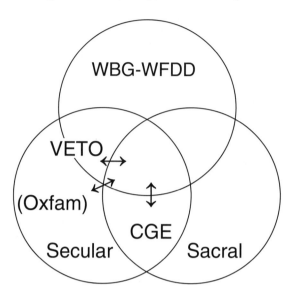

*Figure 6.2    Dynamics of dispute in the contestation phase of the WBG-
WFDD initiative*

behind this change. One possibility was that Oxfam became increasingly
nervous about perceptions of the WFDD's intimate association with the
WBG at a time when debt campaigns and anti-globalization social movements were effective and high profile in their activities. The WFDD may
have also been uncomfortably 'religious' for Oxfam, in the sense that it
advocated a deeper model of engaging religious actors in and through
religious concepts. This was most explicitly evident in the WDR consultation process of the year before. Whereas via Jubilee 2000 secular and
sacral perspectives could meet over the common goal of debt relief, the
WFDD posed a different partnership challenge because 'it is the distinctive nature of the religious communities which is at the heart' of the initiative (WFDD, 2001, p. 22). The secular interests outside the WBG as well
as inside them were thus pulling the initiative away from secular-sacral
integration. This speculative interpretation is represented as 'Oxfam' in
Figure 6.2.

What is more certain is that the net effect of Bryer's decision upon
the WFFD was significant. The move to London did not occur and the
leadership of the WFDD remained interim, via Tyndale and the WFDD
Trustees, until the appointment of Michael Taylor in February 2002
(WFDD-B9, 2001, p. 1). Taylor was as prominent as Bryer in NGO networks, having been the Director of Christian Aid and President of the

Jubilee 2000 Coalition, UK (WFDD-B9, 2001, p.1). Taylor helped establish the Centre for the Study of Global Ethics (CGE) at the University of Birmingham (see Centre for the Study of Global Ethics, n.d.). There were plans to grow the WFDD from its new Birmingham base to a team of six staff (WFDD-B9, 2001, p.1). Significantly, a line of dispute latent in phase one of the WFDD-WBG was now consolidated. The ethos of the CGE was very much shaped by a critical development perspective, and to this end under Taylor's leadership the WFDD-WBG partnership would inherit ideological tensions not dissimilar to those experienced in the WFDD-WCC dialogue. In 2003–04, for instance, the CGE facilitated a seminar series on 'Alternatives to Global Capitalism' that included critical papers from Jubilee and WCC affiliated researchers (for example, Pettifor, 2003; Duchrow, 2004). In March 2003 the WFDD appointed critical development scholar Vineeta Shankar to commence research on 'Faith and the Economic System', and preliminary findings were presented to the CGE 'Alternatives' Seminar on 26 February 2004 (Shankar, 2004). This tension is represented as CGE in Figure 6.2.

Tensions but also empowerment over the theory and practice of development were reflected in the contribution of religious actors to the writing of PRSPs. The PRSP is a 'government-led document that outlines a comprehensive strategy for growth and poverty reduction' (Marshall and Keough, 2004, p.20). Whilst the PRSPs were important for advancing the WBG's access to community development networks (Marshall and Keough, 2004, pp.23–4), the state was once again a factor in determining core aspects of the WBG-WFDD partnership. In a high-level WFDD facilitated meeting of July 2002 to discuss the participation of faith communities in the PRSP process, religious actors acknowledged the constraints that existed within state sovereign domains such as Bangladesh, Sri Lanka and Albania, the distrust of religious communities in contexts such as Cameroon, the disconnection of religious traditions from development priorities in places like Ethiopia, religious resistance to participating in corrupt government programmes in Guatemala. Yet religious actors had also taken important leadership roles in PRSP processes in Ghana, Honduras, Malawi, Mali, Mozambique and Peru (WFDD, 2002, pp.94, 97–103).

Beyond the restrictions and possibilities allowed by state power, important issues of advocacy and perspective emerged for the WFDD. One perspective emanating from religious actors, for instance, was the 'essential gratuitousness' of their fight against poverty: 'it is not because we expect people to be useful that we help them, nor in order that they will become "social capital", but because of themselves, as people made in the image of God. This is important because it implies that we don't consider necessarily either development or wealth as goals' (WFDD, 2002, pp. 98–9). Moreover, where development did galvanize religious actors, they carried with them notions of justice that challenged, for instance, the US Farm Policy and its implication for the poor in Guatemala. It was suggested via the PRSP process that 'the WFDD should be pointing such things out' (WFDD, 2002, p. 104). The important implication here is that the WFDD-led activity held clear potential to increase tensions between the WBG's primary stakeholders, as a general challenge of all state actors via the demands of religious actors, and also as a specific challenge to powerful state actors such as the USA. They reflected the sacral agency at work within an integrated dynamic of development both within and outside the development agenda.

My final description of the phase of contestation focuses on the implementation of a mechanism to try and bring renewed focus to the partnership. In 2002 the WBG identified the need to 'approach and disentangle the various strands of partnership with faith institutions' (World Bank, 2002, p. 12). This was necessitated, in part, by the 'genuine dilemmas' posed by the rapidly emerging fact of the ambivalence of religious actors in development – as both 'a "constituent" or interest group . . . as part of "civil society"' with which the WBG can deal, yet also as critics, as 'key and strong voices for social justice and have often led civil society efforts at country level' (World Bank, 2002, pp. 11–12). In October 2002, within the first year of Taylor's leadership of the WFDD, the WGD and the WFDD signed a MOU in Washington that was aimed, in part, to 'develop clear and dynamic relationships for future partnership' (World Bank, 2002, p. 11).

The MOU held four key aspects in this regard: to extend the PRSP consultation process, to engage faith leaders in the WBG/MDG HIV/AIDS campaign, a WBG review of 'major development institutions and faith communities' and 'pilot efforts on training to help bridge the understanding gap about development institutions' (World Bank, 2002, p. 11). Important work was done in the post-MOU period: the WFDD embarked on an agreed body of case studies on faith-based movement and programmes, and research began on a comment on the first draft of *World Development Report 2004 Making Services for Poor People*.

Yet the case studies, not unlike the outcome of the WBG's own *Voices of the Poor* survey, was celebrated within the bureaucratic discourse of IOs more than it was effecting development practice per se. Moreover, the WFDD consultation on WDR *2004* went unacknowledged in the final release of the report, with a belated version published in June 2004. Whilst the aspiration behind the MOU was high, reflecting aspects of the optimism that existed at the inception of the WFDD in 1998, the larger themes within and surrounding the partnership overwhelmed the potential for direction and clarity.

Within a year, in late 2003, a discussion paper titled 'WFDD – the future' was produced for the Trustees of the WFDD. The paper identified significant constraints and challenges facing the partnership which included confusion about the aims of the WFDD in the tension between 'dialogue, radical criticism and cooperation'; balancing the opportunities and difficulties of a close association with the World Bank; and the perceived marginalization of WFDD staff in important forums, despite a growing expertise in grass-roots engagement with religious development initiatives (WFDD, 2003, pp. 1–2). Each of these concerns expressed the central dynamic of sacral subordination to secular interests in development. Without the realization of an increased agency for sacral actors and interests, the integrated initiative had no future.

There are at least four characteristics that can be drawn from the phase of contestation. The first is the contestation between the WFDD and the WBG that conforms to pre-existing ideological differences in the development space. At a time when Wolfensohn wanted the WBG-WFDD partnership to aid in the establishment of the new synthesis of development, one that was most explicitly carried in the MDGs and the CDF, the WFDD under Taylor gravitated toward established arguments against global capitalism central to a critical development perspective. It could be argued that the agenda emanating from the Birmingham base of the WFDD, whilst utilizing research into religious agency (such as by Shanker), placed an equally important emphasis on religion within a critical development discourse. The differences over religion between the WFDD and the WBG were therefore secondary to those over development ideology.

The second dynamic is the contestation within the WBG that impacted directly upon the WBG-WFDD partnership. The Wolfensohn agenda for broadening the WBG's mission was under intense pressure at the very time when the WFDD initiative was at its most vulnerable. The veto of late 2000 led to a necessary contraction of the faith agenda, and to the need for the WBG to distance – and to be seen to distance – itself from the WFDD (World Bank, 2002, p. 20). Yet the WFDD remained valuable for the very reason that it embodied some of the deepest engagements with 'new' development actors, engagements that embodied the President's agenda most clearly. I therefore argue that the role of the MOU was to at once distance yet contain the WFDD within the WBG's development agenda. The PRSP strategy was also important for achieving this end. PRSPs were held in high regard among faith-based development actors, including by Taylor and the WFDD, having been created as a direct response to Jubilee advocacy. Via the PRSP process religious actors could be used to 'sharpen the strategic focus on poverty reduction and international development support' (Marshall, 2002, p. 18). Within this second dynamic religion has an important instrumental role in the external affairs of the WBG, promoting a grass-roots modus operandi that went beyond assumptions about Washington Consensus development. The WBG went out of its way, for instance, to emphasize the difference between the WFDD and the Bush administration's policy of 'Charitable Choice' a domestic faith-based welfare initiative in the USA (Marshall, 2002, p. 21).

However, challenging these intentions for religion at the WBG, the third dynamic of this period is the role of faith traditions to contest the new orthodoxy both from a traditional critical development perspective. We have emphasized above the ideological differences that were carried by the Birmingham network of the WFDD. That this period of contestation also exists at the height of tensions surrounding the Iraq War should not be underestimated. From a critical development perspective the Iraq campaign represented a textbook case of the hegemony of global capitalism and the continued saliency of the Washington Consensus. Debates about international development, religion and culture were so often subsumed within the larger discourse surrounding the Bush administration's post-9/11 agenda. Religious actors were among the most vocal in opposing the war in Britain and the USA, thus placing the WFDD in a delicate balancing act of condemning the acts of 9/11 whilst calling for a 'deeper reflection on the state of the world and on the role of the religious communities in bringing about peace, security and more equity to all peoples' (WFDD-B9, 2001, p. 2). This latter charge often led the WFDD, with so many others, into a direct (and at times strident) critique of the system so clearly advocated by the WBG as the solution.

Fourth, perhaps the most significant mechanism for the dynamic of contestation was the PRSP consultation process and the country-based partnerships. In short, the closer the PRSP consultations penetrated religious organizations and communities the greater the operation and conceptual differences between them and the WBG became. The formal demands of the WBG were often contrasted by the informal, less rules-based, community dynamics practised by religious actors, such that 'scaling up' to meet these demands threatened to transform religious partners away from their religious moorings. This informality was in many instances held together by the centrality of religious concepts of development that contrasted the secular rubric of the WBG.

### 6.1.3    Phase Three: Disintegration (June 2004–July 2005)

Lengthy discussions were held on the future viability of the WFDD as early as the WFDD Trustees meeting of 9–10 April (WFFD-B13, 2003, p. 15). A more decisive change of direction came in a WFDD Trustees meeting in June 2004 when it was decided to move the WFDD to Washington after Taylor's retirement in July of the same year. A fourth Faith Leaders meeting hosted by the WFDD and the WBG was held in Dublin in January–February 2005. There was a strong consensus 'to persist with faith/development partnerships, but with more clearly defined terms of reference and a more specific work programme' (WFDD-B16, 2005, p. 3). By July 2005 the WFDD was consigned to a transitional status described as 'in hibernation awaiting decisions by its trustees and partners (notably the World Bank)' (World Bank, 2006, p. 1, fn. 1).

I suggest two important dynamics emerge from this last phase of the WFDD (1998–2005). The first relates to the question of autonomy that hung over the WFDD since its inception. I suggest that the aspiration for WFDD autonomy from the WBG was never realized, and indeed became increasingly resisted as the WFDD progressed. These forces of control represent secular interests over sacral ones, and integrated-orthodox interests over integrated-critical concerns. The culmination of this process came with the decision by the trustees of the WFDD to relocate to Washington, DC. Birmingham had proved more distant from Washington in ideological terms than in miles. By contrast, 'the WFDD's new geographical base would be highly relevant to its access to opinion-formers, influence and resources' (WFDD-B16, 2005, p. 2), further embedding the project in the extant development agenda to the exclusion of more critical and arguably more sacral interests. Under such conditions Wolfensohn, 'one of the greatest assets' to the venture, 'made it clear his personal commitment to WFDD and readiness to continue' into the future (WFDD-B16, 2005, p. 2).

The second dynamic to the phase of consignment explains what sort of entity, in the end, the WFDD became. Whereas at its inception the WFDD was a substantial entity with plans for significant expansion, working in partnership with an equally expansive faith unit of the WBG, one the final descriptions of the WFDD was so general as to be almost vacuous: 'The Trustees confirmed that the WFDD was not an agency engaged in the delivery of aid, nor an action group, pressure group or consultation group, but a catalyst for change' (WFDD-B16, 2005, p. 2). The absence of final details on the content of this change, combined with multiple emphases on what the WFDD was not, confirm the increasing levels of control that surrounded the initiative. In an important 2006 assessment paper on the 'history, progress and options' of the faith and ethics agenda of the WBG, it was acknowledged that since 2002 the WFDD was part of a 'Bank-led faith program led from within the institution, aimed at preserving/enhancing global partnerships and country level dialogue between faith communities and policy makers' (World Bank, 2006, p. 5). This is significant in terms of the analysis we have provided above because such an assessment defines the WFDD in terms established by the MOU. Whereas the dynamics of religion 1998–2002 reflected an integrated secular-sacral approach to development, the post-MOU period was framed in more prominently secular terms. This is what the WFDD became to the WBG – a religious reflection of itself. The benefits and costs of such a strategy serve to summarize the challenge that the original WFDD conception posed to the WBG: 'It keeps the initiative within the Bank, simplifies partnership relationships, but also forfeits the opportunities attendant on independence of WFDD and possibilities of greater synergies among development institutions in this area' (World Bank, 2006, p. 5). In other words, secular control was gained to the loss of partnership with sacral actors and interests. Thus, the potential of secular-sacral engagement over the enterprise of development was reduced to a strategic contest between secular-orthodox and integrated-orthodox development agendas. Whilst this may be deemed as a small advance in development practice, it is situated in a very confined space within the religious structure of international development to the exclusion of many other religious dynamics and development outcomes.

### 6.1.4  Religion and the Disintegrated Dynamics of Development Orthodoxy

Formed amidst high expectations of an integrated partnership between secular and sacral interests in development, the WBG-WFDD study highlights the significant and difficult ground that exists between aspiration and implementation. Using the dynamics of religion model I have argued that each phase of the partnership shifted core elements of the WBG-WFDD initiative away from the zone of integration toward distinct and eventually compartmentalized positions within the religious structure of world politics. Three dynamics, situated in Figure 6.3, represent a disintegration process that highlights the challenge of engaging religious actors from within development orthodoxy.

The veto of the Wolfensohn initiative in 2000 by the WBG Governors reinforced the classic secular distinction between religion and the state; the pervading concern about the WFDD's lack of autonomy reinforced suspicions held by some religious actors that the WBG was ideologically closed to their interests; and the attempted consolidation of the partnership in its

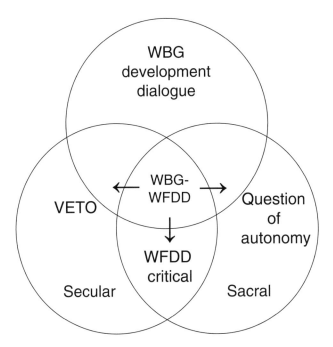

*Figure 6.3   The disintegration of the WBG-WFDD partnership*

latter years reinforced ideological divisions between orthodox and critical schools of development, moving the WFDD toward the latter. The net effect of these dynamics was to pull the initiative in different directions and away from the zone of integration.

## NOTES

1.  Papers at the Johannesburg consultation were given from the perspective of Buddhist, Baha'I and Ismaili (Shi'ite) perspectives on development. See WFDD-OP2 (1999).
2.  For a full list of participants in the WDR process, see WFDD (2001, p. 39).

# 7.   Development and the sacral deficit

> Modernity is secular, not in the frequent, rather loose sense of the word,
> where it designates the absence of religion, but rather in the fact that religion
> occupies a different place, compatible with the sense that all social action takes
> place in profane time.
> Charles Taylor (2004, p. 194)

> Methods, one must repeat ten times, are the essential, as well
> as being the most difficult.
> Nietzsche, *The Antichrist* (cited in Boff, 1987)

Having considered the disintegration of the dynamics of religion from the
perspective of development orthodoxy, I shall conclude by considering the
dynamics of religion at the WBG from a critical development perspective.
The dynamics of religion model is here combined with critical development to produce another reading of the faith and development initiative
of the WBG.

## 7.1   THE DYNAMICS OF RELIGION IN CRITICAL DEVELOPMENT PERSPECTIVE

To reiterate the description previously offered, the aim of critical theory
is to examine the existing order and question how that order has been
formed, and then focus on the ways that the order may be transformed
(Cox, 1996, pp. 89–90). Cox made the distinction between problem solving
theory and critical theory. Unlike problem solving theory which seeks to
explain events using existing structures and actors, a critical approach
does not take institutions or social and power relations as natural or given,
rather critical theory seeks to explore their origins and assess whether they
are in the process of changing (Cox, 1996, pp. 97–9). Critical approaches
explore the potential for alternatives and encourage struggles to achieve
such ends (Linklater, 1992, p. 79). Critical approaches to development
seek to deconstruct and examine the material and ideational power relations that underpin development orthodoxy, yet they also seek to recon-
struct alternatives to that orthodoxy (Matthews, 2004, p. 373), and thus

questions of inclusion and exclusion form an important element of the critical theory approach.

Critical analysts of the opening of the development space have concluded that far from signifying any substantial change in development thinking or practice, the 'new synthesis' demonstrates the hegemony of the international development establishment, particularly IFIs (Ocampo, 2002; I. Taylor, 2004; Girvan, 2006; Guttal, 2006). According to this perspective the opening of the development space to civil society provides limited opportunities and effectively co-opts oppositional actors, particularly through working and funding partnerships between civil society actors and operational agencies. In short, IFIs and other donors fund civil society actors that will not challenge the programmes being implemented, will not destabilize local society and will legitimize the programmes by agreeing to be local partners albeit in a subordinate position (Huddock, 1999; Lewis, 2001). Thus, in a general sense, it has been argued that the relationship between civil society and IFIs and other donors has shifted from an oppositional to a co-operative dynamic (Utting, 2006). This leaves actors attempting to challenge or change the development agenda marginalized in favour of actors supportive of the status quo.

Where might the WBG faith and development programme be situated in relation to these critical development arguments? The very existence of the WBG's partnerships in faith and development provides evidence of an engagement with religion from within the mainstream of development practice. Yet I have now argued that a closer look at the dynamics of religion in the WBG partnerships highlight, in different ways, the disintegration between secular and sacral elements, and the ideological divides that separate many religious actors from a positive engagement with the opening up of the development agenda to civil society actors. I shall explore the exclusion of religious actors further, connecting core assumptions of critical development to basic elements of the dynamics of religion model.

## 7.2   A CRITICAL TYPOLOGY OF RELIGIOUS ACTORS IN DEVELOPMENT[1]

A recent article co-written by the author suggests three broad types of civil society actors emerge from the critical development literature (McDuie-Ra and Rees, 2010, pp. 23–5). I shall outline this typology and then apply it to the current study of the WBG faith and development programme. The first type of actors are formalized civil society organizations based in the North that have access to institutions where the development agenda is set and negotiated, particularly IFIs and UN agencies. They operate in the South often in partnerships with local organizations and their professional development expertise gives them disproportionate power over their Southern partners. The need to implement programmes funded by IFIs and other international donors limits their transformative potential and ensures that they reproduce the development agenda (Murphy, 2005). The second are formalized civil society organizations from the South that work in partnership with Northern organizations, IFIs and often their own national governments. In order to be chosen to work in partnerships these organizations must relinquish their autonomy and ensure that their approach to development reflects that of their financiers and Northern partners. Despite being staffed by and often headed by nationals from the country in question, professional requirements mean that the staff are generally drawn from the social and political elite, limiting their understating of development needs of people from other class and ethnic groups, and ensuring they have an embedded interest in maintaining the broader status quo (Mohan, 2002, p.133; Townsend et al., 2002; Ulvila and Hossain, 2002; Dasgupta and Beard, 2007). The third are local civil society actors that are more deeply involved in communities at the grass-roots. The types of civil society actors funded through IFIs and operational agencies are generally those more able to present themselves as more professionalized which potentially marginalizes smaller and less professionalized actors, some of which may have a deeper understanding of local development needs, but this is not necessarily a given. As distinct from the second type of actors above, they have limited access to the development space and to funds and partnerships whether international or national (Amoore and Langley, 2004, p.99). This third type of actor includes formalized NGOs and philanthropic groups, but also more informal social movements, community groups, networks of activists and collectives. In much of the literature these actors are perceived as having a better understanding of development needs, have more sustainable solutions to development problems and are able to utilize knowledge that is otherwise marginalized by Northern expertise. Though still relatively powerless against the top-down, professionalized, development establishment (White, 1996) they are perceived to provide the best hope for alternative development approaches. It should be noted that this perception has been accused of reifying and romanticizing the grass-roots, glossing over inequalities and homogenizing communities (Agrawal and Sivaramakrishnan, 2001, p.12).

When applied to religious actors involved in development this framework reveals important differences in the status of religious actors and the potential for exclusion from the development space of particular types of religious actors. We illustrate this by classifying religious actors associated with the WBG using the typology of civil society actors constructed above. Groups have been selected because they meet one of three criteria; they have entered into formal partnerships with the WBG, have been involved in specific dialogues with the WBG on development issues or have been identified as prospective development partners by the WBG. Many have featured by name in the studies above. The differentiation of these actors according to the critical development typology is demonstrated in Table 7.1. It is not designed to critique the relative contributions of listed organizations, but to indicate the relative position and type of religious actors in relation to the WBG.

The table highlights three characteristics of the WBG's faith and development agenda. The first is a priority toward formalized organizations. Such an alignment is expected given that the requirements binding the World Bank's ideology for faith and development partnerships lies in a benchmarking activity, measured in the current context by the MDGs (Marshall and Marsh, 2003). Moreover, the institutional requirements of the World Bank favour partnerships of formal activities and reporting. The second is that engagements with religious actors categorized above as informal are more problematic for the WBG. For example, from a WBG perspective the WFDD-sponsored initiative involving the Guatemalan Inter-religious Dialogue on Development (DIRGD) revealed a 'glaring lack of documentation, understanding and use of the rich store of knowledge, work and ideas of faith institutions in development realms' (Marshall and Keough, 2004, p. 88). Similarly, the Ethiopian Interfaith Forum for Development Dialogue and Action (EIFDDA) was hindered by an inability to engage constructively with the economic framework of the World Bank's poverty reduction strategy and its lack of formalized membership resulted in a lack of 'clear strategic direction' (Marshall and Keough, 2004, p. 92). Third, despite its commitment to deep engagements with religious communities, as we have seen, the WFDD experienced difficulties 'especially over how WFDD is perceived by *faith communities* critical of the World Bank, IMF . . . and G7/8' (Taylor et al., 2003, p. 2, emphasis added).

Building on this, I now suggest that a core constraint on faith and development partnerships is produced by the requirement of formality that imposes burdens, not on faith-based organizations (FBOs) as such, but on faith communities (FCs) in particular.

*Table 7.1  Classifying religious actors linked to the World Bank within a
critical development typology of civil society actors*

| Formal Organizations in the North: Setting the Development Agenda | Formal Organizations in the South: Access to the Development Agenda | Informal Actors in the South: Limited Access to the Development Agenda |
|---|---|---|
| World Vision[a] | Community of Sant'Egidio[b] | Guatemalan Inter-religious Dialogue on Development (DIRGD)[e] |
| World Faiths Development[a,b] Dialogue (WFDD) | Council of Anglican Provinces of Africa[c] | Ethiopian Interfaith Forum for Development Dialogue and Action (EIFDDA)[e] |
| World Council of Churches[b] | Sarvodaya Movement[c] | Interfaith health sector dialogue (Tanzania)[e] |
| Spirit of *Fes* Foundation[b] | Vikram Sarabhai Foundation[c] | |
| Women, Faith and Development Alliance (WFDA)[b] | Aga Khan Foundation[c] | |
| Delegates of World Religions[c] | AVENA[d] | |
| Alliance for Religions and Conservation[d] | | |
| Religions for Peace [d] | | |
| World Parliament of Religions[d] | | |
| United Religions Initiative, | | |
| 3iG Int'l Interfaith Investment Group[d] | | |
| Pontifical Counsel on Justice and Peace[d] | | |

*Notes:*
[a]  Civil Society programme partners.
[b]  Partnerships established via the Development Dialogue on Ethics and Values.
[c]  Dialogue and research partners in development.
[d]  Partnerships proposed by the World Bank working paper (2006).
[e]  Community development dialogues facilitated for the World Bank by the WFDD.

*Source:*  World Bank Civil Society Program; World Bank Development Dialogue on Ethics and Values; Marshall and Van Saanen (2007); World Bank (2006); Marshall and Keough (2004); Palmer and Finlay (2003); Belshaw et al. (2001).

## 7.3   DIFFERENTIATING FBOs AND FCs WITH THE DYNAMICS OF RELIGION

A new frontier thus emerges in religion and development research, namely, a critical reading of orthodox development attempts to co-opt religious actors within the formal constraints of the development agenda. Can the dynamics of religion model help to organize this new critical research? I conclude the research with a preliminary argument in the affirmative, based on two basic assertions.

The first is that the difference in capacity between formalized FBOs and informal FCs can be understood in secular-sacral terms. FBOs tend to have access to the political spaces where the international development agenda is negotiated and set. This is not to suggest that such groups cannot challenge the development agenda. The peace-making record of the Community of Sant'Egidio or the advocacy potential of the newly formed Women, Faith and Development Alliance (WFDA) are both examples of this. Yet of equal significance are the limitations that formality places on contesting dominant ideas and practices. The study of the WBG-WFDD highlights the capacity of IFIs to make agreements with religious actors, but at the delivery level of policy the (often necessary) restrictions of formality exclude core religious voices, perspectives and resources. This is particularly important for analysing religious actors in development because religio-cultural dynamics are more deeply rooted in communities than organizations (Thomas, 2004a) – and religious community practice is by nature more sacral than secular. Thomas is correct to see the sacral ground of development embedded in religious communities:

> The 'good', therefore, of the Islamic, Christian, Jewish, Hindu or Buddhist religious tradition, is the formation of a particular kind of community . . . [the] collective attempt to live out the moral life together. (S.M. Thomas, 2005, pp. 238–9)

Moreover, where the institutional formality of the state is failing or corrupt, the poor turn to the structures of religious community. This is a key finding of the WBG's own *Voices of the Poor* study (Narayan, 2001, pp. 43–6) and suggests a divergence between the types of actors included in the development space and the types of actors embedded in sacral communities, especially in the South.

From a WBG perspective it also poses as a significant problem. The informal engagements described in Table 7.1 are attributed by the WBG with a lesser status as 'guideposts' when compared to partnerships with formal organizations which are considered as models (Marshall and

Keough, 2004, p. 87). This may be due to the embryonic nature of initiatives, but also because they constitute attempts by informal networks of sacral actors embedded in communities to engage in grass-roots transformative partnerships (see Tyndale, 2006). Unless an engagement with sacral communities is strategically included, attempts to partner religious actors in development will remain limited to formal secular-oriented engagements.

The recent inclusion of religion in setting the development agenda can thus be read as an expression of the hegemony of Northern interests (Clarke, 2008, pp. 18–21). Aspects of the critical reading of the WBG's faiths and development agenda above encourage such an observation. Yet I also argue that this is not a sufficient point upon which to rest. Religious traditions are best understood as ambivalent (Appleby, 2000, pp. 288–301; Haynes, 2007b, pp. 53–74), and in development practice this means that religious actors offer both limitations to alternative development approaches but also the potential to articulate and gain support for such alternatives.

## 7.4   THE SACRAL DEFICIT

In the foreword to Tyndale's work on religious community and development, Sharma offers the following analogy:

> When the shortcomings of religion were brought to the notice of the Hindu mystic Ramakrishna (1836–86) he remarked: 'Religion is like a cow. It kicks, but it also gives milk.' Modern scholars have only dealt with the kicks; this book highlights that it might give milk, and in a more utopian vision, may even make the land flow with milk and honey. (Sharma in Tyndale, 2006, p. xiv)

Whilst maintaining a traditional suspicion for religious utopias – the talk of milk and honey, for example – critical approaches must now understand the ability for religions to 'give milk' and by this to more fully account for counter-hegemonic activity taking place in the South. Further research needs to be directed toward actors excluded from the development agenda and their sacral agency needs to be re-evaluated. There are numerous examples of this ranging from the role of religious actors in anti-dam movements in Brazil (Rothman and Oliver, 2002), opposition to mining in the Philippines (Holden and Jacobsen, 2007), and promoting neglected aspects of development such as health (Farmer, 2005), water and other basic needs (Patterson, 2007), which can explicitly or implicitly critique dominant development priorities.

The dynamics of inclusion and exclusion in the development space are crucial for analysing the hegemony of the international development agenda and the potential for counter-hegemonic agency. The dynamics of religion model has revealed that the dynamics of inclusion and exclusion can be applied to an examination of the WBG engagement with faith institutions. It has also shown that one key determinant separating these dynamics is the sacral agency of religious actors to contest the development agenda at the community level. Critical development approaches may be better placed to respond to the challenges that this presents. However, a sacral deficit exists in the critical development school that limits an examination of religious agency, despite the importance of sacral communities to development in the South. Understanding the mutually constitutive relationship between secular and sacral elements of the social world will, in turn, enable critical theorists and others to differentiate the effects of religious civil society actors at the international and local levels. The religious structure is therefore an essential component if future analyzes are to consider the full dynamics of religion at work in the realm of international development.

## 7.5   CONCLUSIONS AND DIRECTIONS

This book has attempted to construct a new methodological approach to the study of religion in the field of IR. I have in the first instance argued that secularism and religion be understood as polysemous concepts. Such an approach allows us to situate the elements of religion within reconceived notions of the 'secular' and the 'sacral'. It also challenges binary frameworks that pit secular and sacral interpretations of world politics in a zero-sum relationship. This more integrated assumption that I have adopted is not unique. Indeed, whereas the binary assumption was once the dominant perspective within the social-scientific study of religion, empirical observation and normative arguments of the past decade have led to the emergence of a new orthodoxy which assumes that 'secular' and 'sacral' elements of world politics are, in some way, mutually constitutive. Yet this consensus marks a beginning not an end for religion research in the field, and many significant challenges are yet to be overcome. As Berger suggests below, the uncertain ground that IR religionists must tread is contrasted by the imperative that such a journey must nevertheless be taken:

> Both those that have great hopes for the role of religion in the affairs of the world and those who fear this role must be disappointed by the factual evidence. In assessing this role, there is no alternative to a nuanced, case-by-case

approach. But one statement can be made with great confidence: those who neglect religion in their analyzes of contemporary affairs do so at great peril. (Berger, 1999, p. 18)

Nuance in religion research requires both differentiation and accommodation. In regards to differentiation, the elements of religion need to be recognized and utilized as core resources in the analysis of social world religious phenomena. In regards to accommodation, the elements of religion need to be comprehended within an integrative whole, understanding that discreet elements of religion rarely, if ever, exist in isolation from other competing and/or complementary elements. This book has attempted to balance differentiation and accommodation at the conceptual and applied levels. I shall summarize this effort and suggest some new frontiers that can be anticipated as a result.

### 7.5.1  The Dynamics of Religion in IR

In Chapter 1 three distinct yet overlapping dynamics of religion were identified within the general discourse of IR: the secular, sacral and integrated discourses. These discourses were understood to be constituent elements of the religious structure of world politics. When the dynamics of IR were read into this structure, the differentiation and accommodation of religion could be achieved.

This approach has yielded significant analytical benefit in three ways. First, such an approach resulted in the construction of the dynamics of religion model, a heuristic tool that can be applied to multiple contexts in a way that amicably accommodates (after Madeley, 2003, p. xii) secular and sacral political interests. Second, the model helps us to 'see' political dynamics in new ways by employing the criterion of religious agency as an organizing force (after Hurd, 2008, p. 1) in political analysis. Third, this approach is not constrained or beholden to concerns for the promotion of secularization or sacralization, but instead employs a situative approach that privileges 'where religion is' rather than 'what religion is' in a normative sense.

The benefits so described are the result of an approach that is at once complex yet also quite simple: Is religion a primary, secondary or integrated force in a given political event or context? Are the important dynamics of religion in this context included or excluded from dominant global political agendas? Answers to such questions can be clear, and can lead to further enquiries that broaden or deepen the study of religious dynamics in the political realm.

The dynamics of religion model can be applied and/or modified by IR scholars, be they religion specialists or those confronting religious actors and interests as part of larger research agendas. Moreover, the structural foundations of the model encourage a more systematic approach to the study of religion in the discipline as a whole. Religion is more than a 'special issue' focus, more than a subtopic of terrorism studies or perspectives on global culture. Religion is a structure that influences actor behaviour in world politics as significantly as the structures of international law, global governance, gender, environment, security and even of the system of states. If the structural status of religion is not accepted in the field, it will remain an unrealized analytical resource at a time when it is perhaps needed more than ever.

### 7.5.2    The Dynamics of Religion in International Development

In Chapters 2 to 6 the dynamics of religion model was applied as an organizing tool to study the domain of international development and specifically the recent engagements with religion by the WBG. The application of this model allowed us to perceive the full extent of religious agency – of a primary (sacral), secondary (secular) and integrated nature – and its impact upon the policy domain of the WBG. Applying the model in this way also enabled us to achieve three objectives which are briefly summarized below.

The first benefit was to understand the dynamics that helped create the WBG's engagement with religion. The dynamics of religion model was employed to show that the WBG's engagement with religion was created by a combination of secular, sacral and integrated influences, and by elements of religion that were both internal and external to its institutional domain. This opened the analytical space by situating religion in multiple contexts of the WBG in ways that had not been fully achieved.

The second benefit was to situate and interpret the dynamics of religion within WBG faith and development partnerships. Using the dynamics of religion model to differentiate three faith and development partnerships, the study revealed that the foundational WBG initiatives were primarily influenced by the secular dynamics of religion (*Fes*) or by integrated dynamics that were ideologically oppositional to the WBG mandate (WCC). It was also shown that the WBG evidenced some flexibility to work in an integrated fashion with religious actors where it felt able whilst acknowledging areas where partnership with these same actors remained unlikely (Sant'Egidio). Significantly, areas of incompatibility involved development ideas that were sacral in nature. The study also highlighted the different position the WBG faith and development partnerships occupied compared to the broader WBG engagement with civil society

– religion thus lacked coherent integration into the WBG's policy domain from the outset. These dynamics were magnified in the final study, the WBG-WFDD partnership.

The third benefit was to interpret the dynamics of including and excluding religious actors in the global development agenda. As one of the world's most powerful development institutions the WBG embodies the ideologies and practices that dominate the global development agenda. By studying the WBG's faith and development initiative this study has begun a process of differentiating religious actors relative to the dynamics of the development agenda. Combining the dynamics of religion model with a critical development approach, I argued that formal religious actors which contest the development agenda and informal development associations drawn from religious communities are less likely to succeed in development partnership with the WBG. These perspectives were new, and a direct result of the new analytical approach taken throughout the study.

### 7.5.3   New Agendas for Research

Several new frontiers for IR research into religion opened up as a result of the research direction taken in this book. The first is an analysis of the comparative dynamics of religion across different IOs. Religion has become integrated into the policy initiatives of important actors such as the UN, ILO, WHO as well as the WBG. The present study into the WBG has employed the dynamics of religion model to open new questions about whether the embrace of religion by globalized actors such as IOs limits rather than releases the power of religion. Of particular interest is whether IOs have co-opted – and even helped create – a certain kind of 'multilateral religion' that is palatable to mainstream global interests to the exclusion of more dissident religious views that challenge such interests. As suggested above, the study of partnerships between the WBG and religious actors suggests that the dynamics of co-option do mark central aspects of the WBG engagement with religion. The degree to which this dynamic also constitutes the creation of a certain type of religion remains underexplored. Such an inquiry would be achieved by a more extensive comparative study that sought to situate religion in the policy domains of a range of IOs and regional development organizations. The present study lays the methodological foundation for such a work via the construction of the dynamics of religion model (which could be applied to the study of other actors) and also by offering insights into the international discourse on religion via the WBG study. One further implication of this new research agenda is the potential for insight into the engagement of religion by state actors. As the key stakeholders in the WBG and other IFIs, states play a determining role in development policies that directly impact religious actors and interests. State power (as secular power) was a central determinant, for instance, in the WBG-WFDD study.

The second frontier for new research is the need to extend the critical research agenda to include an examination of the way religious actors contest development orthodoxy. Such a research agenda will continue to challenge the lingering binaries, notably in critical scholarship, that understand the material and the spiritual to be fundamentally oppositional. As McDuie-Ra and Rees note,

> . . . given the importance of religious agency it is imperative that critical theorists not exclude religion from counter-hegemonic praxis. Studies of religious actors in counter-hegemonic movements tend to escape this dilemma by name swapping. For example, religious groups become 'community groups', 'grassroots organizations', or part of 'social movements' when they challenge the hegemony of the development agenda whereas they remain 'religious' when they are associated with the dominant ideas and practices. We argue for a new classification of religious actors. (McDuie-Ra and Rees, 2010, p. 31)

The new classification has been set via the application of the dynamics of religion model in a way that situates religious agency within critical causes and explored within critical assumptions. Yet the investigation remains embryonic and the outcomes of future analysis, importantly and reassuringly, seem almost impossible to predict. Once again, the need to proceed with caution when dealing with religion seems paramount.

Like the present study, which now draws to a close, these new frontiers form part of a focus on religion in IR that is neither naïve toward religious input in political process nor in denial of the ambivalence and ubiquity of religion in the political realm. In moving the research agenda forward, and whatever methodological pitfalls that may await in the attempt, the dynamics of religion must now be considered of central and abiding importance in the study of world politics.

## NOTE

1. This section is an adapted extract from a previously published article (McDuie-Ra and Rees, 2010).

# Appendix: WFDD phases of development (1998–2005)

| Commencement (February 1998–November 2000) | Contestation (November 2000–May 2005) | |
|---|---|---|
| **1998** | **2000–1** | **2003** |
| • WFDD Faith Leaders meeting 1, Lambeth (February) | • Wolfensohn proposal for a 'Directorate on Faith' rejected by WBG Executive Board 24:0 (late 2000) | • Vineeta Shanker joins WFDD and begins research in 'Faith in the Global Economic System' (March) |
| • Wendy Tyndale appointed WFDD Director | • David Bryer (Oxfam) accepts then rejects appointment as CEO of the WFDD (January 2001) | • Regional workshops on FBO service delivery (Autumn) |
| • WDR Dialogue, Buckingham Palace (21 October) | • Structural and staffing problems ensue; WFDD consolidates existing work and WBG faith initiative continues via the DDVE | • WFDD Trustees meeting, Washington. Lengthy discussion on WFDD future and viability (9–10 April) |
| • WDR Dialogue, Rome (December) | | • Paper, 'WFDD – the future' (September 2003) |
| **1999** | | • WFDD involved in WCC-WBG-IMF dialogue, Geneva (September) |
| • WDR Dialogue, Johannesburg (January) | | • Case studies begin to be published (October) |
| • WBG launches CDF (January) | | • WFDD workshop – Ghana (28–29 October) |
| • WDR Dialogue, Berlin (February) | | • WFDD workshop – Tanzania (11–13 November) |
| • WFDD Comment on draft of WDR *2000/01 Attacking Poverty*, World Bank (June) | | • WFDD workshop – Thailand (5–7 December) |
| • IMF/WBG prioritize HIPC and PRSPs (September) | **2002** | **2004** |
| • WFD interfaith working group in Ethiopia commences (February) | • Michael Taylor appointed as WFDD director; Wendy Tyndale begins stepping down as WFDD co-ordinator; plans to increase WFDD to six (February) | • WFDD-CGE Seminar Series 'Alternatives to Global Capitalism' (Autumn 03– Summer 04) |

- WFDD Faith Leaders meeting 2, Washington DC (November)
- Joseph Stiglitz resigns from the WBG
- WFDD-WBG Engagement Groups set up in Tanzania and Ethiopia (October–December)
- WFDD–Veda Vyasa Sabha Trust meeting on Culture and Development, Chennai (3–4 October)
- Publication of *Poverty and Development, an Inter-faith Perspective* (November)
- World Conference on Religion and Peace (WCRP), Amman (24–29 November )
- Parliament of the World's Religions (PWR) Conference, Cape Town (1–8 December)

*2000*

- WFDD interfaith working group in Guatemala established (January)
- WFDD interfaith working group in Tanzania commences (February)
- Bain and Co. Review of the WFDD (April)
- Bain Review discussed and adopted, World Bank (8 May)
- Ravi Kanbur resigns from the WDR (14 June); WFDD expresses regret (July)
- *Poverty and Development* translated into Spanish, French, Hindi, Portuguese, Swedish and Amharic (July)

- WFDD moves from Oxford to University of Birmingham; begins collaborative work with the Centre for Global Ethics (CGE), University of Birmingham (February)
- WFDD visits Malawi and Uganda to observe faith-based actor involvement in the PRSP process (29 April–8 May)
- WFDD hosts Conference on Religious Involvement in the PRSP, Canterbury, UK (28–31 July)
- WFDD attends workshop on spiritual movements and development, Vikram Sarabhai Foundation, New Delhi (September)
- WFDD Faith Leaders meeting 3, Canterbury Cathedral – WFDD research focus on FBOs in WBG/MDG response to HIV/AIDS; WFDD adopts case studies approach aimed to help faith-based communities 'scale-up' development programmes (6–8 October)
- WFDD–WBG MOU signed (October)
- WFDD attends conference 'The Poor Will Help the Poor', Tanzania (November)
- WFDD joins Roundtable discussion titled 'The Challenge of Globalization', hosted by Movement For A Just World, Kuala Lumpur, Malaysia (November)

- WFDD workshop – New Delhi (10 February)
- Vineeta Shanker Paper, 'Faiths in the global economic order', *Alternatives to Global Capitalism Seminar Series*, CGE, University of Birmingham (26 February)
- WFDD funding from the Development Gateway for further programmes to 'scale-up' programmes of faith-based communities
- African workshop funding redirected toward education programmes to African religious leaders on issues of the global economy and development. Seminar scheduled for September 2004 (postponed)
- WFDD contribution to WDR *2004* published late, separate from original (June)

Consignment
(June 2004–July 2005)

- WFDD Trustees meeting, decision to move WFDD to Washington after Michael Taylor's retirement in July (June)
- WFDD seminar on *Visions of Development*, WFDD-WBG panel on faith and economics at the PWR, Barcelona (7–13 July)

*2005*

- WFDD Faith Leaders meeting 4, Dublin (31 January–2 February); plans to move WFDD to Washington affirmed

- WFDD organizes three workshops on Poverty at the Millennium World Peace Summit for Religious and Spiritual Leaders, NY (Aug)
- *WDR 2000/1* published (Sept)
- WFDD affirm commitment to PRSPs
- Interviews for new WFDD CEO (replacing coordinator Wendy Tyndale) begin (November)

- WFDD research begins on comment on first draft of *WDR 2004 Making Services Work for Poor People* (December)
- WFDD joins International Interfaith Network

- James Wolfensohn retires as President of the WBG (31 May); DDVE joins the WBG Human Development Network
- WFDD placed in 'hibernation' pending future developments (July)

*Source:* *WFDD Bulletins* (1–16), World Faiths Development Dialogue (Oxford and Birmingham), 1998–2005; K. Marshall, *The Faiths and Ethics Agenda for the World Bank. Report on Progress and Proposals for Next Steps*, World Bank transcript, April 27, 2002; G. Clarke (2007, p. 82); J. Wolfensohn (2004, pp. 21–2).

# Bibliography

Abercrombie, N., S. Hill and B.S. Turner (1980), *The Dominant Ideology Thesis,* London: Allen & Unwin.

Abou El Fadl, K. (2003), 'Conflict resolution as a normative value in Islamic law: handling disputes with non-Muslims' in D. Johnston (ed), *Faith-Based Diplomacy: Trumping Realpolitik,* Oxford and New York: Oxford University Press, pp. 178–209.

Agarwala, R. (1991), 'A harmonist manifesto', in D. Beckmann, R. Agarwala, S. Burmester and I. Serageldin (eds), in *Friday Morning Reflections at the World Bank: Essays on Values and Development,* Washington, DC: Seven Locks Press, pp. 1–16.

Agrawal, A. and K. Sivaramakrishnan (2001), 'Introduction: agrarian environments', in A. Agrawal and K. Sivaramakrishnan (eds), *Social Nature: Resources, Representations, and Rule in India,* New Delhi: Oxford University Press, pp. 1–22.

Ahmad, K. (2003), 'The challenge of global capitalism: an Islamic perspective', in J.H. Dunning (ed.), *Making Globalisation Good: The Moral Challenges of Global Capitalism,* Oxford: Oxford University Press, pp. 181–209.

Al Akhawayn University (n.d.), 'Founding statement', accessed 30 July 2008 at www.aui.ma/ PresidentsCabinet/aboutaui/about-aui-brief.htm.

Alkire, S. (2006), 'Religion and Development', in D.A. Clark (ed.), *The Elgar Companion to Development Studies,* Cheltenham, UK and Northhampton, MA, USA: Edward Elgar Publishing, pp. 502–10.

Alliance of Religions and Conservation (n.d.), 'About us', accessed 29 October 2008 at www.arcworld.org/about.asp?pageID=2.

Almond, G.A., R.S. Appleby and E. Sivan (eds) (2003), *Strong Religion: The Rise of Fundamentalisms Around the World,* Chicago, IL: University of Chicago Press.

Amin, A. and R. Palan (2001), 'Towards a non-rationalist international political economy', *Review of International Political Economy,* **8** (4), 559–77.

Amoore, L. and P. Langley (2004), 'Ambiguities of global civil society', *Review of International Studies,* **30** (1), 89–110.

Anderson, L. (1991), 'Obligation and accountability: Islamic politics in North Africa', *Daedalus,* **120** (3), 93–112.

Appleby, R.S. (2000), *The Ambivalence of the Sacred: Religion, Violence, and Reconciliation*, Lanham, MD: Rowman and Littlefield.

Appleby, R.S. (2002), 'Retrieving the missing dimension of statecraft: religious faith in the service of peacebuilding', in D. Johnston (ed.), *Faith-Based Diplomacy: Trumping Realpolitik*, Oxford and New York: Oxford University Press, pp. 231–58.

APRODEV (n.d.), 'About Aprodev', accessed 20 February 2008 at www.aprodev.net/main/about_aprodev.htm#mandate.

APRODEV (2001), *European Union Development Co-operation Policies, Between Intentions and Reality: The Problem of Incoherence*, Geneva: APRODEV, accessed 22 March 2009 at www.aprodev.net/files/DevPol/brochureCoherence.pdf.

Armstrong, K. (2000), 'Defending Khomeini', *Australian Financial Review*, 20 October, pp. 1–2, 11.

Armstrong, D. (2008), 'The evolution of international society', in J. Baylis, S. Smith and P. Owens (eds), *The Globalisation of World Politics: An Introduction to International Relations*, 4th edn, Oxford: Oxford University Press, pp. 36–52.

Arnold, D. (1994), 'The colonial prison: power, knowledge and penology in nineteenth-century India', in D. Arnold and D. Hardiman (eds), *Subaltern Studies No.8: Writings on South Asian History and Society*, Delhi: Oxford University Press, pp. 148–87.

Art, R.J. and R. Jervis (2005), *International Politics: Enduring Concepts & Contemporary Issues*, 7th edn, New York: Pearson & Longman.

Asad, T. (2003a), *Formations of the Secular: Christianity, Islam, Modernity*, Stanford, CA: Stanford University Press.

Asad, T. (2003b), *Genealogies of Religion: Discipline and Reasons of Power in Christianity and Islam*, Baltimore, MD: Johns Hopkins University Press.

Asad, T. (2006), 'A single history?', *openDemocracy*, 5 May, accessed 20 June 2008 at www.opendemocracy.net/democracy-fukuyama/single_history_3507.jsp.

Ashley, R.K. (1988), 'Untying the sovereign state: a double reading of the anarchy problematique', *Millennium*, **17** (2), 227–62.

Ayers, R.L. (1983), *Banking on the Poor: The World Bank and World Poverty*, Cambridge, MA: MIT Press.

Azimi, F. (2008), *The Quest For Democracy in Iran*, Cambridge, MA: Harvard University Press.

Baker, J.T. (1971), *Thomas Merton, Social Critic*, Lexington, KY: University Press of Kentucky.

Baker, R.W. (1991), 'Afraid for Islam: Egypt's Muslim centrists between pharaohs and fundamentalists', *Daedalus*, **120** (3), 41–68.

Barnett, M. (2005), 'Social constructivism', in J. Baylis, S. Smith and P. Owens (eds), *The Globalization of World Politics: An Introduction to International Relations*, 3rd edn, Oxford: Oxford University Press, pp. 251–70.

Barnett, M.N. and M. Finnemore (1999), 'The politics, power and pathologies of international organizations', *International Organization*, **53** (4), 699–732.

Baylis, J., S. Smith and P. Owens (eds) (2008), *The Globalization of World Politics: An Introduction to International Relations,* 3rd edn, Oxford: Oxford University Press.

Beattie, T. (2007), 'Religion's cutting edge: lessons from Africa', *openDemocracy*, 14 February, accessed 22 June 2008 at www.opendemocracy.net/node/4347.

Bechert, H. (1973), 'Sangha, state, society, "nation": persistence of traditions in "post-traditional" Buddhist societies', *Daedalus*, **102** (1), 85–96.

Beckford, J.A. (1991), 'Politics and religion in England and Wales', *Daedalus* **120** (3), 179–202.

Beckmann, D. (1991) 'Sober prospects and Christian hope', in D. Beckmann, R. Agarwala, S. Burmester and I. Serageldin, *Friday Morning Reflections at the World Bank: Essays on Values and Development*, Washington, DC: Seven Locks Press, pp. 17–36.

Beckmann, D., R. Agarwala, S. Burmester and I. Serageldin (1991), *Friday Morning Reflections at the World Bank: Essays on Values and Development*, Washington, DC: Seven Locks Press.

Belshaw, D., R. Calderisi, and C. Sugden, (2001), *Faith in Development: Partnership Between the World Bank and the Churches of Africa*, Oxford and Washington, DC: Regnum Books and the World Bank.

Benedetti, C. (2006), 'Islamic and Christian inspired relief NGOs: between tactical collaboration and strategic diffidence?', *Journal of International Development*, **18** (6), 849–59.

Benjamin, B. (2007), *Invested Interests: Capital, Culture, and the World Bank*, Minneapolis, MN: University of Minnesota Press.

Berger, P.L. (1967), *The Sacred Canopy: Elements of a Sociological Theory of Religion*, New York: Doubleday/Anchor.

Berger, P.L. (1968), 'A bleak outlook is seen for religion', *New York Times*, 25 April.

Berger, P.L. (1999), 'The desecularisation of the world: a global overview', in P. Berger (ed.), *The Desecularisation of the World: Resurgent Religion and World Politics,* Grand Rapids, MI: Eerdmans, pp. 1–18.

Berger, P.L. (2007), 'Religion and development', in B. Klein Goldewijk (ed.), *Religion, International Relations and Development Cooperation*, Wageningen, Netherlands: Wageningen Academic, pp. 237–46.

Berkeley Center for Religion, Peace and World Affairs (n.d.), accessed 20 August 2009 at www.berkleycenter.georgetown.edu/pages/home.

Berkeley Center for Religion, Peace and World Affairs (2007a), 'Faith-Inspired Organisations and Global Development Policy: US and international perspectives. "Mapping" faith-based development work in the United States – a background review', Georgetown University Luce/ SFS Program on Religion and International Affairs working paper, 9 April, accessed 16 October 2007 at http://berkleycenter.georgetown.edu.

Berkeley Center for Religion, Peace and World Affairs (2007b), *Report of the Symposium on Faith-inspired Organizations and Global Development Policy: US and International Perspectives*, The Luce/SFS Program on Religion and International Affairs, 16 April, Georgetown University, accessed 10 July 2008 at http://berkleycenter.georgetown.edu/ publications/176.

Berlin, I. (1999 Henry Hardy (ed.)), *The Roots of Romanticism: The A.W. Melon Lectures in Fine Arts, 1965, the National Gallery of Art, Washington, DC*, London: Pimlico.

Berryman, P. (1987), *Liberation Theology: The Essential Facts About the Revolutionary Movement in Latin America and Beyond*, New York: Pantheon Books.

Bhargava, R. (1998a), *Secularism and Its Critics*, New Delhi: Oxford University Press.

Bhargava, R. (1998b), 'What is secularism for?', in R. Bhargava (ed.), *Secularism and Its Critics*, New Delhi: Oxford University Press, pp. 486–542.

Bilgrami, A. (2003), 'The clash within civilizations', *Daedalus*, **132** (3), 88–94.

Birdsall, N. (ed.) (2006), *Rescuing the World Bank: A C.D.G. Working Group Report and Selected Essays*, Washington, DC: Centre for Global Development.

Bøås, M. and D. McNeill (2004), 'Introduction, power and ideas in multilateral institutions: towards an interpretive framework', in M. Bøås and D. McNeill (eds), *Global Institutions and Development: Framing the World?*, London and New York: Routledge, pp. 1–12.

Boff, C. (1987), *Theology and Praxis: Epistemological Foundations*, New York: Orbis Books.

Boff, L. and C. Boff (1987), *Introduction to Liberation Theology*, London: Burns and Oats.

Bonino, J. (1975), *Doing Theology in a Revolutionary Situation*, Philadelphia, PA: Fortress Press.

Booth, K. and T. Dunne (eds) (2002), *World in Collision: Terror and the Future of Global Order*, New York: Palgrave Macmillan.

Brooks, D. (2008), 'Obama, gospel and verse', *New York Times*, 27 April, accessed 30 June 2009 at http://select.nytimes.com/2007/04/26/opinion/26brooks.html?_r=1&scp=2&sq=Niebuhr&st=cse.

Brown, C. (2002), 'Narratives of religion, civilization and modernity', in K. Booth and T. Dunne (eds), *World in Collision: Terror and the Future of Global Order*, New York: Palgrave Macmillan, pp. 293–302.

Brown, P. (1972), *Religion and Society in the Age of Saint Augustine*, New York: Harper and Row.

Brown, R. (1984), *Unexpected News: reading the Bible with Third World Eyes*, Philadelphia, PA: Westminster Press.

Bruce, S. (ed.) (1992), *Religion and Modernization: Sociologists and Historians Debate the Secularization Thesis*, Oxford: Clarendon Press.

Bruce, S. (2002), *God is Dead: Secularisation in the West,* Oxford: Blackwell.

Bull, H. (1977), 'Introduction: Martin Wight and the study of international relations', in M. Wight (ed.), *Systems of States*, Leicester: Leicester University Press, pp. 1–20.

Bull, H. (1984), 'The revolt against the West', in H. Bull (ed.), *The Expansion of International Society*, Oxford: Clarendon Press, pp. 217–28.

Burleigh, M. (2006), *Sacred Causes: Religion and Politics from the European Dictators to Al Qaeda*, London: Harper Perennial.

Burmester, S. (1991), 'Can the twilight of the gods be prevented?', in D. Beckmann, R. Agarwala, S. Burmester and I. Serageldin (eds), *Friday Morning Reflections at the World Bank: Essays on Values and Development*, Washington, DC: Seven Locks Press, pp. 37–54.

Busby, J. (2007), 'Bono made Jesse Helms cry: Jubilee 2000, debt relief, and moral action in international politics', *International Studies Quarterly*, **51** (2), 247–75.

Butler, J. (2000), *Religion in Colonial America,* Cary, NC: Oxford University Press.

Calderisi, R. (2001), 'The World Bank and Africa', in D. Belshaw, R. Calderisi and C. Sugden (eds), *Faith in Development: Partnership Between the World Bank and the Churches of Africa*, Oxford and Washington, DC: Regnum Books and the World Bank, pp. 57–64.

Campbell, C. (2003), *Glimmer of a New Leviathan: Total War in the Realism of Niebuhr, Morgenthau, and Waltz*, New York: Columbia University Press.

Camdessus, M. (2001), 'The IMF at the beginning of the twenty-first century: can we establish a humanized globalisation?', *Global Governance*, **7**, 363–70.

Carbone M. and M. Lister (2006), *New Pathways in International Development: Gender and Civil Society in EU Policy*, Aldershot: Ashgate.

158    *Religion in international politics and development*

Cardim de Carvalho, F.J. (2000–01), 'The IMF as crisis manager: an assessment of the strategy in Asia and its criticisms', *Journal of Post Keynesian Economics*, **23** (2), 235–66.

Carroll, J. (2003), 'Why religion still matters', *Daedalus*, **132** (3), 9–13.

Casanova, J. (1994), *Public Religions in the Modern World*, Chicago, IL: University of Chicago Press.

Cassell, P. (ed.) (1993), *The Giddens Reader*, London: Macmillan.

Centre for the Study of Global Ethics (n.d.), accessed 15 August 2005 at www.globalethics.bham.ac.uk /index.shtml.

Chan, S. (2000), 'Writing sacral IR: an excavation involving Küng, Eliade and illiterate Buddhism', *Millennium*, **29** (3), 565–90.

Chehabi, H.E. (1991), 'Religion and politics in Iran: how theocratic is the Islamic Republic?', *Daedalus*, **120** (3), 69–92.

Clarke, G. (2006), 'Faith matters: faith-based organisations, civil society and international development', *Journal of International Development*, **18** (6), 835–48.

Clarke, G. (2007), 'Agents of transformation? Donors, faith-based organisations and international development', *Third World Quarterly*, **28** (1), 77–96.

G. Clarke and M. Jennings (eds) (2008a), *Development, Civil Society and Faith-based Organisations: Bridging the Sacred and the Secular*, New York: Palgrave Macmillan.

Clarke, G. (2008b), 'Faith-based organisations and international development: an overview', in G. Clarke and M. Jennings (eds), *Development, Civil Society and Faith-based Organisations: Bridging the Sacred and the Secular,* New York: Palgrave Macmillan, pp. 17–45.

Clevenot, M. (1985) *Materialist Approaches to the Bible*, translated by W. Nottingham, New York: Orbis Books.

Cohen, I.J. (1996), 'Theories of action and praxis', in B. Wilson (ed.), *The Blackwell Companion to Social Theory*, Oxford: Blackwell, pp. 73–111.

Cohen, J.L. and A. Arato (1992), *Civil Society and Political Theory*, Cambridge, MA: MIT Press.

Cohn, T. (2005), *Global Political Economy: Theory and Practice*, New York: Pearson Longman.

Comblin, J. (1989), *The Holy Spirit and Liberation*, London: Burns & Oats.

Community of Sant'Egidio (2003), 'War and peace: faiths and cultures in dialogue', accessed 21 March 2008 at www.santegidio.org/uer/2003/int_425_EN.htm.

Connolly, W.E. (1999), *Why I Am Not A Secularist*, Minneapolis, MN: University of Minnesota Press.

Cowen, M.P. and R.W. Shenton (1996), *Doctrines of Development*, London and New York: Routledge.

Cox, B. and D. Philpott (2003), 'Faith-based diplomacy: an ancient idea newly emergent', *Review of Faith and International Affairs*, **1** (2), 31–40.

Cox, R.W. (1986), 'Social forces, states and world order: beyond international relations theory', in R. Keohane (ed.), *Neorealism and its Critics*, New York: Columbia University Press, pp. 204–54.

Cox, R. (1987), *Production, Power and World Order: Social Forces in the Making of History*, New York: Columbia University Press.

Cox, R.W. (1986), 'Social forces, states, and world order: beyond international relations theory' in R. Keohane (ed.), *Neorealism and its Critics*, New York: Columbia University Press, pp. 85–123.

Craig, C. (2003), *Glimmer of a New Leviathan: Total War in the Realism of Niebuhr, Morgenthau, and Waltz*, New York: Columbia University Press.

Darlington, S. (1998), 'The ordination of a tree: the Buddhist ecology movement in Thailand', *Ethnology*, **37** (1), 1–15.

Dasgupta, A. and V. Beard (2007), 'Community driven development, collective action and elite capture in Indonesia', *Development and Change*, **38** (2), 229–49.

DDVE (n.d.), 'The World Bank', accessed 24 February 2007 at http://web.worldbank.org/WBSITE/EXTERNAL/EXTABOUTUS/PARTNERS/EXTDEVDIALOGUE/0,,menuPK:64193238~pagePK:64192526~piPK:64192494~theSitePK:537298,00.html.

DDVE (2005), 'Organisations', accessed 17 March 2005 at http://web.worldbank.org/WBSITE/EXTERNAL/ EXTABOUTUS/PARTNERS/EXTDEVDIALOGUE/0,,contentMDK:21955855~menuPK:5554941~pagePK:64192523~piPK:64192458~theSitePK:537298,00.html.

Demerath III, N.J. (1991), 'Religious capital and capital religions: cross-cultural and non-legal factors in the separation of church and state', *Daedalus* **120** (3), 21–40.

Derrida, J. (1995), *Points de suspension: Interviews, 1974–1994*, Elisabeth Weber ed., Peggy Kamuf trans., Stanford, CA: Stanford University Press.

Dionne Jr, E.J., K.M. Drogosz and J.B. Elshtain (2004), 'The paradoxes of religion and foreign policy: an introduction', in B. Hehir (ed.), *Liberty and Power: A Dialogue on Religion and US Foreign Policy in an Unjust World*, Washington, DC: Brookings Institution Press, pp. 1–10.

Dievine, F. (2002), 'Qualitative research', in D. Marsh and G. Stoker (eds), *Theory and Methods in Political Science*, New York: Palgrave Macmillan, pp. 197–215.

Dodge, D. and J. Murray (2006), 'The evolving international monetary order and the need for an evolving IMF', *Global Governance*, **12**, 361–72.

Duchrow, U. (2004), 'Property for people – not for profit. Alternatives to the global tyranny of capital', paper presented, to the Centre for the Study of Global Ethics, 16 February, accessed 20 July 2006 at www.globalethics.bham.ac.uk/index.shtml

Dunne, T. and B.C. Schmidt (2005), 'Realism', in J. Baylis and S. Smith (eds), *The Globalization of World Politics: An Introduction to International Relations*, 3rd edn, Oxford: Oxford University Press, pp. 161–84.

Dunning, J.H. (2003), 'The moral imperatives of global capitalism: an overview' in J.H. Dunning (ed.), *Making Globalisation Good: The Moral Challenges of Global Capitalism*, Oxford: Oxford University Press, pp. 11–40.

Eade, D. (ed.) (2002), *Development and Culture: A Development in Practice Reader*, London: Oxfam GB and WFDD.

Ebadi, S. (2006), *Iran Awakening*, New York: Random House.

*The Economist* (2006), 'Keeping the faith: mixing religion and development raises soul-searching questions', 19 August, p. 62.

Einhorn, J. (2001), 'The World Bank's mission creep', *Foreign Affairs*, **80** (5), 22–37.

Einstadt, S.N. (1973), 'Post-traditional societies and the continuity and reconstruction of tradition', *Daedalus*, **102** (1), 1–28.

Einstadt, S.N. (2000), 'The reconstruction of religious arenas in the framework of "Multiple Modernities"', *Millennium*, **29** (3), 591–612.

Elliott, J.J. (1993), *Social-scientific Criticism of the New Testament*, London: SPCK/Augsburg Fortress.

Elshtain, J.B. (1999), 'Really existing communities', *Review of International Studies*, **25**, 141–46.

Elshtain, J.B. (2003), 'Against liberal monism', *Daedalus*, **132** (3), 78–9.

Enloe, C. (1989), *Bananas, Beaches and Bases: Making Feminist Sense of International Politics*, Berkeley, CA: University of California Press.

Escobar, A. (1995), *Encountering Development: The Making and Unmaking of the Third World*, Princeton, NJ: Princeton University Press.

Escobar, A. (2004), 'Beyond the Third World: imperial globality, global coloniality and anti-globalisation social movements', *Third World Quarterly*, **25** (1), 207–30.

Esposito, J.L. and J.O. Voll (2000), 'Islam and the West: Muslim voices of dialogue', *Millennium*, **29** (3), 613–40.

Esposito, J.L. and M. Watson (eds) (2000), *Religion and Global Order*, Cardiff: University of Wales Press.

Farmer, P. (2005), *Pathologies of Power: Health, Human Rights, and the New War on the Poor*, Berkeley, CA: University of California Press.

Farrell, B. (2003), 'The role of international law in the Kashmir conflict', *Penn State International Law Review*, **21** (2), 293–318.

Fawcett, L. (2005), *International Relations of the Middle East*, Oxford: Oxford University Press.

Feldman, N. (2003), *After Jihad: America and the Struggle for Islamic Democracy*, New York: Farrar/Strauss & Giroux.

Filali-Ansary, A. (1996), 'Islam and liberal democracy: the challenge of secularisation', *Journal of Democracy*, 7 (2), 76–80.

Finnemore, M. (1996a), *National Interests in International Society*, Ithaca, NY: Cornell University Press.

Finnemore, M. (1996b), 'Norms, culture, and world politics: insights from sociologies institutionalism', *International Organisation*, **50** (2), 325–47.

Finnemore, M. and K. Sikkink (1998), 'International norm dynamics and political change', *International Organization*, **52** (4), 887–917.

Fomerand, J. (2002), 'Recent UN textbooks: suggestions from an old-fashioned practitioner', *Global Governance*, **8**, 383–403.

Forman, S. and D. Segaar (2006), 'New coalitions for global governance: the changing dynamics of multilateralism', *Global Governance*, **12**, 205–25.

Fox, J. (2001), 'Religion as an overlooked element of international relations', *International Studies Review*, **3** (3), 53–73.

Fox, J. (2008), *A World Survey of Religion and the State*, Cambridge, MA: Cambridge University Press.

Fox, J. and S. Sandler (2006), *Bringing Religion in International Relations*, New York: Palgrave Macmillan.

Frank, A.G. (1979), *Dependent Accumulation and Underdevelopment*, New York: Monthly Review Press.

Freeden, M. (1996), *Ideologies and Political Theory*, Oxford: Clarendon Press.

Freeden, M. (2003), *Ideology: a very short introduction*, Oxford, UK: Oxford University Press.

Friday Morning Group (The World Bank) (n.d.), accessed 12 September 2008 at www.dgroups.org/groups/worldbank/FMG.

Fukuyama, F. (1989/2006), *The End of History and the Last Man*, New York: Free Press.

Fukuyama, F. (2002), 'Has history started again?', *Policy*, **18** (2), 3–7.

Fukuyama, F. (2006), 'After the "End of History"' *openDemocracy*, 2 May, accessed 24 June 2008 at www.opendemocracy.net/democracy-fukuyama/revisited_3496.jsp.

Galston, W. (2003), 'Jews, Muslims, and the prospects for pluralism', *Daedalus*, **132** (3), 73–7.

Galvan, D. (2004), *The State Must Be Our Master of Fire: How Peasants Craft Culturally Sustainable Development in Senegal,* Berkeley, CA: University of California Press.

Geertz, C. (1973), *The Interpretation of Cultures: Selected Essays by Clifford Geertz*, London: Hutchinson.

Gellner, E. (1992), *Postmodernism, Reason and Religion*, London: Routledge.

Genest, M.A. (2004), *Conflict and Cooperation: Evolving Theories of International Relations,* 2nd edn, Belmont, CA: Thomson & Wadsworth Publishing.

George, S. and F. Sabelli (1994), *Faith and Credit: The World Bank's Secular Empire,* London: Penguins Books.

Gibbins, J.R. and B. Reimer (1999), *The Politics of Postmodernity: An Introduction to Contemporary Politics and Culture*, London: Sage.

Gilpin, R. (2003), 'The Nature of political economy', in C.R. Goddard, P. Cronin and K.C. Dash (eds), *International Political Economy: State-market Relations in a Changing Global Order,* 2nd edn, Boulder, CO: Lynne Rienner, pp. 1–24.

Girvan, N. (2006), 'The search for policy autonomy in the global south' in P. Utting (ed.), *Reclaiming Development Agendas: Knowledge, Power and International Policy Making*, Basingstoke and New York: Palgrave Macmillan, pp. 73–89.

Global Policy Forum (2000), 'Statement on Ravi Kanbur's resignation as World Development Report lead author', accessed 14 March 2008 at www.globalpolicy.org/socecon/bwi-wto/critics/2000/kanbur2.html.

Goldstein, J. (2003), *International Relations*, 5th edn, New York: Longman.

Gore, C. (2000), 'The rise and fall of the Washington Consensus as a paradigm for developing countries', *World Development*, **28** (5), 789–804.

Gopin, M. (2003) 'The peacemaking qualities of Judaism as revealed in sacred scripture', in D. Johnston (ed.), *Faith-based Diplomacy: Trumping Realpolitik*, Oxford and New York: Oxford University Press, pp. 102–23.

Gould, W. (2004), *Hindu Nationalism and the Language of Politics in Late Colonial India,* New York: Cambridge University Press.

Gould, W. (2005), 'Contesting secularism in colonial and postcolonial North India between the 1930s and 1950s', *Contemporary South Asia*, **14** (4), 481–94.

Gourevitch, P.A. (2002), 'Interacting variables: September 11 and the role of ideas and domestic politics', *Dialogue-IO*, **1**(1), 71–80.

Graubard, S.R. (1991), 'Preface to the issue "Religion and Politics"' *Daedalus*, **120** (3), v–viii.

Gray, J. (2000), *The Two Faces of Liberalism*, New York, USA: The New Press.

Griffiths, B. (2003), 'The challenge of global capitalism: a Christian perspective', in J.H. Dunning (ed.), *Making Globalisation Good: The Moral Challenges of Global Capitalism*, Oxford: Oxford University Press, pp. 159–80.

Griffiths, M. and T. O'Callaghan (2002), *International Relations: The Key Concepts*, London: Routledge.

Guha, R. (1997), 'Introduction', in R. Guha (ed.), *A Subaltern Studies Reader, 1986–1995*, Minneapolis, MN: University of Minnesota Press, pp. ix–xxii.

Guthrie, W. (2003), *The Later Thirty Years War: From the Battle of Wittstock to the Treaty of Westphalia*, Westport, CT: Greenwood Press.

Gutiérrez, G. (1973), *A Theology of Liberation: History, Politics, and Salvation*, London: SCM Press.

Gutner, T.L. (2003), *Banking on the Environment: Multilateral Development Banks and their Environmental Performance in Central and Eastern Europe*, Cambridge, MA: MIT Press.

Guttal, S. (2006), 'Challenging the knowledge business', in P. Utting (ed.), *Reclaiming Development Agendas: Knowledge, Power, and International Policy Making*, Basingstoke: Palgrave Macmillan/UNRSID, pp. 25–42.

Hall, I. (2006), *International Political Thought of Martin Wight*, Basingstoke: Palgrave Macmillan.

Hall, M. and P.T. Jackson (eds) (2007), *Civilizational Identity: The Production and Reproduction of 'civilizations' in International Relations*, New York: Palgrave Macmillan.

Halliday, F. (2005), 'Nationalism', in J. Baylis and S. Smith (eds), *The Globalization of World Politics: An Introduction to International Relations*, 3rd edn, Oxford: Oxford University Press, pp. 521–38.

Hanson, E.O. (1987), *The Catholic Church in World Politics*, Princeton, NJ: Princeton University Press.

Hanson, E.O. (2006), *Religion and Politics in the International System Today*, Cambridge and New York: Cambridge University Press.

Haque, M.S. (1999), *Restructuring Development Theories and Policies*, New York: State University of New York Press.

Harb, M. (2008), 'Faith-based organisations as effective development partners? Hezbollah and post-war reconstruction in Lebanon', in G. Clarke and M. Jennings (eds), *Development, Civil Society and Faith-based Organisations: Bridging the Sacred and the Secular*, New York: Palgrave Macmillan, pp. 214–39.

Harcourt, W. (2003), 'Editorial: clearing the path of collective compassion', *Development*, **46** (4), 3–5.

Hashmi S.H. (2002), 'Islamic ethics in international society', in J. Miles and S.H. Hashmi (eds), *Islamic Political Ethics: Civil Society, Pluralism, and Conflict*, Princeton, NJ and Oxford: Princeton University Press, pp. 148–72.

Hassner, P. (1997), 'Morally objectionable, politically dangerous', *The National Interest*, **46**, 63–9.

Hauerwas, S. (1983), *The Peaceable Kingdom*, Notre Dame, IN: University of Notre Dame Press.

Haynes, J. (1994), *Religion in Third World Politics*, Boulder, CO: Lynne Rienner.

Haynes, J. (1995), '"The Revenge of Society?" Religious responses to political disequilibrium in Africa', *Third World Quarterly*, **16** (4), 728–36.

Haynes, J. (2000), 'Renaissance of political religion in the Third World in the context of global change', in J.L. Esposito and M. Watson (eds), *Religion and Global Order*, Cardiff: University of Wales Press, pp. 167–89.

Haynes, J. (2006), *The Politics of Religion*, London and New York: Routledge.

Haynes, J. (2007a), *An Introduction to International Relations and Religion*, London: Longman.

Haynes, J. (2007b), *Religion and Development: Conflict or Cooperation?*, New York: Palgrave Macmillan.

Helleiner, E. (2002), 'Economic nationalism as a challenge to economic liberalism', *International Studies Quarterly*, **46** (3), 307–29.

Henry, C.M. (2005), 'The clash of globalisations in the Middle East', in L. Fawcett (ed.), *International Relations of the Middle East*, Oxford: Oxford University Press, pp. 105–30.

Hermassi, E. (1973), 'Political traditions of the Maghrib', *Daedalus*, **102** (1), 207–24.

Hillman, R. (2004) 'Endgame in Tehran', *Australian Financial Review*, 13 February, p. 3.

Hinman, L.M. (1998), *Ethics: A Pluralist Approach to Moral Theory*, Belmont, CA: Thomson & Wadsworth.

Hiro, D. (2005), *Iran Today*, New York: Nation Books.

Hitchens, C. (2003), 'The future of an illusion', *Daedalus*, **132** (3), 83–7.

Hobden, S. and R. Wyn Jones (2005), 'Marxist theories of international relations', in J. Baylis and S. Smith, (eds), *The Globalization of World Politics: An Introduction to International Relations* 3rd edn, Oxford and New York: Oxford University Press, pp. 225–50.

Holden, W. and R. Jacobsen (2007), 'Ecclesial opposition to mining in Mindanao: neoliberalism encounters the Church of the Poor in the land of promise', *Worldviews: Environment, Culture, Religion*, **11** (2), 155–202.

Hollis, R. (2005), 'Europe in the Middle East' in L. Fawcett (ed.), *International Relations of the Middle East*, Oxford: Oxford University Press, pp. 314–16.

Holmes, S. (2006), 'Logic of a blocked history', *openDemocracy*, 23 May, accessed 26 June 2008 at www.opendemocracy.net/democracy-fukuyama/history_blocked_3573.jsp.

Hoogvelt, A. (1997), *Globalisation and the Postcolonial World: The New Political Economy of Development*, London: Macmillan.

Hoornaert, G. (1989), *The Memory of the Christian People*, London: Burns and Oats.

Hoover, D. (2006), 'Getting religion', *Review of Faith and International Affairs*, **4** (1), 1.

Huddock, A. (1999), *NGOs and Civil Society: Democracy by Proxy?*, Cambridge: Polity Press.

Huntington, S.P. (1993), 'The clash of civilizations?', *Foreign Affairs*, **72** (3), 22–49.

Huntington, S.P. (1996), *The Clash of Civilizations and the Remaking of World Order*, New York: Simon and Schuster.

Hurd, E.S. (2008), *The Politics of Secularism in International Relations*, Princeton, NJ: Princeton University Press.

Ibrahim, S.E. (2006), 'Politico-religious cults and the "End of History"', *openDemocracy* 10 May, accessed 14 June 2008 at www.opendem ocracy.net/democracy-fukuyama /cults_3523.jsp.

International Institute for Labour Studies (n.d.), 'Decent work: a development paradigm', accessed 24 March 2008 at www.ilo.org/public/english/bureau/inst/research/paradigm.htm.

International Labour Organization (2008), 'ILO governing body concludes 301st session – considers labour situation in Myanmar, Colombia and other countries, welcomes growing links with World Bank', press release 20 March, accessed 23 March 2008 at www.ilo.org/global/About_the_ILO/Media_and_public_information/Press_releases/lang--en/WCMS_091563/index.htm.

International Monetary Fund (2004), *Evaluation of the IMF's Role in Poverty Reduction Strategy Papers and the Poverty Reduction and Growth Facility*, Washington, DC: International Monetary Fund Independent Evaluation Office.

ISA (International Studies Association) (2006), *47th International Studies Association Convention Program*, San Diego, CA: International Studies Association.

Jackson, R.H. and P. Owens (2005), 'The evolution of international society', in J. Baylis and S. Smith (eds), *The Globalization of World Politics: An Introduction to International Relations,* 3rd edn, Oxford: Oxford University Press, pp. 52–5.

Jain, D. and A. Sen (2005), *Women, Development and the UN: A Sixty-year Quest for Equality and Justice,* Indianapolis, IN: Indiana University Press.

Jakobsen, J.R. and A. Pellegrini (2000), 'World secularisms at the millennium', *Social Text,* 64, **18** (3), 1–27.

Jarvis, D.S.L. (2002), 'Toward an understanding of the Third Debate: international relations in the new millennium', in D.S.L. Jarvis (ed.), *International Relations and the 'Third Debate',* Westport, CT: Praeger, pp. 1–13.

Jeffery, R. (2006), *Hugo Grotius in International Thought,* New York: Palgrave Macmillan.

Jennings, M. and G. Clarke (2008), 'Conclusion: faith and development – of ethno-separatism, multiculturalism and religious partitioning?', in G. Clarke and M. Jennings (eds), *Development, Civil Society and Faith-based Organisations: Bridging the Sacred and the Secular,* New York: Palgrave Macmillan, pp. 260–72.

Johnson, M.G. and J. Symonides (1998), *The Universal Declaration of Human Rights: A History of its Creation and Implementation, 1948–1998,* Paris: UNESCO Publishing.

Johnston, A.I. (2001), 'Treating international institutions as social environments', *International Studies Quarterly,* **45**, 487–515.

Johnston, D. (ed.) (2003), *Faith-based Diplomacy: Trumping Realpolitik,* Oxford and New York: Oxford University Press.

Johnston, D. and B. Cox (2003), 'Faith-based Diplomacy and Preventative Engagement', in D. Johnston (ed.), *Faith-based Diplomacy: Trumping Realpolitik,* Oxford and New York: Oxford University Press, pp. 11–29.

Johnston, D. and C. Sampson (eds) (1995), *Religion: The Missing Dimension of Statecraft,* New York: Oxford University Press.

Juergensmeyer, M. (1993), *The New Cold War? Religious Nationalism Confronts the Secular State,* Berkeley, CA: University of California Press.

Juergensmeyer, M. (1996), 'Religious nationalism: a global threat?', *Current History,* **95** (604), 372–76.

Kapoor, I. (2002), 'Capitalism, culture, agency: dependency versus postcolonial theory', *Third World Quarterly,* **23** (4), 647–64.

Kapur, D. (2002), 'The changing anatomy of governance at the World Bank', in J.R. Pincus and J.A. Winters (eds), *Reinventing the World Bank,* Ithaca, NY: Cornell University Press, pp. 54–75.

Kapur, D., J.P. Lewis and R. Webb (1997), *The World Bank: Its First Half Century*, vol. 1, Washington, DC: Brookings Institution Press.

Keane, J. (1998), *Civil Society: Old Images, New Visions*, Oxford: Blackwell Publishing.

Keane, J. (2003), *Global Civil Society?* Cambridge: Cambridge University Press.

Keddie, N.R. (1995), *Iran and the Muslim World: Resistance and Revolution*, London: Macmillan Press.

Keddie, N.R. (2003), 'Secularism and its discontents', *Daedalus*, **132** (3), 14–31.

Keddie, N.R. and M.J. Gasiorowski (1990), *Neither East Nor West. Iran, the Soviet Union and the United States*, New Haven, CT and London: Yale University Press.

Kegley, C.W. Jr, and G.A. Raymond (1999), *How Nations Make Peace*, London: Macmillan Press.

Kegley, C.W. Jr and E.R. Wittkopf (2005), *World Politics: Trends and Transformation*, 10th edn, Belmont, CA: Thomson and Wadsworth Publishing.

Kennedy, E. (2006), *Secularism and Its Opponents from Augustin to Solzhenitsyn*, New York: Palgrave Macmillan.

Keohane, R.O. (1998), 'Beyond dichotomy: conversations between international relations and feminist theory', *International Studies Quarterly*, **42** (1), 193–7.

Keohane, R.O. (2002) 'The globalisation of informal violence, theories of world politics, and the "Liberalism of Fear"', *Dialogue-IO, 1*, 29–43.

Keohane, R.O. and J.N. Nye (2000), 'Globalisation: what's new? What's not? (and so what?)', *Foreign Policy*, **118**, 104–19.

Keough, L. and K. Marshall (2006), 'Mozambique's battle against HIV/AIDS and the DREAM Project', *HIV/AIDS – Getting Results*, May, Washington, DC: World Bank Global HIV/AIDS Program.

Kingsbury, D. (2004) 'Introduction' in D. Kingsbury, J. Remenyi, J. McKay and J. Hunt (eds), *Key Issues in Development*, Sydney, NSW and New York: Palgrave Macmillan, pp. 1–22.

Kingsbury, D., J. Remenyi, J. McKay and J. Hunt (2004), *Key Issues in Development*, Sydney, NSW and New York: Palgrave Macmillan.

Kitching, G. (2001), *Seeking Social Justice Through Globalisation: Escaping a Nationalist Perspective*, University Park, PA: Pennsylvania State Press.

Kitching, G. (2006), 'The modernisation myth', *openDemocracy*, 30 May, accessed 22 June 2008 at www.opendemocracy.net/democracy-fukuyama/modernisation_3597.jsp.

Korany, B. (2005), 'The Middle East since the Cold War: torn between

168      *Religion in international politics and development*

geopolitics and geoeconomics', in L. Fawcett (ed.), *International Relations of the Middle East*, Oxford: Oxford University Press, pp. 59–78.

Kosmin, B.A. and S.P. Lachman (1993), *One Nation Under God: Religion in Contemporary American Society*, New York: Crown Publishers.

Kramer, M. (1998), 'The moral logic of Hizballah', in W. Reich (ed.), *Origins of Terrorism. Psychologies, Ideologies, Theologies, States of Mind*, Washington, DC: Woodrow Wilson Centre Press, pp. 131–57.

Krasner, S. (1985), *Structural Conflict: The Third World Against Global Liberalism*, Berkeley, CA: University of California Press.

Krasner, S. (2001) 'Rethinking the sovereign state model', *Review of International Studies*, **27**, 17–42.

Krygier, M. (2005), *Civil Passions. Selected Writings*, Melbourne, VIC: Black Inc Publishing.

Kubalkova, V. (2000), 'Towards an international political theology', *Millennium*, **29** (3), 675–705.

Kung, H. (2003), 'An ethical framework for the global market economy', in J.H. Dunning (ed.), *Making Globalisation Good: The Moral Challenges of Global Capitalism*, Oxford: Oxford University Press, pp. 145–58.

Kurtz, S. (2002), 'The future of history', *Policy Review*, **113**, 43–58.

Lal, V. (2006), 'The beginning of a history', *openDemocracy* 25 May, accessed 16 June 2008 at www.opendemocracy.net/democracy-fukuyama/beginning_3585.jsp.

Lausten, C.B. and O. Waever (2000), 'In defence of religion: sacred referent objects for securitisation', *Millennium,* **29** (3), 705–39.

Leach, E. (1973), 'Buddhism in the post-colonial order in Burma and Ceylon', *Daedalus*, **102** (1), 29–54.

Lewis, D. (2001), *The Management of Non-governmental Development Organisations: An introduction*, London and New York: Routledge Press.

Linden, I. (2008), 'The language of development: what are international development agencies talking about?', in G. Clarke and M. Jennings (eds), *Development, Civil Society and Faith-based Organisations: Bridging the Sacred and the Secular,* New York: Palgrave Macmillan, pp. 72–93.

Linklater, A. (1992), 'The question of the next stage in international relations: a critical theoretical point of view', *Millennium*, **21** (1), 77–98.

Linz, J.J. (1991), 'Church and state in Spain from the civil war to the return of democracy', *Daedalus*, **120** (3), 159–78.

Liotta, G., L. Palombi, G. Guidotti et al. (2005), 'Mother-to child transmission in limited-resource Settings: the role of HAART in the DREAM programme', 14th International Conference on AIDS and Sexually Transmitted Infections in Africa (ICASA), 4–9 December, Abuja, Nigeria, and Treatment Acceleration Program, Regional Advisory Panel meeting, Addis Ababa, 12–13 December.

Lipscutz, R. (2005), 'Power, politics and global civil society', *Millennium*, **33** (3), 747–69.

Little, R. and M. Smith (2005), *Perspectives on World Politics,* 3rd edn, London: Routledge.

Loy, D. (2003), 'The poverty of development: Buddhist reflections', *Development*, **46**, 7–14.

Luciani, G. (2005), 'Oil and political economy in the international relations of the Middle East', in L. Fawcett (ed.), *International Relations of the Middle East*, Oxford: Oxford University Press, pp. 79–104.

Lumsdaine, D.H. (2009), 'Evangelical Christianity and democratic pluralism in Asia: an introduction', in D.H. Lumsdaine (ed.), *Evangelical Christianity and Democracy in Asia*, Oxford: Oxford University Press, pp. 3–42.

Lynch, C. (2000), 'Dogma, praxis, and religious perspectives on multiculturalism', *Millennium*, **29** (3), 741–60.

MacAnulla, S. (2002), 'Structure and agency' in D. Marsh and G. Stoker (eds), *Theory and Methods in Political Science,* 2nd edn, New York: Palgrave Macmillan, pp. 271–91.

MacDonald, M. (1998), *Shared Hope: Environment and Development Agendas for the 21st Century*, London: Routledge.

Madan, T.N. (2003), 'The case of India', *Daedalus*, **132** (3), 62–6.

Madavo, C. (2001), 'Serving the poor in Africa', in D. Belshaw, R. Calderisi and C. Sugden (eds), *Faith in Development: Partnership Between the World Bank and the Churches of Africa*, Oxford and Washington, DC: Regnum Books and the World Bank, pp. 51–6.

Madeley, J.T. (2003), 'Introduction', in J.T. Madeley (ed.), *Religion and Politics*, Burlington, VT: Ashgate, pp. ix–xxiv.

Maier, C.S. (2006), 'The intoxications of history', *openDemocracy*, 18 May, accessed 16 June 2008 at www.opendemocracy.net/democracy-fukuyama/intoxication_3560.jsp

Mallaby, S. (2004), *The World's Banker*, Sydney, NSW: University of New South Wales Press.

Mandle, J. (2003), *Globalisation and the Poor*, New York: Cambridge University Press.

Mardin, S. (1973), 'Centre-periphery relations: a key to Turkish politics?', *Daedalus*, **102** (1), 169–90.

Marsh, D. and P. Furlong (2002), 'A skin not a sweater: ontology and epistemology in political science', in D. Marsh and G. Stoker (eds), *Theory and Methods in Political Science*, New York: Palgrave Macmillan, pp. 17–44.

Marshall, K. (2001), 'Development and religion: a different lens on development debates', *Peabody Journal of Education*, **76** (3/4), 339–75.

Marshall, K. (2004), 'Treating HIV/AIDS in Africa: a challenge for a new humanism' in *Comunita di Sant'Egidio*, accessed 21 February 2008 at www.santegidio.org/uer/2004/int_00659_EN.htm.

Marshall, K. (2005), *A Feast of Cultures: The Fes Festival of World Sacred Music*, Washington, DC: The World Bank.

Marshall, K. (2006), 'Introductory remarks at meeting of Catholic organisations engaged in HIV and AIDS response', 23–26 January, Geneva, Switzerland, accessed 19 February 2008 at web.worldbank.org/ WBSITE/EXTERNAL/EXTABOUTUS/PARTNERS/EXTDEVDIA LOGUE/0,,contentMDK:20805165~menuPK:64192472~pagePK:641 92523~piPK:64192458~theSitePK:537298,00.html.

Marshall, K. and L. Keough (2004), *Mind, Heart and Soul in the Fight Against Poverty*, Washington, DC: The World Bank.

Marshall, K. and L. Keough (2005), *Finding Global Balance: Common Ground Between the Worlds of Development and Faith*, Washington, DC: The World Bank.

Marshall, K. and R. Marsh (eds) (2003), *Millennium Challenges for Faith Development and Faith Institutions*, Washington, DC: The World Bank.

Marshall, K. and M. Van Saanen (2007), *Development and Faith: Where Mind, Heart and Soul Work Together*, Washington, DC: The World Bank.

Martin, D. (1978), *A General Theory of Secularization*, New York: Harper and Row.

Martin, H.P. and H. Schumann (1997), *The Global Trap: Globalization and the Assault on Prosperity and Democracy*, Pretoria, Sydney, Bangkok and London: HRSC/RGN, Pluto Press, White Lotus and Zed Books.

Martin, L.L. and B. Simmons (1998), 'Theories and empirical studies of international institutions', *International Organization*, **52** (4), 729–57.

Marty, M.E. (2003), 'Our religio-secular world', *Daedalus*, **132** (3), 42–8.

Marty, M.E. and R.S. Appleby (eds) (1991), *Fundamentalisms and the State: Remaking Politics, Economies and Militance*, The Fundamentalism Project Series vol. 3, Chicago, IL: University of Chicago Press.

Marty, M.E. and R.S. Appleby (1992), *The Glory and the Power: The Fundamentalist Challenge in the Modern World*, Boston, MA: Beacon Press.

Marty, M.E. and R.S. Appleby (eds) (1994), *Fundamentalisms Observed*, The Fundamentalism Project Series vol. 1, Chicago, IL: University of Chicago Press.

Marty, M.E. and R.S. Appleby (eds) (2004), *Fundamentalisms Comprehended*, The Fundamentalism Project Series vol. 5, Chicago, IL: University of Chicago Press.

Marty, M.E., R.S. Appleby, N.T. Ammerman, R.E. Frykenberg, S.C. Heilman and J. Piscatori (eds) (2004), *Accounting for Fundamentalisms: The Dynamic Character of Movements*, The Fundamentalism Project Series vol. 4, Chicago, IL: University of Chicago Press.

Mathy, J.-P. (2004), 'French-American relations and the war in Iraq: anything new or business as usual?', *Contemporary French and Francophone Studies,* **8** (4), 415–24.

Matthews, S. (2004), 'Post-development theory and the question of alternatives: a view from Africa', *Third World Quarterly*, **25** (2), 373–84.

Mayall, J. (1990), *Nationalism and International Theory*, Cambridge: Cambridge University Press.

McAnnulla, S. (2002), 'Structure and agency', in D. Marsh and G. Stoker (eds), *Theory and Methods in Political Science*, New York: Palgrave Macmillan, pp. 271–91.

McDuie-Ra, D. and J.A. Rees (2010), 'Religious actors, civil society and the development agenda: the dynamics of inclusion and exclusion', *Journal of International Development*, **22**, 20–36.

McNeill, D. (2004), 'Social capital and the World Bank', in M. Bøås and D. McNeill (eds), *Global Institutions and Development: Framing the World?*, London and New York: Routledge, pp. 108–23.

Merton, T. (1948), *The Seven Storey Mountain*, San Diego, CA: Harcourt Brace.

Merton, T. (1996), *Turning Toward the World: The Journals of Thomas Merton Vol. 4 (1960–1963)*, V. Kramer (ed.), New York: HarperCollins.

Miguez, N. (2006), 'Latin American reading of the Bible: experiences, challenges and its practice', *Expository Times*, **118** (3), 120–9.

Mihevc, J. (1995), *The Market Tells Them So: The World Bank and Economic Fundamentalism in Africa*, London: Zed Books.

Miranda, J. (1974), *Marx and the Bible*, New York: Orbis Books.

Mishra, P. (2002) 'Present at the creation of Hinduism: on the British midwife at the birth of India's nationalist religion', *Australian Financial Review*, 30 August, pp. 4–5.

Mitchell, M. (2002), '"Living Our Faith": the Lenten pastoral letter of the bishops of Malawi and the shift to multiparty democracy, 1992–1993', *Journal for the Social Scientific Study of Religion*, **41** (1), 5–18.

Mohan, G. (2002), 'The disappointments of civil society: the politics of NGO intervention in northern Ghana', *Political Geography,* **21** (1), 125–54.

Moltmann, J. (1999), *God for a Secular Society: The Public Relevance of Theology*, Minneapolis, MN: Fortress Press.

Mumford, R. (2006), 'Religion and international development: interview with Katherine Marshall', *The Pew Forum on Religion and Public Life*, 6 March, accessed 22 March 2008 at http://pewforum.org/events/index.php?EventID=100.

Munson, H. (2003), '"Fundamentalism" ancient and modern', *Daedalus*, **132** (3), 31–41.

Murden, S. (2000), 'Religion and the political and social order in the Middle East', in J.L. Esposito and M. Watson (eds) (2000), *Religion and Global Order*, Cardiff: University of Wales Press, pp. 149–66.

Murden, S. (2005), 'Culture in world affairs', in J. Baylis and S. Smith (eds), *The Globalization of World Politics: An Introduction to International Relations*, 3rd edn, Oxford: Oxford University Press, pp. 539–53.

Murden, S. (2008), 'Culture in world affairs', in J. Baylis, S. Smith and P. Owens (eds), *The Globalisation of World Politics: An Introduction to International Relations* 4th edn, Oxford: Oxford University Press, pp. 420–33.

Murphy, C.N. (2000) 'Global governance: poorly done and poorly understood', *International Affairs*, **76** (4), 789–804.

Murphy, J. (2005), 'The World Bank, INGOs, and civil society: converging agendas? The case of universal basic education in Niger', *Voluntas: International Journal of Voluntary and Nonprofit Organisations*, **16** (4), 353–74.

Nandy, A. (2002), *Time Warps: The Insistent Politics of Silent and Evasive Pasts*, London: Hurst & Company.

Narayan, D. (2001), 'Voices of the poor', in D. Belshaw, R. Calderisi and C. Sugden (eds), *Faith in Development. Partnership Between the World Bank and the Churches of Africa*, Oxford and Washington, DC: Regnum Books/World Bank, pp. 39–48.

Narayan, D., R. Patel, K. Schafft, A. Rademacher and S. Koch-Schulte (2000), *Can Anyone Hear Us? Voices of the Poor*, New York: Oxford University Press.

Nasr, V. (2003), 'Lessons from the Muslim world', *Daedalus*, **132** (3), 67–72.

Nasr, V. (2006), *The Shia Revival: How Conflicts with Islam will Shape the Future*, New York: Norton Publishing.

Norris, P. and R. Inglehart (2004), *Sacred and Secular: Religion and Politics Worldwide*, New York: Cambridge University Press.

Norton, A.R. (2005), 'The puzzle of political reform in the Middle East', in L. Fawcett (ed.), *International Relations of the Middle East*, Oxford: Oxford University Press, pp. 131–49.

O'Brien, R. and M. Williams (2004), *Global Political Economy*, New York: Palgrave Publishing.

Ocampo, J. (2002), 'Rethinking the development agenda', *Cambridge Journal of Economics,* **26** (3), 393–407.

O'Donovan, O. and J. Lockwood O'Donovan (1999), *From Irenaeus to Grotius: A Sourcebook in Christian Political Thought,* Grand Rapids, MI: William B. Eerdmans.

O'Loughlin, E. (2004), 'Love of cash unites bickering hardliners', *Sydney Morning Herald,* 28–29 February, p. 22.

Öniş, Z. and F. Şenses (2005), 'Rethinking the emerging post-Washington Consensus', *Development and Change,* **36** (2), 263–90.

Osborne, C. (2004), *Presocratic Philosophy: A Very Short Introduction,* Oxford: Oxford University Press.

Osiander, A. (2000), 'Religion and politics in Western civilisation: the ancient world as matrix and mirror of the modern', *Millennium,* **29** (3), 761–90.

Osiander, A. (2001), 'Sovereignty, international relations, and the Westphalian myth', *International Organization,* **55** (2), 251–87.

PACANet (Pan-African Christian AIDS Network) (2005), 'The Church's role in strengthening the family in an era of HIV/AIDS', 14th International Conference on AIDS and Sexually Transmitted Infections in Africa (ICASA), Abuja, Nigeria, 4–9 December.

Pagden, A. (2006), 'The end of history, or history all over again?', *open-Democracy,* 7 May, accessed 21 June 2008 at www.opendemocracy.net/democracy-fukuyama/again_3514.jsp.

Pallas, C.L. (2005), 'Canterbury to Cameroon: a new partnership between faiths and the World Bank', *Development in Practice,* **15** (5), 677–84.

Palmer, M. and V. Finlay (2003), *Faith in Conservation: New Approaches to Religions and the Environment,* Washington, DC: The World Bank.

Park, S. (2004), 'How transnational advocacy networks reconstitute IO identities', *Seton Hall Journal of International Relations and Diplomacy,* **5** (2), 79–93.

Park, S. (2005a), 'How transnational environmental advocacy networks socialise IFIs: a case study of the international finance corporation', *Global Environmental Politics,* **5** (4), 95–119.

Park, S. (2005b), 'Norm diffusion within international organisations: a case study of the World Bank', *Journal for International Relations and Development,* **8** (2), 114–41.

Park, S. (2006), 'Theorising norm diffusion within international organisations', *International Politics,* **43**, 342–61.

Parker, J., L. Mars, P. Ransome and H. Stanworth (2003), *Social Theory: A basic Tool Kit,* New York: Palgrave Macmillan.

Parliament of the World's Religions (n.d.), accessed 27 March 2009 at www.worldspiritforum.org/en/.

Parliament of the World's Religions (1993), 'Declaration toward a global ethic', 4 September, accessed 29 January 2009 at www.parliamentofreligions.org/_includes/FCKcontent/File/TowardsAGlobalEthic.pdf.

Parrott, D. (2004), 'The Peace of Westphalia', *Journal of Early Modern History*, **8** (1–2), 153–59.

Patterson, A. (2007), 'Civil society organisations: the search for empowerment', in J. Senghor and N. Poku (eds), *Towards Africa's Renewal*, Aldershot: Ashgate, pp. 255–78.

Pease, K.-K.S. (2003), *International Organisations: Perspectives on Governance in the Twenty-first Century*, Upper Saddle River, NJ: Pearson Education.

Peccoud, D. (ed.) (2004), *Philosophical and Spiritual Perspectives on Decent Work,* Geneva: International Labour Organization.

Peet, R. (1999), *Theories of Development*, New York: The Guildford Press.

Pender, J. (2001), 'From "Structural Adjustment" to "Comprehensive Development Framework": conditionality transformed?', *Third World Quarterly*, **22** (3), 397–411.

Petras, J. (2003), *The New Development Politics: The Age of Empire Building and New Social Movements,* Aldershot and Burlington, VT: Ashgate.

Pettifor, A. (2003), 'The coming First World debt crisis', paper presented, Centre for the Study of Global Ethics, 17 November, accessed 10 February 2005 at www.globalethics .bham.ac.uk/index.shtml.

Pettman, R. (2002), 'What is religion for? Sacral alternatives to world affairs', conference paper, New Zealand Association for the Study of Religion Conference, Victoria University, Wellington, 11–13 December.

Pettman, R. (2004), *Reason, Culture, Religion: The Metaphysics of World Politics*, New York: Palgrave Macmillan.

Pfanner T. (2005), 'Editorial', *International Review of the Red Cross*, **858**, 237–41.

Philpott, D. (2000), 'The religious roots of modern international relations', *World Politics*, **52** (2), 206–45.

Philpott, D. (2002), 'The challenge of September 11 to secularism in international relations', *World Politics*, **55** (1), 66–95.

Picciotto, R. (2003), 'International trends and development evaluation: the need for ideas', *American Journal of Evaluation*, **24** (2), 227–34.

Piggott, L. (2005), 'Tribalism in the Arab MENA Region', *Policy*, **21** (1), 15–20.

Pincus, J.R. and J.A. Winters (2002), 'Reinventing the World Bank', in

J.R. Pincus and J.A. Winters (eds), *Reinventing the World Bank,* Ithaca, NY: Cornell University Press, pp. 1–25.

Pine, F. and J. de Pina-Carbral (eds) (2008), *On the Margins of Religion,* New York and Oxford: Berghahn Books.

Piscatori, J. (2000), 'Religious transnationalism and global order', in J. Esposito and M. Watson (eds), *Religion and Global Order*, Cardiff: University of Wales Press, pp. 66–99.

Poethig, K. (2002), 'Moveable peace: engaging the transnational in Cambodia's dhammayietra', *Journal for the Social Scientific Study of Religion*, **41** (1), 19–28.

Pollins, B.M. (2007), 'Beyond logical positivism: reframing King, Keohane and Verba', in R. Lebow and M.I. Lichbach (eds), *Theory and Evidence in Comparative Politics and International Relations,* New York: Palgrave Macmillan, pp. 87–106.

Postel, D. (2006), 'The "End of History" revisited: Francis Fukuyama and his critics', *openDemocracy* 2 May, accessed 24 June, 2008 at www.opendemocracy.net/democracy-fukuyama/intro_3493.jsp.

PovertyNet (The World Bank) (n.d.), 'Poverty reduction strategies', accessed 22 January 2009 at http://web.worldbank.org/WBSITE/EXTERNAL/TOPICS/EXTPOVERTY/EXTPRS/0,,contentMDK:20 228278~pagePK:210058~piPK:210062~theSitePK:384201,00.html.

Rees, J.A. (2004), '"Really existing" scriptures: on the use of sacred text in international affairs', *Review of Faith and International Affairs*, **2** (1), 17–26.

Rees, J.A. (2006), 'The Shi'ites, the West and the future of democracy: reframing political change in a religio-secular world', *Portal: Journal of Multidisciplinary International Studies*, **3** (1), 1–22.

Rees, J.A. (2007), 'Book reviews in religion and politics', *Millennium,* **35** (3), 813–17.

Remenyi, J. (2004), 'What is development?', in D. Kingsbury, J. Remenyi, J. McKay and J. Hunt (eds), *Key Issues in Development*, New York: Palgrave Macmillan, pp. 22–44.

Rich, B. (1994), *Mortgaging the Earth: The World Bank, Environmental Impoverishment and the Crisis of Development,* London: Earthscan Books.

Rich, B. (2002), 'The World Bank under James Wolfensohn', in J.R. Pincus and J.A. Winters (eds), *Reinventing the World Bank,* Ithaca, NY: Cornell University Press, pp. 26–53.

Rich, B. (2003), 'Still waiting: the failure of reform at the World Bank', in C.R. Goddard, P. Cronin and K.C. Dash (eds), *The International Political Economy: State-Market Relations in a Changing Global Order,* Boulder, CO: Lynne Rienner, pp. 353–66.

Rist, G. (2008), *The History of Development: From Western Origins to Global Faith*, translated by P. Camiller, London and New York: Zed Books.

Rittberger, V. and B. Zangl (2006), *International Organization: Polity, Politics and Policies,* New York: Palgrave Macmillan.

Roberts, G. (1984), *Questioning Development*, London: Returned Volunteer Action.

Roberts, R.H. (2002), *Religion, Theology and the Human Sciences*, Cambridge: Cambridge University Press.

Rosenau, J. (1996), 'Probing puzzles persistently: a desirable but improbable future for IR theory', in S. Smith, K. Booth and M. Zalewski (eds), *International Theory: Positivism and Beyond,* Cambridge: Cambridge University Press, pp. 309–27.

Rosencrance, R. (1998), 'Book review: the clash of civilizations and the remaking of world order, by Samuel P. Huntington (1996) (New York: Simon & Schuster)', *American Political Science Review*, **92** (4), 978–80.

Rothman, F. and T. Oliver (2002), 'From local to global: the anti-dam movement in southern Brazil, 1979–1992', in J. Smith and H. Johnston (eds), *Globalization and Resistance: Transnational Dimensions of Social Movements,* Lanham, MD: Rowman and Littlefield, pp. 115–32.

Rowland, C. (ed.) (2007), *The Cambridge Companion to Liberation Theology*, Cambridge: Cambridge University Press.

Roy, O. (1997), 'Islamists in power', in M. Kramer and D. Brumberg (eds), *The Islamism Debate*, Dayan Center Papers, no. 120, Tel Aviv: Universitat Tel-Aviv, pp. 69–83.

Roy, O. (2006), 'The end of history and the long march of secularisation', *openDemocracy*, 16 May, accessed 22 June 2008 at www.opendemocracy.net/node/3546.

Royal, R. (1997), 'The seven-storied Thomas Merton', *First Things*, **70**, 34–8.

Ruether, R. (1983), *Sexism and God-talk: Towards a Feminist Theology*, London: SCM Press.

Ruether, R. and McLaughlin E. (eds) (1979), *Women of Spirit: Female Leadership in the Jewish and Christian Traditions,* New York: Simon & Schuster.

Ruggie, J.G. (1998a), 'What makes the world hang together? Neo-utilitarianism and the social constructivist challenge', *International Organization*, **52** (4), 729–57.

Ruggie, J.G. (1998b), *Constructing World Polity: Essays on International Institutionalisation*, New York: Routledge.

Rushdie, S. (1982), *Midnight's Children,* London: Picador.

Rushdie, S. (2000), 'Ghandi, now', in S. Rushdie, *Step Across This Line. Collected Non-fiction 1992–2002,* London: Jonathan Cape, pp. 180–5.

Sacks, J. (1997), *The Politics of Hope,* London: Random House.

Sacks, J. (2003), 'Global covenant: a Jewish perspective', in J.H. Dunning (ed.), *Making Globalization Good: The Moral Challenges of Global Capitalism,* Oxford: Oxford University Press, pp. 210–31.

Said, E. (2001), 'The clash of ignorance', *The Nation,* 22 October, accessed 14 March 2002 at www.thenation.com/doc/20011022/said.

Samuel, V. (2001), 'The World Bank and the churches: reflections at the outset of a new partnership', in D. Belshaw, R. Calderisi and C. Sugden (eds), *Faith in Development. Partnership Between the World Bank and the Churches of Africa,* Oxford and Washington, DC: Regnum Books/The World Bank, pp. 237–43.

Sassen, S. (2006), 'A state of decay', *openDemocracy,* 3 May, accessed 24 June, 2008 at www.opendemocracy.net/democracy-fukuyama/decay_3500.jsp.

Saul J.R. (1997), *The Unconscious Civilization,* Harmonsworth: Penguin.

Scholte, J.A. (2002), 'Civil society and democracy in global governance', *Global Governance,* **8** (3), 281–305.

Scholte, J.A. (2005), *Globalisation: A Critical Introduction,* New York: Palgrave Macmillan.

Schüssler Fiorenza, E. (1983), *In Memory of Her: A Feminist Theological Reconstruction of Christian Origins,* New York: Crossroad.

Scott, D. (2006), 'Fukuyama's crossroads: the poetics of location', *openDemocracy,* 12 May, accessed 24 June 2008 at www.opendemocracy.net/democracy-fukuyama/crossroads_3532.jsp.

Scott, D. and C. Hirschkind (eds) (2006), *Powers of the Secular Modern,* Stanford, CA: Stanford University Press.

Scott, J.C. (1998), *Seeing Like A State: How Certain Schemes to Improve the Human Condition have Failed,* New Haven, CT and London: Yale University Press.

Scott, N.A. (1963), *Reinhold Neibuhr,* University of Minnesota pamphlets on American writers no. 31, Minneapolis, MN: University of Minnesota Press.

Seiple, R.A. and D.R. Hoover (eds) (2004), *Religion and Security: The New Nexus in International Relations,* Lanham, MD: Rowman and Littlefield.

Sen, A. (1998), 'Secularism and its discontents', in R. Bhargava (ed.), *Secularism and Its Critics,* New Delhi: Oxford University Press, pp. 454–85.

Sen, A. (1999), *Development As Freedom,* New York: Knopf.

Sen, A. (2003), 'Democracy and its global roots', *The New Republic*, **6** (October), 28–35.

Serageldin, I. (1991), 'The justly balanced society', in D. Beckmann, R. Agarwala, S. Burmester and I. Serageldin (eds), *Friday Morning Reflections at the World Bank: Essays on Values and Development*, Washington, DC: Seven Locks Press, pp. 55–74.

Shankar, V. (2004), 'Faiths in the global economic order – response of Hindus, Muslims, Buddhists and Christians', paper presented, 26 February, Centre for the Study of Global Ethics, accessed 10 February 2005 at www.globalethics.bham.ac.uk/index.shtml.

Shiva, V. (1992), *Staying Alive: Women, Ecology and Development* 5th edn, New Dehli: Zed Books/Kali for Women.

Simon, D. (2007), 'Beyond antidevelopment: discourses, convergences, practices', *Singapore Journal of Tropical Geography*, **28**, 205–18.

Singer, D.J. (1961), 'The level-of-analysis problem in international relations', *World Politics*, **14** (1), 77–92.

Sivaramakrishnan, K. and A. Agrawal (2003a), 'Regional modernities in stories and practices of development', in K. Sivaramakrishnan and A. Agrawal (eds), *Regional Modernities: The Cultural Politics of Development in India*, Oxford: Oxford University Press, pp. 1–61.

Sivaramakrishnan, K. and A. Agrawal (eds) (2003b), *Regional Modernities: The Cultural Politics of Development in India,* Oxford: Oxford University Press.

Sjoberg, L. (2008), 'Scaling IR theory: geography's contribution to where IR takes place', *International Studies Review*, **10**, 472–500.

Skorupski, J. (2007), *Why Read Mill Today?*, London: Routledge.

Sluglett, P. (2005), 'The Cold War in the Middle East', in L. Fawcett (ed.), *International Relations of the Middle East,* Oxford: Oxford University Press, pp. 44–60.

Smith, A.D. (2000), 'The "Sacred" dimension of nationalism', *Millennium*, **29** (3), 791–814.

Smith, A.D. (2001), *Nationalism: Key Concepts*, Cambridge: Polity Press.

Smith, D.E. (ed.) (1974), *Religion and Political Modernisation,* New Haven, CT and London: Yale University Press.

Smith, S. (2000), 'The discipline of international relations: still an American social science?', *British Journal of Politics and International Relations*, **2** (3), 374–402.

Smith, S. and P. Owen (2005), 'Alternative approaches to international theory', in J. Baylis and S. Smith (eds), *The Globalization of World Politics: An Introduction to International Relations*, 3rd edn, Oxford: Oxford University Press, pp. 270–93.

St Clair, A.L. (2006), 'The World Bank as a transnational expertised institution', *Global Governance*, **12**, 77–95.

Stark, R. (1999), 'Secularisation, R.I.P.', *Sociology of Religion*, **60** (3), 249–73.

Staudt, K. (1991), *Managing Development: State, Society, and International Contexts*, Newbury Park, CA: Sage.

Steele, D.A. (2003), 'Christianity in Bosnia-Herzegovina and Kosovo: from ethnic captive to reconciling agent', in D. Johnston (ed.), *Faith-based Diplomacy: Trumping Realpolitik,* Oxford: Oxford University Press, pp. 124–77.

Stiglitz, J.E. (2003a), 'Democratising the International Monetary Fund and the World Bank: governance and accountability', *Governance: An International Journal of Policy, Administrations and Institutions*, **16** (1), 111–39.

Stiglitz, J.E. (2003b), 'Towards a new paradigm of development', in J.H. Dunning (ed.), *Making Globalisation Good: The Moral Challenges of Global Capitalism,* Oxford: Oxford University Press, pp. 76–107.

Stout, J. (2004), *Democracy and Tradition,* Princeton, NJ and Oxford: Princeton University Press.

Suh, D. (1991), *The Korean Minjung in Christ,* Hong Kong: The Christian Conference of Asia.

Swatos, W.H. (1992), 'Religion and the social order: new developments in theory and research', *Journal for the Scientific Study of Religion*, **31** (4), 537–38.

Swatos, W.H. (1999), 'Secularisation theory: the course of a concept', *Sociology of Religion*, **60** (3), 209–28.

Tambiah, S.J. (1973), 'The persistence and transformation of tradition in Southeast Asia, with special reference to Thailand', *Daedalus*, **102** (1), 55–84.

Tambiah, S.J. (1998), 'The crisis of secularism in India', in R. Bhargava (ed.), *Secularism and Its Critics,* New Delhi: Oxford University Press, pp. 418–53.

Tamimi, A.S. (2001), *Rachid Ghannouchi: A Democrat Within Islamism,* Oxford: Oxford University Press.

Tamimi, A.S. (2003), 'The renaissance of Islam', *Daedalus*, **132** (3), 51–8.

Taylor, C. (1998), 'Modes of secularism', in R. Bhargava (ed.), *Secularism and Its Critics,* New Delhi: Oxford University Press, pp. 31–53.

Taylor, C. (2004), *Modern Social Imaginaries,* Durham, NC and London: Duke University Press.

Taylor, C. (2007), *The Secular Age,* Cambridge, MA: Belknap/Harvard University Press.

Taylor, I. (2004), 'Hegemony, neoliberal "Good governance" and the

International Monetary Fund: a Gramscian perspective', in M. Bøås and D. McNeill (eds), *Global Institutions and Development: Framing the World?*, London and New York: Routledge, pp. 124–35.

Taylor, M. (1995), *Not Angels But Agencies: The Ecumenical Response to Poverty – A Primer*, Geneva: WCC Publications.

Taylor, M. (2005), *Eat Drink and Be Merry, For Tomorrow We Live: Studies in Christianity and Development*, Edinburgh: T&T Clarke.

Taylor, M., W. Tyndale, V. Shanker and M. Clay (2003), 'WFDD – The Future', 24 September, accessed 19 August 2007 at www.wfdd.org.uk/programmes/futurediscdec_03.pdf.

Thomas, C. (2005), 'Poverty, development, and hunger', in J. Baylis and S. Smith (eds), *The Globalization of World Politics: an introduction to International Relations*, 3rd edn, Oxford: Oxford University Press, pp. 645–68.

Thomas, S.M. (2000), 'Taking religious and cultural pluralism seriously: the global resurgence of religion and the transformation of international society', *Millennium*, **29** (3), 815–41.

Thomas, S.M. (2001), 'Faith, history and Martin Wight: the role of religion in the historical sociology of the English School of international relations', *International Affairs*, **77** (4), 905–29.

Thomas, S.M. (2004a), 'Building communities of character: foreign aid policy and faith-based institutions', *SAIS Review of International Affairs*, **24** (2), 133–48.

Thomas, S.M. (2004b), 'Faith and foreign aid, or how the World Bank got religion and why it matters', *Review of Faith and International Affairs*, **2** (2), 21–30.

Thomas, S.M. (2005), *The Global Resurgence of Religion and the Transformation of International Relations*, New York: Palgrave Macmillan.

Tibi, B. (2000), 'Post-bipolar order in crisis: the challenge of politicised Islam', *Millennium*, **29** (3), 843–60.

Tickner, A. (2006), 'On the frontlines or sidelines of knowledge and power? Feminist practices of responsible scholarship', *International Studies Review*, **8**, 383–95.

Tony Blair Faith Foundation (n.d.), accessed 10 August 2009 at http://tonyblairfaithfoundation.org/.

Tosteson, D.C. (2003), 'Religion and the plague of war', *Daedalus*, **132** (3), 80–1.

Toussaint, E. (2008), *The World Bank: A Critical Primer*, London: Pluto Press.

Townsend, J., G. Porter and E. Mawdsley (2002), 'The role of the transnational community of nongovernment organisations: governance or poverty reduction?', *Journal of International Development*, **14** (6), 829–39.

Tschannen, O. (1991), 'The secularisation paradigm: a systematisation', *Journal for the Scientific Study of Religion*, **30** (4), 395–415.

Turner, B.S. (1983), *Religion and Social Theory: A Materialist Perspective*, London: Heinemann Educational Books.

Turner, D. (2007), 'Marxism, liberation theology and the way of negation', in C. Rowland (ed.), *The Cambridge Companion to Liberation Theology*, Cambridge: Cambridge University Press, pp. 229–47.

Tyndale, W. (2002), 'Faith and economics in "development": a bridge across the chasm?', in D. Eade (ed.), *Development and Culture: A Development in Practice Reader*, London: Oxfam GB/WFDD, pp. 45–59.

Tyndale, W. (2003), 'Idealism and practicality: the role of religion and development', *Development*, **46** (4), 22–8.

Tyndale, W. (ed.) (2006), *Visions of Development: Faith-based Initiatives*, Aldershot: Ashgate.

Uchitelle, L. (1999), 'World Bank economist felt he had to silence criticism or quit', *New York Times*, 2 December, accessed 30 May 2007 at www.nytimes.com/1999/12/02/business/world-bank-economist-felt-he-had-to-silence-his-criticism-or-quit.html.

Ulvila, M. and F. Hossain (2002), 'Development NGOs and political participation of the poor in Bangladesh and Nepal', *Voluntas – International Journal of Voluntary and Nonprofit Organizations*, **13** (2), 149–63.

UNCTAD (United Nations Commission on Trade and Development) (n.d.), 'A brief history of UNTAD', accessed 21 March 2008 at www.unctad.org/Templates/Page.asp?intItemID=3358&lang=1.

UNCTAD (2003), 'List of non-governmental organizations participating in the activities of UNTAD', 13 January, accessed 20 February 2008 at www.unctad.org/en/docs/ tbngolistd5_en.pdf.

UNECA (United Nations Economic Commission for Africa) (2005), *Treatment Acceleration Program: Tripartite Meeting (World Bank, WHO and UNECA)*, Nairobi, Kenya, 23–24 June, accessed 23 March 2008 at www.uneca.org/tap/rap3/TAP-Nairobi-Meeting-reportV3.pdf.

Utting, P. (2006), 'Introduction: reclaiming development agendas', in P. Utting (ed.), *Reclaiming Development Agendas: Knowledge, Power, and International Policy Making*, Basingstoke: Palgrave Macmillan/ UNRSID, pp. 1–24.

Valley, P. (1990), *Bad Samaritans: First World Ethics and Third World Debt*, London: Hodder & Stoughton.

Ver Beek, K.A. (2002), 'Spirituality: a development taboo', in D. Eade (ed.), *Development and Culture: A Development in Practice Reader*, London: Oxfam GB/WFDD, pp. 60–77.

Volf, M. (2000), 'Forgiveness, reconciliation and justice: a theological contribution to a more peaceful social environment', *Millennium*, **29** (3), 861–78.

Volpi, F. (2004), 'Pseudo-democracy in the Muslim world', *Third World Quarterly*, **25** (6), 1061–78.

Wade, R. (1997), 'Greening the bank: the struggle over the environment 1970–1995', in D. Kapur, J.P. Lewis and R. Webb (eds), *The World Bank: Its First Half Century, Vol. 2, Perspectives*, Washington, DC: Brookings Institution, pp. 611–734.

Wade, R.H. (2002), 'US hegemony and the World Bank: the fight over people and ideas', *Review of International Political Economy*, **9** (2), 215–43.

Waever, O. (1996), 'The rise and fall of the inter-paradigm debate', in S. Smith, K. Booth and M. Zalewski (eds), *International Theory: Positivism and Beyond*, Cambridge: Cambridge University Press, pp. 149–85.

Wallerstein, I. (1974), *The Modern World System*, vol. 1, New York: Academic Press.

Wallerstein, I. (1979), *The Capitalist World Economy*, Cambridge: Cambridge University Press.

Waltz, K. (1979), *Theory of International Politics*, Reading, MA: Addison-Wesley.

Ward, H. (2002), 'Rational choice', in D. Marsh and G. Stoker (eds), *Theory and Methods in Political Science*, New York: Palgrave Macmillan, pp. 65–89.

Warren, H. (1997), *Theologians of a New World Order: Reinhold Niebuhr and the Christian Realists, 1920–1948*, New York: Oxford University Press.

Weber, M. (1930), *The Protestant Ethic and the Spirit of Capitalism*, translated by T. Parsons, London: Allen & Unwin.

Wendt, A. (1998), 'On constitution and causation in international relations', *Review of International Studies*, **24** (4), 101–17.

Wendt, A. (1999), *Social Theory of International Politics*, New York: Cambridge University Press.

Westerlund, D. (1996), *Questioning the Secular State: The Worldwide Resurgence of Religion and Politics*, London: I.B. Taurus.

WFDD (2000), *Exploring a Dialogue: A Report on Progress, July 1998–December 2000*, Oxford: WFDD.

White, S. (1996), 'Depoliticising development: the uses and abuses of participation', *Development in Practice*, **6** (1), 6–15.

Wight, M. (1987), 'An anatomy of international thought', *Review of International Studies*, **13**, 221–7.

Wilber, C.K. and K.P. Jameson (1980), 'Religious values and the social limits to development', *World Development*, **8**, 467–79.

Wilson, B.R. (1992), 'Reflections on a many-sided conversation', in S. Bruce (ed.), *Religion and Modernisation: Sociologists and Historians Debate the Secularisation Book*, Oxford: Clarendon Press, pp. 195–210.

Wolfensohn, J. (2004), 'Millennium challenges for faith and development: new partnerships to reduce poverty and strengthen conservation', Third Annual Richard Snowdon Lecture, Interfaith Conference of Metropolitan Washington, Trinity College, Washington, DC, 30 March, accessed 22 April, 2009 at http://go.worldbank.org/OAX42ODDR0.

Woods, N. (2001), 'Making the IMF and the World Bank more accountable', *International Affairs*, **77** (1), 83–100.

Woods, N. (2005), 'International political economy in an age of globalisation', in J. Baylis and S. Smith (eds), *The Globalization of World Politics: An Introduction to International Relations*, 3rd edn, Oxford: Oxford University Press, pp. 277–98.

Woods, N. (2006), *The Globalizers: The IMF, the World Bank and their Borrowers*, Ithaca, NY and London: Cornell University Press.

World Bank (n.d. a), 'Multi-country HIV/AIDS Project', accessed 24 March 2008 at http://web.worldbank.org/WBSITE/EXTERNAL/ COUNTRIES/AFRICAEXT/EXTAFRHEANUTPOP/EXTAFRRE GTOPHIVAIDS/0,,contentMDK:20415735~menuPK:1001234~page PK:34004173~piPK:34003707~theSitePK:717148,00.html.

World Bank (n.d. b), 'DDVE: WFDD', accessed 17 March 2005 at http://wbln0018.worldbank.org/developmentdialogue/developmentdia- logueweb.nsf/weblinks.

World Bank (1999a), *World Development Report 1999/2000: Entering the 21st Century,* Washington, DC: The World Bank.

World Bank (1999b), 'News and broadcast – final statement by the co- chairs Second Meeting of the World Faiths Development Dialogue November 11, 1999', accessed 23 January 2007 at http://web.world- bank.org/WSITE/EXTERNAL/NEWS.

World Bank (2000), *World Development Report 2000/1: Attacking Poverty*, Washington, DC: The World Bank.

World Bank (2002), *The Faith and Ethics Agenda for the World Bank: Report on Progress and Proposals for Next Steps*, status report (K. Marshall), DDVE on values and ethics, 27 April.

World Bank (2003), *World Development Report 2004: Making Services for Poor People*, Washington, DC: The World Bank.

World Bank (2006), 'Faiths and ethics agenda in the World Bank: history, progress and options', K. Marshall and the Human Development Network working paper, 15 March, Washington, DC: The World Bank.

World Bank (2008), *World Bank Annual Report: Year in Review*, Washington, DC: The World Bank Group.

World Council of Churches (n.d.), 'The WCC and the Ecumenical Movement', accessed 22 January 2008 at www.oikoumene.org/en/who-are-we/background.html.

World Council of Churches (2001), *Lead Us Not Into Temptation: Churches' Response to the Policies of International Financial Institutions*, Rogate R. Mshana (ed.), 31 December, accessed 23 October 2008 at www.oikoumene.org/fileadmin/files/wcc-main/documents/p3/lead_us_not_in to_temptation.pdf.

World Council of Churches (2004a), 'WCC encounters Bretton Woods institutions: through critical engagement, making sure the cries of the people most affected are heard', media release, 22 October, accessed 22 February 2008 at www2.wcc-coe.org/pressreleasesen.nsf/index/pu-04-52.html.

World Council of Churches (2004b), 'The WCC-IMF-WB high-level encounter, 22 October 2004', accessed 26 February 2008 at www.oik oumene.org/en/resources/documents/wcc-programmes/public-witness-addressing-power-affirming-peace/poverty-wealth-and-ecology/trade/22-10-04-wcc-imf-wb-high-level-encounter.html.

World Economic Forum (2008a), 'Belief systems: to what extent do they guide us?', panel discussion with members John Chew Hiang Chea, Garth C. Japhet, Brian McLaren, Ingrid Mattson, Baroness Neuberger, Robert M. Winston, moderated by David Bodanis, 24 January, accessed 20 February, 2008 at www.weforum.org/en/know ledge/KN_SESS_SUMM_23412?url=/en/knowledge/KN_SESS_SUMM _23412.

World Economic Forum (2008b), *Islam and the West: Annual Report on the State of the Dialogue, January 2008*, Davos, Switzerland: World Economic Forum.

World Economic Forum (2008c), 'Faith and modernization', Panel discussion with members Abdullah Ahmad Badawi, Mahdi Hadavi, David A. Harris, Cardinal Theodore McCarrick, Rick Warren, chaired by Tony Blair, 24 January, accessed 20 February 2008 at www.weforum. org/en/knowledge/KN_SESS_SUMM_23765?url=/en/knowledge/KN_ SESS_SUMM_23765.

WFDD (World Faiths Development Dialogue) (n.d. a), accessed August, 2009 at www.developmentandfaith.org.

WFDD (n.d. b), 'About WFDD: what we are', accessed 18 March 2005 at www.wfdd.org.uk/aboutus.html.

WFDD (1998), 'Key issues for development: a discussion for the contribution by the World Faiths Development Dialogue to the World Bank's World Development Report 2001', WFDD occasional paper no.1, W. Tyndale (ed.), Oxford: WFDD.

WFDD (1999a), 'Papers presented by Faiths' Delegates at the Consultation on the World Bank's World Development Report 2000/1 on the themes of values, norms and poverty', Johannesburg, 12–14 January, WFDD occasional paper no. 2, P.D. Premasiri, M. Weinberg and A. Lakhani (eds), Oxford: WFDD.

WFDD (1999b), 'A new direction for world development?', WFDD occasional paper no. 3, Oxford: WFDD.

WFDD (1999c), *Poverty and Development: An Inter-faith Perspective*, Oxford: WFDD.

WFDD (2001), *Exploring a Dialogue. A Report on Progress July 1998–December 2000*, Birmingham: WFDD.

WFDD (2002a), *Report on Visit to Malawi and Uganda, 29 April–8 May 2002*, Birmingham: WFDD.

WFDD (2002b), *World Faiths Development Dialogue Report 2001–2*, Birmingham: WFDD.

WFDD (2002c), *Meeting of World Leaders on Faith and Development, Canterbury, England, October 6–8, 2002*, Birmingham: WFDD.

WFDD (2003), *WFDD – The Future*, Birmingham: WFDD.

WFDD-B(1–16) (various years), World Faiths Development Dialogue Bulletins nos 1–16, accessed June 2007 at www.wfdd.org.uk.

WFDD-OP(1–5) (various years), World Faiths Development Dialogue Occasional Papers nos 1–5, accessed June 2007 at www.wfdd.org.uk.

World Spirit Forum (n.d.), accessed 28 January 2009 at www.worldspiritforum.org/en/.

Wright, R. (1996), 'Islam and liberal democracy: two visions of reformation', *Journal of Democracy*, **7** (2), 64–75.

Wuthnow, R. (1991), 'Understanding religion and politics', *Daedalus*, **120** (3), 1–20.

Yavuz, M.H. (2003), 'The case of Turkey', *Daedalus*, **132** (3), 59–61.

Youngs, G. (2004), 'Feminist international relations: a contradiction in terms? Or why women are essential to understanding the world "we live in"', *International Affairs*, **80** (1), 75–87.

# Index